Nietzsche and Metaphor

Nietzsche and Metaphor

Sarah Kofman

Translated, with an Introduction,
Additional Notes, and a Bibliography
by Duncan Large

THE ATHLONE PRESS
LONDON

First published 1993 by
The Athlone Press
1 Park Drive, London NW11 7SG

First published in France 1972
© Editions Galilée 1983 *Nietzsche et la métaphore*
English translation and Introduction, Notes and Bibliography
© 1993 The Athlone Press

Publisher's Note

The publishers wish to record their thanks to the French Ministry
of Culture for a grant towards the cost of translation.

British Library Cataloguing in Publication Data
*A catalogue record for this book is available
from the British Library*

ISBN 0 485 11422 4 hb
     0 485 12098 4 pb

Typeset by Saxon Graphics Ltd, Derby
Printed and bound in Great Britain by
the University Press, Cambridge

Contents

Translator's Introduction

Nietzsche et la métaphore – Sarah Kofman's second book, and her first on Nietzsche – was first published in France in 1972 (bib., 1972a), so it has taken over twenty years for a complete English translation to appear. In the intervening period, and over the course of a prolific output which includes some twenty-three books to date – not to mention articles, reviews, and interviews (see Bibliography) – she has firmly established herself, in Andrew Benjamin's words, as 'one of France's most important contemporary philosophers'.[1] Building on an early and decisive engagement with the work of Nietzsche, Freud, and Derrida, she has developed her ideas over a remarkable range of areas as diverse as aesthetics, literary criticism, the history of philosophy from the 'Pre-Socratics' to Derrida, Freudian psychoanalysis, feminism, autobiographical writing, art and film criticism, as well as providing her own drawings to illustrate a number of her more recent works. Nietzsche has continued to remain at the forefront of her interests, though, and it is ironic that the publication of *Nietzsche and Metaphor*, Kofman's first book on Nietzsche to appear in English translation, should coincide with the publication in France of her fourth, *Explosion II: Les enfants de Nietzsche*, the second and concluding part of her monumental and definitive study of *Ecce Homo* (1992a, 1993a).

Kofman's reception in the English-speaking world has been hampered, then, by the sometimes inordinate time-lag between the publication of her books in French and the appearance of English translations. Other countries and other languages have fared better: a Spanish translation of her first book, *L'enfance de l'art* (1970a), appeared as early as 1973, and by now her work has been translated into nine languages besides French. Although a section from *Nietzsche et la métaphore* was included in *The New Nietzsche*, David B. Allison's influential collection of translated articles and excerpts, which first appeared in 1977[2] and was the first piece by Kofman to be translated into English, this was not followed up, and it took until the second half of the 1980s for her work to become at all widely known in the English-speaking world, where her reputation has grown up almost exclusively around her writings on 'the question of woman' in philosophical and psychoanalytical texts. Her work in this area was relatively quick to be translated: between 1980 and 1982, the years which saw the publication in France of *L'énigme de la femme* and *Le respect des femmes* respectively (1980a and 1982a), four excerpts from them appeared in English translation (1980a, 1980d, 1982a). *The Enigma of Woman* was then published complete a further three years later in 1985 (see 1980a) – the first of Kofman's books to come out in English translation[3] – and since then the momentum has gradually been building up, with *The Childhood of Art* in 1988 (see 1970a) and *Freud and Fiction* in 1991 (see 1974a).

The feminist and psychoanalytical sides to her work have begun to be appreciated, then, thanks also to the support of a number of journals, most notably *SubStance* and *Diacritics*, which have played an important role in promoting her writings. But her work in other areas has yet to make a corresponding impact – key books, from *Camera obscura* (1973a) through *Lectures de Derrida* (1984a) and *Mélancolie de l'art* (1985a) to *Socrate(s)* (1989a), remain to be translated, or translated in full. So it is to be hoped that this translation of

Nietzsche and Metaphor, as well as affording the English-speaking reader access to one of the most important pieces of Nietzsche criticism from the last thirty years, will also contribute, simply by adding to the corpus of available material, to a more rounded assessment of Kofman's work in the English-speaking world. This introductory essay is not intended as a critical assessment of the book, for which the reader is referred to a number of recent English-language studies that have begun to debate Kofman's positions.[4] The essay which follows is aimed rather at resituating *Nietzsche and Metaphor* in the historical context in which it originally appeared, at the high-water mark during an extraordinary surge of interest in 'the new Nietzsche' which swept over France in the 1960s and early 1970s, and of which *Nietzsche and Metaphor* is one of the most important products.

THE FRENCH CONTEXT: DELEUZE AND AFTER

Having begun her philosophy-teaching career at a lycée in Toulouse (1960–63), Kofman moved back to Paris in 1963 to take up a post at the Lycée Claude-Monet (1963–70) and later to begin a doctoral thesis on 'The Concept of Culture in Nietzsche and Freud' under Jean Hyppolite at the Collège de France in 1966. The decisive nature of these moves becomes apparent if one considers that her previous work – which resulted in her first publication, 'Le problème moral dans une philosophie de l'absurde' in 1963 (see bib.) – had been on Sartre. She recently republished this article as an appendix to the collection *Séductions* (1990a), commenting by way of introduction: 'It seemed to me interesting to insert this first publication on Sartre into this collection of more recent texts, as a sort of strange vestige of a philosophical past in which "I" hardly recognize "myself" any longer' (p.167). The crucial, 'self'-estranging break came after this first article, then, over a formative five-year period during which the regulations concerning French doctoral dissertations in force at the time precluded the pre-publication of any excerpts derived from thesis work. The years 1963–68 thus mark a hiatus of unique proportions in Kofman's otherwise steady stream of publications, and the first work to appear after this 'publishing purdah' clearly signals her new orientation, especially since it appeared in the same journal as her first piece, the *Revue de l'enseignement philosophique*. A spin-off from the thesis in progress, this article is her first piece on Nietzsche, and discusses his analysis in *The Antichrist* of the historical transition from Judaism to Christianity in terms of will to power (1968).

Working in Paris, Kofman was ideally placed to participate in the extraordinary intensification of interest in Nietzsche which gripped the French intellectual scene over the period of roughly a dozen years following the publication of Heidegger's *Nietzsche* in 1961 and especially Deleuze's seminal *Nietzsche et la philosophie* in 1962.[5] In tracing the post-war emergence of the new Nietzsche, one would undoubtedly have to consider the contributions of Georges Bataille[6] and Maurice Blanchot,[7] as well as of Jean Wahl, whose Sorbonne lecture series *La pensée philosophique de Nietzsche des années 1885–1888* was published in 1959,[8] the same year as *Nietzsche devant ses contemporains*, edited by Geneviève Bianquis, the most outstanding Nietzsche translator and interpreter of the pre-war generation.[9] Deleuze himself credits Pierre Klossowski with having rekindled interest in Nietzsche through two important essays,[10] though it would be difficult to overestimate Deleuze's own contribution to the definition of the new Nietzsche. Kofman acknowledges his contribution in the foreword to her second book on Nietzsche, *Nietzsche et la scène philosophique* (1979b, p.7); in *Explosion II* she reveals that it was a course by Deleuze on *On the Genealogy of Morals*, which she followed when she was studying for the 'agrégation' examination, that first inspired her interest in Nietzsche, and indeed Deleuze took over the supervision of Kofman's thesis work in 1971 after Jean Hyppolite had died in 1968. A recent issue of the *Magazine littéraire* devoted to 'Les vies de

Nietzsche' remarks that without Deleuze's various contributions in the 1960s, 'Nietzsche would not be what he has become for us today',[11] and it opens its Nietzsche dossier with a section from Deleuze's latest Nietzsche study as a mark of his continued importance.

Before Deleuze, and despite the 'home-grown' productions just mentioned, the reception of Nietzsche in France after the war had been largely determined by translations of key German works: in particular those by Karl Jaspers,[12] Karl Löwith,[13] Karl Schlechta,[14] and Martin Heidegger.[15] The impact of Deleuze as the first French writer of importance is marked by Jean Wahl in his 1963 review of *Nietzsche et la philosophie*, in which he already feels able to add Deleuze's book to the pantheon of major studies so far – all of those he cites being German.[16] Deleuze's study decisively breaks with existentialist and, in particular, Hegelian readings of Nietzsche, and the celebratedly magisterial opening – 'Nietzsche's most general project is the introduction of the concepts of sense and value into philosophy' (p. 1) – gives an immediate indication of the fundamental nature of Deleuze's revaluation. Deleuze deliberately chooses as the basis for his study *On the Genealogy of Morals*, 'Nietzsche's most systematic book' (p. 87), and he presents Nietzsche's philosophy as a continuation and radicalization of the Kantian project of critique (p. 1),[17] yet his account does not shy away from accommodating Nietzsche's 'grand doctrines' of will to power and the eternal return. These latter thus come into their own at last and need no longer be either bracketed as inconvenient metaphysical residues or – the Heideggerian move – espoused as the cornerstones of Nietzsche's philosophy yet only at the expense of relegating Nietzsche to the status of 'last of the metaphysicians'. Perhaps most influentially, Deleuze stresses that Nietzsche's model of the world as will to power makes for an affirmation of difference, of the play of (interpretative, appropriative) active and reactive *forces*.[18]

Kofman makes relatively frequent references to Deleuze in *Nietzsche and Metaphor*, and to a variety of other works besides *Nietzsche and Philosophy*, too.[19] Thus the fact that there is only one explicit reference to this latter work (in the context of 'active' and 'reactive' forgetting – cf. section III, n.31) should not lead us to ignore other Deleuzian echoes in Kofman's study. These are particularly apparent if the first two parts of section V, on forces of 'appropriation' and on 'genealogical etymology' respectively – passages where, uncoincidentally, *On the Genealogy of Morals* assumes centre stage – are considered in the light of a passage such as the following, from the beginning of *Nietzsche and Philosophy*:

> We will never find the sense of something [...] if we do not know the force which appropriates the thing, which exploits it, which takes possession of it or is expressed in it. A phenomenon is not an appearance or even an apparition but a sign, a symptom which finds its meaning in an existing force. The whole of philosophy is a symptomatology, and a semiology. (p.3)

We can see Deleuze's new emphasis on a reading of Nietzsche which privileges forces and difference coming through already in Derrida's pioneering early rebuttal of Jean Rousset's classic 1962 structuralist study *Forme et signification*, 'Force and Signification', now best known as the opening essay of *Writing and Difference*, but initially published in *Critique* in 1963.[20] Here we find Derrida arguing: '*Form* fascinates when one no longer has the force to understand force from within itself' (p.4), and he concludes on a stirring and explicitly Nietzschean note, quoting from *Philosophy in the Tragic Age of the Greeks* and *Twilight of the Idols*, and ending with a long quotation from *Thus Spoke Zarathustra*.

After *Nietzsche and Philosophy*, Deleuze continued to set the agenda for French Nietzsche reception through the

1960s. Further writings followed – a second *Nietzsche* in 1965 (a short introduction and selection of texts) as well as an article in 1966, 'Renverser le platonisme'[21] – and he also played an instrumental role in organizing the first of the major Nietzsche conferences of the period, the 'Colloque de Royaumont' in July 1964.[22] The list of contributors to this conference indicates the extent to which it can be seen as a watershed, for on the one hand the 'old guard' is still represented in the shape of Karl Löwith, Gabriel Marcel, and Jean Wahl, for example, but on the other hand the new generation is also making its presence felt, its Nietzsche heard: Deleuze himself, Klossowski, Michel Foucault, and Gianni Vattimo.

One particularly significant contribution to the 1964 conference is a report from Giorgio Colli and Mazzino Montinari concerning the state of the Nietzsche manuscripts.[23] Their critical edition – which gives as reliable a version of the unpublished notes as will likely be possible – began to appear in 1967[24] and is at last nearing its 30-volume completion; most importantly, the German volumes have been 'shadowed' all along by translations into French and Italian (in marked contrast to the state of affairs in the English-speaking world where, although an agreement to translate the edition has been reached, we are still some way from the publication of the first volume). The importance the new edition was accorded in France is indicated by the calibre of those involved with the project from the outset, some of the most prominent of the 'new Nietzscheans'. The first text to appear in the new critical edition was *The Gay Science* (with the notes from the same period), translated by Klossowski and accompanied by an introductory essay from Deleuze and Foucault, the original French editors.[25] By the time of the publication of *Nietzsche and Metaphor* in 1972, four volumes were already out[26] – and this is quite apart from the burgeoning number of reprints of earlier translations of Nietzsche's works, by Henri Albert, Geneviève Bianquis, and Alexandre Vialatte, among others.[27]

Even though Michel Foucault's work has been of little direct importance to Kofman, his contribution to French Nietzsche reception in the 1960s went far beyond coediting the new Colli-Montinari edition and deserves consideration here. Foucault is one of those thinkers – among whom one can also include Jean-François Lyotard – who may have written relatively little specifically on Nietzsche, but whose projects would be inconceivable without Nietzsche's influence, and Foucault's central importance to the definition of the new style of interpretation has been recognized by Luc Ferry and Alain Renaut in their polemical book *French Philosophy of the 60s*, where he is discussed as the sole representative of 'French Nietzscheanism'.[28] The paper which Foucault contributed to the 1964 Royaumont conference, on 'Nietzsche, Freud, Marx',[29] went a long way toward establishing the pre-eminence throughout the period under discussion of that particular triumvirate, dubbed by Paul Ricœur the 'masters of suspicion'.[30] It is the primacy of the notion of interpretation in the work of these three writers which serves as the common denominator for Foucault, but despite his celebrated defence of what he characterizes as Nietzsche's hermeneutics against its *'ferocious enemy'*, semiology,[31] it is broadly speaking a semiological interest in Nietzsche which will come to hold sway over the next decade and is distinctive of the 'new Nietzscheanism'.

In his 1966 *The Order of Things*, Foucault himself highlights the importance of 'Nietzsche the philologist' as 'the first to connect the philosophical task with a radical reflection upon language.'[32] However, the 'linguistic turn' in French Nietzsche reception had already been inaugurated at least as early as *Nietzsche and Philosophy*, in which, as we saw above, Deleuze portrays a Nietzsche who argues that '[t]he whole of philosophy is a symptomatology, and a semiology' (*Nietzsche and Philosophy*, p.3), who characterizes philosophy as 'active philology [...] active linguistics' (p.74).[33] What is more, the new theoretical approach was increasingly backed up during this period by the publication of further new primary materials – aside from the first volumes of the new critical edition – which had previously been unavailable in French translation. Especially important were two early Nietzsche texts dating from the early 1870s, either side of the publication of *The Birth of Tragedy* in 1872, written during the early years of Nietzsche's teaching at the University of Basle and reflecting his early intense engagement with the question of the relation between philosophy and language.

In 1969, Angèle Kremer-Marietti published a parallel text edition of the so-called *Philosophenbuch* or *Philosopher's Book* (see section II, n.14), which was to prove a major influence on 'Sarah Kofman's Nietzsche'. For in 1971 Kofman reviewed it, along with the earlier Bianquis translations of *The Birth of Tragedy* and *Philosophy in the Tragic Age of the Greeks*, and it was this review (1971b) which was to provide the backbone of the second and third sections of *Nietzsche and Metaphor* – the crucial theoretical sections where Kofman argues for the 'strategic status' of metaphor, drawing precisely on these early texts. The second important translation to be published in this period was that by Philippe Lacoue-Labarthe and Jean-Luc Nancy of selections from Nietzsche's early notebooks on 'Rhetoric and Language', the material he used for his lecture courses in Basle on Greek rhetoric.[34] This material was published in the same 1971 issue of *Poétique* that contained the first published version of 'Nietzsche et la métaphore', in abridged article form (as well as two other key texts by Derrida and Lacoue-Labarthe – see section II, n.3★), but Kofman had the opportunity to incorporate references into the final, book-length version of *Nietzsche and Metaphor*.

NIETZSCHE, FREUD, MARX

All the activity of translation and commentary so far mentioned resulted in an unparalleled interest in Nietzsche in France and a surge of production, in the form of books and articles, biographies,[35] and special journal numbers[36] devoted to him – quite apart from more unusual items in the form of fiction[37] and drama.[38] The culmination was reached with the second big Nietzsche conference of the period, the 'Colloque de Cerisy-la-Salle' of July 1972 entitled 'Nietzsche aujourd'hui?', which saw contributions from virtually every major French Nietzsche critic writing at the time.[39] The general intensity of this activity is reflected by one of the contributors to the 'Nietzsche aujourd'hui?' conference, Pierre Boudot – himself the author of three books on Nietzsche in the space of five years.[40] His *Nietzsche et les écrivains français* opens with a comparison between the current (1970) state of interest in Nietzsche and the situation in 1929, when Geneviève Bianquis published her authoritative overview of *Nietzsche en France*:

> Nietzsche had not yet reached the intelligence of the general public. There were many who did not think as we do nowadays that the contemporary mind must give either Marx or Nietzsche as its references. Young people were not as ambiguously infatuated with him then as they are now. Philosophers were not concerned with his statements from a technical point of view and were not looking to see whether his poetic words might be hiding a theory of knowledge. (p.19f.)

By this stage, then, reference to Nietzsche for one's philosophical credentials had become almost *de rigueur*, although Kofman's commitment to Nietzsche patently exceeds the contemporary modishness; she would also resist the pull exerted by Marx on so many of her intellectual generation. She has described herself in a recent interview as 'an heir to 1968',[41] yet she balked at following Deleuze or Lyotard on their paths to overtly politicized Nietzsches, to the kind of Freudo-Marxist Nietzschean-isms of *Anti-Oedipus* or *Libidinal Economy*.[42] Kofman pays her respects to Marx in *Nietzsche and Metaphor*, with a number of footnote references pointing up analogies and differences between his work and Nietzsche's (see section III, nn.3, 9, 18; section IV, n.1; section V, n.3), and in *Camera obscura* (1973a) she devotes a whole chapter to Marx, developing one of the earlier references. That is as far as she will go in this direction, though, and hers is a different trajectory – one mapped in this respect by the 'Philosophie en effet' group in general, and paralleled by Jean-Michel Rey who, in his *L'enjeu des signes*, dutifully quotes Marx and invokes the trinity in a manner reminiscent of Foucault,[43] but is much more interested in Nietzsche and Freud than in Marx.[44]

If we return to pick up the thread of Kofman's own output around 1970, we can see that her work from this period reflects the now central position in her thinking of the nexus of Nietzsche and Freud, on whom at this point she begins publishing in earnest. After the first article on Nietzsche in 1968, mentioned above, over the next three years Kofman publishes a further three pieces on him preparatory to *Nietzsche and Metaphor*: the article in *Poétique* and the review of Kremer-Marietti's translation of the *Philosophenbuch* (1971a and 1971b), as well as the pioneering review of Jean Granier's *Le problème de la vérité dans la philosophie de Nietzsche* (1970b), which is reproduced here as an appendix. In attacking Granier's reading – a monolithic, 650-page study drawing mainly on Heideggerian ontology and on Ricœur, which had been fêted since its first publication in 1966 – Kofman was very much writing against the grain (the book had already run to a second edition by 1969). This became apparent from the difficulty she had in placing her review, before Jean Piel finally accepted it for *Critique* in April 1970, when it was the first piece to earn her a degree of prominence.

Concurrently with this early series of pieces on Nietzsche, though, over the period 1969–74 Kofman was also publishing on Freud – a series of readings which would lead to *Quatre romans analytiques* in 1974 (1974a), as well as her 'petite thèse' on Freud's aesthetics, *L'enfance de l'art* (1970a). This latter was her first book, and coincided with her move to the post of *maître-assistant de philosophie* at her Alma Mater, the Sorbonne (Paris I), where she has remained since and was at last appointed to a chair (not without considerable institutional opposition) in 1991. Her publications on Nietzsche and Freud coincided with an abandonment of her thesis in its original form, though she was to gain a 'thèse sur travaux' in 1976 on the basis of submitted published work.[45] The early pattern of working on Nietzsche and Freud 'in tandem' has been sustained: *Nietzsche et la scène philosophique* appeared in 1979 (1979b) and was closely followed in 1980 by her third book on Freud, *L'énigme de la femme* (1980a); in 1986 the article 'Nietzsche et l'obscurité d'Héraclite' (1986c) accompanied *Pourquoi rit-on?* (1986a); latterly *'Il n'y a que le premier pas qui coûte'* (1991b) was followed in 1992 by 'Nietzsche et Wagner' (1992c) and *Explosion I* (1992a); and in 1993 'Un autre Moïse ou la force de la loi' (1993c) was followed by *Explosion II* (1993a).

'A REAL ENCOUNTER' – THE RELATION TO DERRIDA

The Nietzsche–Freud nexus in Kofman's writing is already evident from the number of references to Freud in *Nietzsche and Metaphor*, but by this stage in her development her 'two "great" thinkers'[46] had become a triumvirate with the addition of Jacques Derrida: as she makes clear in the acknowledgements for *Nietzsche and Metaphor*, she gave a first version of the book to Derrida's seminar on philosophical method at the École Normale Supérieure in the academic session 1969–70. Kofman's relation to Derrida is rather more complex than has generally been perceived – in a recent interview she has explained her position thus:

> I worked in total isolation until 1969. The first text I published was on Sartre in 1962 [*sic*]. Then I worked

alone on Nietzsche and Freud and published my first texts on these two authors before having either read or met Derrida. My later reading of Derrida allowed me to generalize the type of reading I had done in isolation on these two authors. At that time there was a fascination on my part that introduced a certain mimeticism into my writing, which I think I have done away with now. So I have never been a 'disciple' of Derrida in the proper sense of the word.[47]

This is typical of the somewhat exasperated tone she has adopted in recent interviews, where she has been increasingly assertive of her independence from Derrida in the face of attempts – as in the above interview – to categorize her as 'a philosopher and a Derridean'.[48] 'I am troubled by your qualifier "Derridean",' Kofman responds, 'not because I want to hide my strong ties to Derrida – a real encounter – but because [...] [i]f I think "as a Derridean", just then I'm not thinking any more.'[49]

Unfortunately, despite her protestations, Kofman did rapidly become pigeon-holed as precisely such a 'Derridean' acolyte – even Andrew Benjamin feels obliged to preface the critical appreciation quoted at the beginning of this essay with: 'It must be said, of course, that the paper ['Beyond Aporia?'] is not a simple essay in applying Derrida's work to Platonic texts. Kofman is an important thinker in her own right.'[50] However, Kofman did not make things easy for herself in this respect by the adulatory tone of her reception of Derrida's paper to the 1972 Cerisy conference, for example,[51] by the 'mimeticism' in her writing – which is particularly evident in the period shortly after *Nietzsche and Metaphor*, in a piece such as her first essay on Derrida, 'Un philosophe "unheimlich"' (1973c) – or by her subsequent affiliation to various groups which were publicly perceived as very much Derrida-led.[52] What is more, for years after the 1969–70 session, Kofman continued to attend Derrida's rue d'Ulm seminar regularly and to present first versions of other works there: not just *Nietzsche et la métaphore*, but her next book, too – *Camera obscura* (1973a, cf. p.76, n.70), which is co-dedicated to Derrida – and, even as late as 1982, *Le respect des femmes* (1982a, cf. p.150, n.121). Kofman has always been generous in her recognition of the importance of Derrida's seminar, and apart from the occasions when she read versions of her works at it, there are further references to the seminar peppered throughout her published writings.[53]

To trace Kofman's divergence from Derrida one would probably have to begin with her resistance to Heidegger and her sustained attempt to 'de-Heideggerianize' Nietzsche,[54] though such an analysis falls outside the ambit of this essay. It is certainly the case that by 1969, when Kofman first met Derrida, he had established a leading position in French philosophy, even if his position in French Nietzscheanism was not consolidated until the publication of his first text specifically on Nietzsche, his paper to the Cerisy conference on 'La question du style'.[55] As we have seen, Derrida was using Nietzsche strategically in his published works as early as 1963, and in other key texts published through the 1960s he will continue to establish his brand of the nascent post-structuralism firmly under the sign of Nietzsche.[56] Concurrently he is also developing his investigation of the status of metaphor which will culminate in the 1969–70 seminar: the relation between the metaphorical and the 'proper' goes back in Derrida's writing at least as far as 'the metaphysics of a proper subjectivity' in 'La parole soufflée',[57] and 'originary metaphor' occupies an important place in the discussion in *Of Grammatology*.[58]

'White Mythology', Derrida's main text on metaphor, was published in 1971 in the same issue of *Poétique* as the first version of *Nietzsche and Metaphor*, and as with the 'Rhetoric and Language' notes in the same issue, Kofman had the opportunity to incorporate references to it into the final version of the book (cf. section III, n.3 and section V, n.3). What is more, given that 'White Mythology' is a kind of synopsis of the 1969–70 seminar, it is hardly surprising that *Nietzsche and Metaphor* should share a good many of its terms of reference and cite many of the same 'proper names'. So there is a common canon which emerged from Derrida's seminars and was adopted to a greater or lesser extent by those who attended them – including, of course, Derrida himself. In the cases of Artaud (cf. section II, n.7), Bataille (cf. section VI, n.7*) and in particular Rousseau, Kofman appears to be drawing on Derrida in *Nietzsche and Metaphor*, for although she goes on to subject Rousseau to her own searching analyses (1982a and 1985b) after this book, nevertheless at this stage she is still working with the Rousseau of *Of Grammatology*. Yet on the other hand the fact that the 'traffic' at Derrida's seminars was two-way can be judged at least in some measure from the scant and somewhat cryptic 'global' acknowledgement Derrida delivers at the outset of 'La question du style' to those (including Kofman, as a footnote makes clear) whose recent readings of Nietzsche provided the backdrop to his 'sally'.[59]

NIETZSCHE AND METAPHOR – AND BEYOND

In 'White Mythology', Derrida sketches out a vast history of 'metaphor in the text of philosophy', from Plato and Aristotle to Lenin, Heidegger, and Lacan, in the space of seventy-five pages. Nietzsche is marshalled along with all the rest in this 'mobile army' of proper names, with references to *Philosophy in the Tragic Age of the Greeks* and *Daybreak*, and two quotations from the essay which more than any other attracted the attention of the new French Nietzsche critics in the wake of Kremer-Marietti's 1969 translation, 'On Truth and Lies in a Nonmoral Sense'.

Kofman's focus in *Nietzsche and Metaphor* is deliberately more concentrated, and yet it is not merely this restriction in the object of her analysis which constitutes the specificity of her study – it is also the nature of her method, as the first section makes clear. Her aim is to give a 'faithfully' Nietzschean reading of Nietzsche – an appropriate appropriation – and one of the main results is that, for all the 'penetration' of Kofman's treatment, her overriding interest in the textuality of Nietzsche's writing requires a strategic, deconstructive indulgence in the 'surface' at the expense, specifically, of addressing Nietzsche's 'grand doctrines'. Whereas the eternal return, for example, had been one of the major preoccupations of the 1960s – in Deleuze's *Nietzsche and Philosophy*, and especially in the work of Klossowski[60] – it impinges hardly at all on *Nietzsche and Metaphor* (at the beginning of section III, section III, n.16, and the end of section VI), and the same holds true for the overman or *amor fati*. Kofman uses *Thus Spoke Zarathustra* here very sparingly indeed, and even will to power, interpreted as an heuristic principle of interpretation, does not make a full appearance until section V.

In return for the return, Kofman gives us the concept of metaphor – and the concept as metaphor – in a series of microtextual analyses. What is more, because her aim is 'to write conceptually in the knowledge that a concept has no greater value than a metaphor and is itself a condensate of metaphors', the polysemy of the concept and the originary nature of metaphor inevitably surface periodically in her own writing in the form of puns. Apart from presenting problems to the translator (documented as far as possible in the translator's notes), such language-play exemplifies the speciousness of the very distinction between the literal and the metaphorical – with the concomitant denigration and subordination of the latter – which Nietzsche himself is out to deconstruct. Kofman's play with the 'literal', 'proper', 'clean', 'appropriate' (etc.) meanings of the term 'propre' (see section II, n.5), for example, vitiates any use it might have within the binary oppositions of a rigid categorization.

On the other hand, pointing out the 'metaphorical' nature of the term 'metaphor' itself is such a rigorous *reductio* that the self-referential paradox which results is too unstable to be catered for by the establishment of 'the originary nature of metaphor'. As Kofman points out, with such a generalization of metaphor and effacement of its binary opposite – the strong claim in 'On Truth and Lies' (couched in metaphorical language) that all language is ultimately metaphorical – a need arises for a new terminology. Hence aporia is avoided when the strategic use of metaphor which she discerns in Nietzsche's early texts, where his philological preoccupations are still uppermost, gives way to more general notions of 'text' and 'interpretation', and ultimately to 'will to power'. Once she has sketched out these moments on Nietzsche's 'conceptual' itinerary, then, from section IV, which is largely based on a close reading of the 'On Truth and Lies' essay, Kofman fills out this developmental model and turns to a typology of the principal Nietzschean metaphors and their modulations. The argument culminates, typically, in the 'strategic' final footnote, where she stresses that Nietzsche is concerned not so much with inventing new metaphors as with revaluating and subverting some of the most traditional of philosophical tropes – the 'naked truth', knowledge as vision, the 'tree of knowledge', and so on.

After *Nietzsche and Metaphor*, the development of 'Sarah Kofman's Nietzsche' is rich and complex and can only be sketched in here. This first book, and the two other pieces, both published in 1973, which result from the same bout of intense engagement with Nietzsche's texts – 'Le/les "concepts" de culture dans les "Intempestives" de Nietzsche' (1973b) and the *Camera obscura* chapter on him (1973a) – are followed in 1975 by 'Baubô' (1975b), an analysis of the figure of woman in Nietzsche's writing. This study prefigures Kofman's later discussions of the question of woman in the texts of philosophy, psychoanalysis, and literature, and is reproduced as an annexe to her *Nietzsche et la scène philosophique* (1979b). Here, in a succession of essays which reflect her teaching and submit selected passages of

Nietzsche to particularly close readings, Kofman situates him in relation to 'the philosophical tradition' with which he himself was engaging. Starting with his revaluation of the '"Pre-Socratics"' (whom he prefers to call 'the ancient masters of Philosophy', as Kofman reminds us (p.17)), Kofman focuses on the ancient Greeks whilst ranging widely through Descartes, Spinoza, Pascal, Rousseau, Kant, Hegel, and Schopenhauer. This book marks a temporary quietus with Nietzsche, as Kofman's attention then switches predominantly to Freud and to 'the question of woman', but from 1986 she began producing a further series of studies on Nietzsche's relationship to specific figures: 'Nietzsche et l'obscurité d'Héraclite' (1986c), 'Les Socrate(s) de Nietzsche: "Qui" est Socrate?', in *Socrate(s)* (1989a), and latterly 'Nietzsche et Wagner' (1992c). With these, and especially with the two *Explosion* volumes (1992a and 1993a), Kofman has re-established her position at the very forefront of Nietzsche criticism.

'FREDDY'S BACK!'

The appearance of *Nietzsche et la métaphore* in translation is in many ways timely in its untimeliness. For the combination of circumstances which marked its original appearance in France is one which is being curiously reproduced in the English-speaking world only now, twenty years on – even down to the current vogue for Georges Bataille.[61] As far as Nietzsche's notebooks are concerned, we have had a selection in translation (including the *Philosophenbuch*) since Daniel Breazeale's *Philosophy and Truth* came out in 1979;[62] in 1983, Carole Blair published a translation of the same selection of early lecture notes as Lacoue-Labarthe and Nancy translated in 1971,[63] but an English translation of the full series did not appear till 1989.[64] Not only will an English translation of the Colli–Montinari edition begin appearing soon (with luck), but we now also have Heidegger's *Nietzsche* complete in English translation, though we had to wait till 1987 for the final volume.[65]

All this activity of translation and commentary is being reflected in what Richard Schacht calls 'a veritable explosion of interest in Nietzsche'.[66] To anyone familiar with the French scene around 1970, the story sounds strangely familiar, and his report continues: 'Nearly every major university and scholarly press has now published books dealing with him; and they are appearing at a rate that makes it difficult to keep up with them. [...] Prominent journals likewise are publishing articles on Nietzsche with growing frequency.' What is more, as in France the interest being shown in Nietzsche in the English-speaking world is not restricted to the pages of scholarly presses and journals. To quote Schacht again: 'Interest in Nietzsche is manifesting itself in an astonishing range of contexts these days',[67] and although the attention which is nowadays being paid to Nietzsche's music, for example, is new, the fictional treatments which have recently appeared[68] mirror the popularization which took place a generation ago in France.

The new British magazine *Philosophy Now* succinctly encapsulates the renewed interest in Nietzsche – as well as embodying it – with a recent cover which proclaims: 'Freddy's Back!'[69] Indeed the sense of urgency with which lost time is being made up is particularly noticeable in Britain, where the Friedrich Nietzsche Society was inaugurated in 1990 (the North American Nietzsche Society predating it by a decade). A notable feature of this renewed interest in Nietzsche in the English-speaking world, and particularly in Britain, is the erosion of resistance to 'the new Nietzsche'. For a long time 'Derrida's Nietzsche' (along with the pieces in *The New Nietzsche*) held sway as representative of the new interpretations issuing from France simply because other texts were yet to be translated; *Nietzsche and Metaphor*, and the other works which are now being translated, will at last allow English speakers to appreciate the sheer wealth of material which emerged in such an extraordinarily concentrated burst at that particular historical conjunction. It has taken the same

length of time for an English translation of Kofman's
Nietzsche and Metaphor to appear as it did for Deleuze's
Nietzsche and Philosophy. Perhaps in that light one should
see it as a good omen.

D.L.
Swansea
April 1993

NOTES

1 'Introduction', in *Post-structuralist Classics*, ed. by
  Andrew Benjamin (London and New York: Routledge,
  1988), p.4.
2 'Metaphor, Symbol, Metamorphosis', trans. by David
  B. Allison, in *The New Nietzsche: Contemporary Styles of
  Interpretation* (hereafter *TNN*), ed. by David B. Allison
  (New York: Dell, 1977; 2nd edn Cambridge, Mass. and
  London: MIT Press, 1985), pp.201–14.
3 Kofman relates the circumstances surrounding the
  translation in a recent interview: 'Cynthia Chase [...]
  attended one of my courses at the Sorbonne, on the
  enigma of woman in Freud's work. She and her
  husband, Jonathan Culler, had *L'Énigme de la femme*
  translated in the USA' ('Subvertir le philosophique *ou*
  Pour un supplément de jouissance' (1993b), p.17).
4 Favourable accounts are given by Alexander Nehamas
  (in *Nietzsche: Life as Literature* (Cambridge, Mass.:
  Harvard University Press, 1985), pp.15–17, 60, 72,
  124f.), Alan D. Schrift (in *Nietzsche and the Question of
  Interpretation: Between Hermeneutics and Deconstruction*
  (New York and London: Routledge, 1990), pp.85–94,
  166–68), and Andrzej Warminski (in *Readings in Inter-
  pretation* (Minneapolis: University of Minnesota Press,
  1987)). For less positive readings, cf. Maudemarie
  Clark, *Nietzsche on Truth and Philosophy* (Cambridge:
  Cambridge University Press, 1990), pp.15–18, and
  Richard H. Weisberg, 'De Man Missing Nietzsche', in

Nietzsche as Postmodernist: Essays Pro and Contra, ed. by Clayton Koelb (Albany: State University of New York Press, 1990), pp. 111–24 (pp. 112–20). For further discussions of French Nietzsche reception, cf. Rudolf Künzli, 'Nietzsche und die Semiologie: Neue Ansätze in der französischen Nietzsche-Interpretation', *Nietzsche-Studien*, 5 (1976), 263–88, and David Couzens Hoy, 'Philosophy as Rigorous Philology? Nietzsche and Poststructuralism', *New York Literary Forum*, 8–9 (1981), 171–85.

5 Martin Heidegger, *Nietzsche*, 2 vols (Pfullingen: Neske, 1961), and Gilles Deleuze, *Nietzsche et la philosophie* (Paris: P.U.F., 1962; 7th edn 1988) (English trans. by Hugh Tomlinson, *Nietzsche and Philosophy* (London: Athlone, 1983)).

6 Cf. *L'expérience intérieure* (Paris: Gallimard, 1943) and especially *Sur Nietzsche: volonté de chance* (Paris: Gallimard, 1945), which was republished in 1967. Bataille first read Nietzsche in 1922, and his pre-war writings, often with a strongly Nietzschean flavour, began to be republished in the late 1960s (cf. especially 'La "vieille taupe" et le préfixe *sur* dans les mots *surhomme* et *surréaliste*', which Kofman cites in *Nietzsche and Metaphor* and which was published in *Tel Quel*, 34 (Summer 1968) before being reprinted in the first volume of the *Œuvres complètes*, which began to appear in 1970 under the editorship of Denis Hollier). For Bataille's relationship to Nietzsche, cf. Bernard Sichère, 'Le "Nietzsche" de Georges Bataille', *Stanford French Review*, 12/1 (Spring 1988), 13–30, Takeshi Sakai, 'Bataille et Nietzsche', *Études de Langue et Littérature Françaises*, 54 (1989), 65–81, and Jean-François Pradeau, 'Bataille: l'expérience extatique', *Magazine littéraire*, 298 (April 1992: 'Les vies de Nietzsche') (hereafter *ML*), 67–69.

7 Cf. three essays in *L'entretien infini* (Paris: Gallimard, 1969, though apparently dating in part from a decade earlier (p. 202n.)): 'Nietzsche, aujourd'hui' (pp. 201–15),

'Passage de la ligne' (pp.215–27) and 'Nietzsche et l'écriture fragmentaire' (pp.227–55). Françoise Collin discusses 'Blanchot's Nietzsche' in 'Blanchot: le surhomme et le dernier homme' (in *ML*, 80–82).

8 Paris: 'Les cours de Sorbonne'. Cf. also: *L'avant-dernière pensée de Nietzsche* (Paris: C.D.U., 1961). Jean Wahl's greatest influence in publicizing Nietzsche was through the reviews of the most important German studies which he published in the early 1960s in the *Revue de métaphysique et de morale* (hereafter *RMM*), the journal he edited: 'Le cas Nietzsche', 66/3 (1961), 306–11 (review of 1960 trans. of Karl Schlechta, *Der Fall Nietzsche*); 'Le problème du temps chez Nietzsche', 66/4 (1961), 436–56 (review of Joan Stambaugh, *Untersuchungen zum Problem der Zeit bei Nietzsche*); 'Le Nietzsche de Fink', 67/4 (1962), 475–89 (review of Eugen Fink, *Nietzsches Philosophie*).

9 Monaco: Éditions du Rocher. Cf. also Geneviève Bianquis (ed.), *Nietzsche: Études et témoignages du cinquantenaire 1900–1950* (Paris: Flinker, 1950) and 'Pour une révision des écrits posthumes de Nietzsche', *RMM*, 67/1 (1962), 110–15. The 'grande dame' of French Nietzscheanism, Bianquis had been active since long before the war, with her translations and two important studies: *Nietzsche en France: L'influence de Nietzsche sur la pensée française* (Paris: Alcan, 1929) and *Nietzsche* (Paris: Rieder, 1933).

10 'Nietzsche, le polythéisme et la parodie', *RMM*, 63/2–3 (1958), 325–48 (republished in *Un si funeste désir* (Paris: Gallimard, 1963), pp.185–228), and 'Oubli et anamnèse dans l'expérience vécue de l'éternel retour du même', his presentation on the eternal return to the 'Colloque de Royaumont' in 1964 (see n.60, below). Deleuze cites Klossowski in *Différence et répétition* (Paris: P.U.F., 1968, p.81f., quoted in Schrift, *Nietzsche and the Question of Interpretation*, p.204, n.2); Klossowski returns the compliment by dedicating his major work

of Nietzsche criticism, *Nietzsche et le cercle vicieux* (Paris: Mercure de France, 1969; 2nd edn 1975), to Deleuze. Cf. Michel Balzamo, 'Klossowski et le "cas nietzsche"', *Revue des Sciences Humaines*, 50/197 (January–March 1985), 23–34, and Michel Onfray, 'Klossowski: un mystique chez l'antéchrist', in *ML*, 73–75.

11 François Ewald, in *ML*, 20. Cf. also François Zourabichvili, 'Deleuze: le négatif destitué', in *ML*, 85–87. Although this issue of the *Magazine littéraire* evidently intends to give the general reader an introduction to the most significant aspects of Nietzsche reception, and it concentrates on the situation in France, it unfortunately succeeds in omitting any reference to a great many of the best French writers on Nietzsche in the last twenty-five years. Thus not only Kofman, but the whole 'Philosophie en effet' group (Derrida, Kofman, Philippe Lacoue-Labarthe, and Jean-Luc Nancy) are conspicuous by their absence.

12 *Nietzsche et le christianisme* (German: f.p. 1946), trans. by Jeanne Hersch (Paris: Minuit, 1949), and *Nietzsche: Introduction à sa philosophie* (German: 1936), trans. by Henri Niel, with an introductory letter-preface by Jean Wahl (Paris: Gallimard, 1950). Cf. Fauzia Assaad-Mikhaïl, 'Jaspers interprète de Nietzsche', *RMM*, 71/3 (1966), 307–38.

13 The first post-war article on Nietzsche in the *RMM*, which appeared as late as 1956 and is entitled simply 'Nietzsche', is by Löwith (trans. by Claude Chabod, *RMM*, 61/3–4, 328–45). Cf. also 'Le concept de l'histoire chez Nietzsche', in *Les grands philosophes* (Paris: Lucien Mazenod, 1956), and *De Hegel à Nietzsche* (German: 1941), trans. by Rémi Laureillard (Paris: Gallimard, 1969). Löwith's main work, *Nietzsches Philosophie der ewigen Wiederkunft des Gleichen* (German: 1935), was only recently translated: *Nietzsche: philosophie de l'éternel retour du même*, trans. by Anne-Sophie Astrup (Paris: Calmann-Lévy, 1991).

14 Schlechta's three-volume German edition of Nietzsche
    was published in 1956 (Munich: Hanser) and is dis-
    cussed by Angèle Kremer-Marietti in her 'Nietzsche et
    quelques-uns de ses interprètes actuels' (*RMM*, 64/4
    (1959), 456–68). Schlechta's *Der Fall Nietzsche* (German:
    1958) came out rapidly in French translation as *Le cas
    Nietzsche* (trans. by André Cœuroy (Paris: Gallimard,
    1960)).

15 Martin Heidegger: 'Qui est le Zarathoustra de
    Nietzsche?' (German: 1954), in *Essais et conférences*
    (trans. by André Préau (Paris: Gallimard, 1958),
    pp.116–47), and 'Le mot de Nietzsche "Dieu est mort"'
    (German: 1949), in *Chemins qui ne mènent nulle part*
    (trans. by Wolfgang Brokmeier (Paris: Gallimard,
    1962), pp.253–322).

    The impact of the 'Freiburg Nietzsche' of Heidegger
    and his disciple Eugen Fink (who lectured in Freiburg
    with Heidegger, 1946–71) continued to be felt through-
    out the period of the 1960s and early 1970s. Fink's
    Nietzsches Philosophie was published in German in 1960
    (Stuttgart: Kohlhammer), reviewed by Jean Wahl in
    1962 (see n.8, above) and published in French transla-
    tion (by H. Hildenbrand and A. Lindenberg) in 1965
    (Paris: Minuit), in which form it proved if anything
    more influential than in German. Heidegger's 1936–40
    lectures on Nietzsche, published in German in 1961,
    again had an impact on the French scene early, even
    before they appeared in Klossowski's French transla-
    tion in 1971 (*Nietzsche*, 2 vols (Paris: Seuil)). Cf. Jean
    Beaufret, 'Heidegger et Nietzsche: le concept de val-
    eur', in *Nietzsche*, ed. by Gilles Deleuze (Paris: Minuit
    ('Cahiers de Royaumont'), 1967), pp.245–64), Fauzia
    Assaad-Mikhaïl, 'Heidegger interprète de Nietzsche',
    RMM, 73/1 (1968), 16–55, and Michel Haar, 'Heideg-
    ger: une lecture ambivalente', in *ML*, 94–96. Jean
    Granier's *Le problème de la vérité dans la philosophie de
    Nietzsche* (Paris: Seuil, 1966; 2nd edn 1969) uses many

Heideggerian formulations, as Kofman points out (see Appendix).

16 'Nietzsche et la philosophie', *RMM*, 68/3 (1963), 352–79 (p.352).

17 Kofman quotes this Deleuzian line with approval in the foreword to *Nietzsche et la scène philosophique* (p.7).

18 For further discussion of 'Deleuze's Nietzsche', cf. James A. Leigh, 'Deleuze, Nietzsche, and the Eternal Return', *Philosophy Today* (Fall 1978), 206–23, Vincent P. Pecora, 'Deleuze's Nietzsche and Post-Structuralist Thought', *SubStance*, 48 (1986), 34–50, Steven Best and Douglas Kellner, 'Deleuze's Nietzsche', in *Postmodern Theory: Critical Investigations* (Basingstoke and London: Macmillan, 1991), pp.79–85, Ronald Bogue, 'Deleuze's Nietzsche: Thought, will to power, and the eternal return', in *Deleuze and Guattari* (London and New York: Routledge, 1989), pp.15–34, and especially Michael Hardt, 'Nietzschean Ethics: From Efficient Power to an Ethics of Affirmation', in *Gilles Deleuze: An Apprenticeship in Philosophy* (London: UCL Press, 1993), pp.26–55.

19 *The Logic of Sense* (section VI, n.12) and *Expressionism in Philosophy: Spinoza* (section V, n.23). Cf. also the extra reference to *The Fold: Leibniz and the Baroque* (section VI, n.4).

20 'Force and Signification', in *Writing and Difference*, trans. by Alan Bass (Chicago: University of Chicago Press; London: Routledge and Kegan Paul, 1978), pp.3–30.

21 Gilles Deleuze, *Nietzsche* (Paris: P.U.F., 1965; 2nd edn 1968; 8th edn 1988); 'Renverser le platonisme (Les simulacres)', *RMM*, 71/4 (1966), 426–38.

22 The proceedings were later published as *Nietzsche*, ed. by Gilles Deleuze (Paris: Minuit ('Cahiers de Royaumont'), 1967) (hereafter *CR*).

23 'État des textes de Nietzsche' (trans. by H. Hildenbrand and A. Lindenberg), in *CR*, 127–40.

24 *Nietzsche: Werke Kritische Gesamtausgabe*, 30 vols (Berlin and New York: De Gruyter, 1967–   ).

25 Foucault was succeeded in 1970 by Maurice de Gandillac.

26 *The Gay Science* was followed in 1968 by *Human, All Too Human* (with fragments), in 1970 by *Daybreak* (with fragments), and in 1971 by *Beyond Good and Evil* with *On the Genealogy of Morals*; *Thus Spoke Zarathustra* appeared in 1972. In 1977 the edition was relaunched as Nietzsche's 'Œuvres complètes', with a new translation of *The Birth of Tragedy* (with fragments) by Lacoue-Labarthe, Michel Haar, and Nancy.

27 A number of major Parisian publishers were bringing Nietzsche out in their paperback series during this period: they included Aubier–Flammarion ('Bilingue'), U.G.E. ('10/18'), Denoël–Gonthier ('Médiations'), and latterly Le Livre de Poche. Particularly worthy of mention here are the titles published in Gallimard's popular 'Idées' series: Bianquis's translations of *Philosophy in the Tragic Age of the Greeks* (1969) and *The Birth of Tragedy* (1970) joined Vialatte's *The Gay Science* (1964) and Albert's *On the Genealogy of Morals* (1967); de Gandillac's *Thus Spoke Zarathustra* followed in 1972.

28 Luc Ferry and Alain Renaut, *French Philosophy of the 60s: An Essay on Antihumanism*, trans. by Mary H. Cattani (Amherst: University of Massachusetts Press, 1990).

29 *CR*, pp.183–92; trans. by Alan D. Schrift, in *Transforming the Hermeneutic Context: From Nietzsche to Nancy*, ed. by Gayle L. Ormiston and Alan D. Schrift (Albany: State University of New York Press, 1990), pp.59–67. The only other piece Foucault published directly on Nietzsche was 'Nietzsche, la généalogie, l'histoire', in *Hommage à Jean Hyppolite* (Paris: P.U.F., 1971), pp.145–72 (trans. by Donald F. Bouchard and Sherry Simon as 'Nietzsche, Genealogy, History', in Michel Foucault, *Language, Counter-Memory, Practice: Selected Essays and Interviews*, ed. by Donald F. Bouchard (Oxford: Blackwell, 1977), pp.139–64. Cf. Judith Revel, 'Foucault: l'apprentissage de la déprise', in *ML*, 83–85.

30 *Freud and Philosophy: An Essay on Interpretation*, trans. by Denis Savage (New Haven and London: Yale University Press, 1970), p.33. David Brett-Evans prefers the term 'Makers of the Twentieth Century': cf. *Makers of the Twentieth Century: Marx, Nietzsche, Freud*, ed. by David Brett-Evans (Englewood Cliffs, NJ: Prentice-Hall, 1968).

31 'Nietzsche, Freud, Marx', in *Transforming the Hermeneutic Context*, p.67.

32 *Les mots et les choses* (Paris: Gallimard, 1966), trans. by Alan Sheridan-Smith as *The Order of Things: An Archaeology of the Human Sciences* (London: Tavistock, 1970), p.305, quoted in Schrift, *Nietzsche and the Question of Interpretation*, p.205, n.13.

33 Jean-Michel Rey quotes this last phrase in his *L'enjeu des signes* (Paris: Seuil, 1971, p.32, n.15) as an indication that 'G. Deleuze is one of the few Nietzschean commentators to place the emphasis on linguistics, which he quite rightly calls "active"'. The characterization of philosophy as a 'symptomatology' and a 'semiology' or 'semiotics' is one which Kofman, also following Deleuze, repeatedly stresses (cf. section IV, n.3; section V, p.87).

34 'Rhétorique et langage', in *Poétique*, 5, 99–142. Cf. section III, n.15★.

35 Charles Andler's definitive *Nietzsche: sa vie et sa pensée* had been reissued in 1958 (2nd edn, 3 vols (Paris: Gallimard)), but the major new contribution was Georges Morel's three-volume *Nietzsche: Introduction à une première lecture* (Paris: Montaigne, 1970–71). Lou Andreas-Salomé's biography – which Wahl referred to with approval in his 1963 review of *Nietzsche and Philosophy* ('Nietzsche et la philosophie', p.352) – also appeared in French translation in 1971, as *Frédéric Nietzsche* (London and New York: Gordon and Breach, 1971). Daniel Halévy's *Nietzsche* was not reissued until 1977 (Paris: Grasset).

36 *Bulletin de la société française de philosophie*, 4 (1969: 'Nietzsche et ses interprètes'), *Poétique*, 5 (1971: 'Rhétorique et philosophie'), *Revue Philosophique*, 96 (1971/3: 'Nietzsche'), and *Critique*, 313 (1973: 'Lectures de Nietzsche').

37 *Nietzsche sera content*, a novel by Jacques Neubourg (Paris: Calmann-Lévy, 1968).

38 *Ainsi parlait Zarathoustra, adaptation pour la scène de Jean-Louis Barrault*, trans. by Arthur Goldschmidt (Paris: Gallimard, 1975).

39 The proceedings were published as *Nietzsche aujourd'hui?*, 2 vols (Paris: U.G.E. ('10/18'), 1973) (hereafter *NAH*).

40 Boudot had been publishing on Nietzsche through the 1960s ('Nietzsche et Valéry', *Revue des Lettres Modernes*, 76/77 (1962/63), 57–62; 'Nietzsche et la volonté de puissance', *Les Temps Modernes*, 20/225 (February 1965), 1493–1506), but his books came in a flurry from 1970: *Nietzsche et l'au-delà de la liberté* (Paris: Montaigne, 1970; 2nd edn (as *Nietzsche et les écrivains français: 1930 à 1960*) Paris: Aubier-Montaigne ('10/18'), 1975), *L'ontologie de Nietzsche* (Paris: P.U.F., 1971), and *Nietzsche en miettes* (Paris: P.U.F., 1973).

41 'Subvertir le philosophique', p.19f.

42 *Anti-Oedipus*, trans. by Robert Hurley, Mark Seem, and Helen R. Lane (Minneapolis: University of Minnesota Press, 1977); *Libidinal Economy*, trans. by Iain Hamilton Grant (London: Athlone, 1993). Cf. also Lyotard's 'Notes sur le Retour et le Kapital', in *NAH*, I, 141–57 (trans. by Roger McKeon as 'Notes on the Return and Kapital', in *Semiotext(e)*, 3/1 (1978), 44–53). Other critics of the period exploring the Nietzsche-Marx link include Paul Valadier (*Essais sur la modernité: Nietzsche et Marx* (Paris: Éditions du Cerf, 1974)) and Henri Lefèbvre (*Hegel-Marx-Nietzsche, ou le royaume des ombres* (Tournai-Paris: Casterman, 1975)).

43 'Nietzsche's text can be read in parallel with the other great texts of modernity, those of Freud (the closeness

of which we are attempting to demonstrate) and Marx (the exemplary rigour of which is marked by the important work of L. Althusser). What the three perhaps have in common is a mode of *reading*, a certain plunging into the thick of signs which inscribes these texts (with all their differences) outside a theological space, the limits of which they themselves *circumscribe*' (*L'enjeu des signes*, p.29, n.12).

44 Rey's *Parcours de Freud* appeared in 1974 (Paris: Galilée), though already in *L'enjeu des signes* – especially in chapter 5 ('Texte, symptôme et généalogie', pp.152–217) – he presents a powerful comparison between Nietzsche and Freud. For further analysis of the relation between Nietzsche and Freud, cf. also Édouard Gaède, 'Nietzsche précurseur de Freud?', in *NAH*, II, 87–113, Louis Corman, 'Nietzsche précurseur de Freud', in *Nietzsche: psychologue des profondeurs* (Paris: P.U.F., 1982), pp.206–27, and Paul-Laurent Assoun, *Freud et Nietzsche* (Paris: P.U.F., 1982) and 'L'héritage de la psychanalyse', in *ML*, 99–101.

45 'The concept of culture' was not lost sight of: it is the subject of Kofman's contribution to the 'Nietzsche aujourd'hui?' conference: 'Le/les "concepts" de culture dans les "Intempestives" ou la double dissimulation' (1973b).

46 In a recent interview, Kofman defines her position after rejecting the questioner's attempt to attribute her to a 'school': 'In fact I detest this notion of a school; one should rather speak of the people I feel closest to, like the "Philosophie en effet" group, to which one would have to add Blanchot [...]. As for Freud and Nietzsche (on whom I have worked most constantly), these are my two "great" thinkers: both of them have left a profound impression on me, and they have given me the most, from a philosophical and psychological point of view. But they are not masters. I prevent Freud from gaining mastery through Nietzsche, and I prevent

Nietzsche from gaining mastery through Freud. I deconstruct the one with the other. I have no master – that is extremely important.' ('Subvertir le philosophique', p.12). Cf. also 'La question des femmes: une impasse pour les philosophes' (1992b): 'My method of reading draws on Freud and Nietzsche, but it does not leave these two authors intact – neither of them really has the last word, since I play the one off against the other' (p.66).

47 'Sarah Kofman' (1991f), p.108.

48 ibid., p.111.

49 The phrase 'a real encounter' ('une véritable rencontre') is evidently Kofman's preferred designation: cf. 'Subvertir le philosophique', p.11: 'there was a real encounter with him [Derrida], in the way in which I worked and in which he worked'.

50 *Post-structuralist Classics*, loc. cit.

51 'I wanted firstly to thank Jacques Derrida for having given such a fine paper. He spoke with really supreme authority, and there is nothing to say after him' (*NAH*, I, 288).

52 The extent to which the 'Philosophie en effet' group and later the 'Groupe de Recherches sur l'Enseignement Philosophique', and their publications, were regarded as vehicles for Derrida can be seen from the introduction to the (group) interview published in *La Quinzaine Littéraire* in 1976 (1976c) on the book which more than any other established the 'Philosophie en effet' group as a group, *Mimesis des articulations* (Paris: Aubier-Flammarion ('La philosophie en effet'), 1975). Here, initially, it sounds for all the world as if the book were by Derrida alone: '*La Quinzaine Littéraire* has reviewed Jacques Derrida's texts [...] on several occasions, but it has never yet organized a round-table discussion on any of them. It has chosen to do so to correspond with the appearance of a collective work: *Mimesis des articulations*' (p.19).

53 For example: 'Un philosophe "unheimlich"' (1973c),
p.148, n.3, and 'Beyond Aporia?' (1983a), p.43f., n.20.
The piece by Rodolphe Gasché on Bataille ('L'avorton
de la pensée') which Kofman cites in *Nietzsche and
Metaphor* (section VI, n.7) was also presented in a first
version to Derrida's 1969–70 seminar, as was Bernard
Pautrat's *Versions du soleil: Figures et système de Nietzsche*
(Paris: Seuil, 1971, cf. p.10, n.1).

54 Cf. section V, n.17. On the term 'deconstruct', for
example, she remarks: 'For my part, I'm not borrowing
that word from Derrida, who borrowed it from
Heidegger, but from Nietzsche' ('Sarah Kofman',
p.112).

55 *NAH*, I, 235–87, later reworked and published sepa-
rately as *Éperons: Les styles de Nietzsche* (Paris: Flam-
marion, 1978), trans. by Barbara Harlow as *Spurs:
Nietzsche's Styles/Éperons: Les Styles de Nietzsche* (Chi-
cago and London: University of Chicago Press, 1979).
Derrida has since published only two other pieces on
Nietzsche: 'Otobiographies: The Teaching of
Nietzsche and the Politics of the Proper Name' (in *The
Ear of the Other: Otobiography, Transference, Translation.
Texts and Discussions with Jacques Derrida*, ed. by Christie
V. McDonald, trans. by Avital Ronell (New York:
Schocken, 1985), and 'Interpreting Signatures
(Nietzsche/Heidegger): Two Questions' (trans. by
Diane Michelfelder and Richard E. Palmer, in *Looking
After Nietzsche*, ed. by Laurence A. Rickels (Albany:
State University of New York Press, 1990), pp.1–17).

56 As far as other texts published in *Writing and Difference*
are concerned: Nietzsche surfaces again in 'La parole
soufflée' (1965, p.184), 'The Theater of Cruelty and the
Closure of Representation' (1966, pp.232–50 (*passim*)),
and in the celebrated conclusion to 'Structure, Sign, and
Play in the Discourse of the Human Sciences' (1966,
p.292). In *Of Grammatology* (trans. by Gayatri
Chakravorty Spivak (Baltimore and London: Johns

Hopkins University Press, 1976)), the emblematic
epigraph to the first chapter is from Nietzsche:
'Socrates, he who does not write' (1967, p.6; cf. p.19).
In those texts later collected in *Margins of Philosophy*
(trans. by Alan Bass (Brighton: Harvester, 1982)):
'Differance' quotes Deleuze's *Nietzsche and Philosophy*
on force in Nietzsche (1968, p.17), 'The Ends of Man'
discusses Nietzsche's conception of the last man (1968,
p.135f.), and 'The Supplement of Copula: Philosophy
before Linguistics' (1971, pp.177–79) quotes from the
Philosophenbuch, 'On Truth and Lies in a Nonmoral
Sense', and *La volonté de puissance*. For further discussion of Derrida's relation to Nietzsche, cf. Ernst
Behler, *Derrida-Nietzsche – Nietzsche-Derrida* (Munich,
Paderborn, Vienna, Zurich: Schöningh, 1988).

57 *Writing and Difference*, p.183.
58 *Of Grammatology*, pp.270–80.
59 It is difficult to avoid reading these elliptical-paraliptical
remarks as other than disingenuous: 'what I shall put
forth here is already a part of that space which certain
readings, in launching a new phase in the process of
deconstructive (i.e. affirmative) interpretation, have
demarcated during the last two years. I owe these
readings a great debt and it is neither through omission
nor in a spirit of presumptuous independence that I do
not refer to them individually (not even to *Versions du
soleil* which provided the title for this text). But,
because they have opened up that problematic field to
the very margin in which (aside from those moments
when I deviate from it) I shall remain, that debt itself
should not be fragmented here, but at each moment
presupposed in its totality' (*Spurs/Éperons*, p.37). The
footnote reveals: 'The "authors" of these works (Sarah
Kofman, Philippe Lacoue-Labarthe, Bernard Pautrat,
Jean-Michel Rey) were present at that lecture' (p.146).
The convenience of this strategy – which capitalizes on
'the death of the author' so as to dispatch the authors –

contrasts markedly with Kofman's more candid recognition of her indebtedness the other way around. A
footnote in 'Le facteur de la vérité' (*The Post Card: From
Socrates to Freud and Beyond*, trans. by Alan Bass
(Chicago and London: Chicago University Press,
1987), pp.411–96) shows Derrida to be rather less coy in
acknowledging Kofman's work on Freud, at least: 'As
concerns Freud, I refer throughout to the works of
Sarah Kofman' (p.420, n.4).

60 Cf. especially his paper to the Royaumont conference:
'Oubli et anamnèse dans l'expérience vécue de l'éternel
retour du même' (*CR*, pp.227–35), included in *Nietzsche
et le cercle vicieux* (pp.93–103) and subsequently re-
excerpted in *TNN* as 'Nietzsche's Experience of the
Eternal Return' (pp.107–20).

61 Cf. *Georges Bataille: Visions of Excess. Selected Writings,
1927–1939*, ed. by Allan Stoekl, trans. by Allan Stoekl,
Carl R. Lovitt, and Donald M. Leslie, Jr (Minneapolis:
University of Minnesota Press, 1983; Manchester:
Manchester University Press, 1985). After almost fifty
years, Bataille's *On Nietzsche* has also recently been
published at last in English translation (trans. by Bruce
Boone (London: Athlone, 1992)). As far as critical
studies are concerned, recent works include Stoekl's
own *Politics, Writing, Mutilation: The Cases of Bataille,
Blanchot, Roussel, Leiris and Ponge* (Minneapolis: University of Minnesota Press, 1985) and *On Bataille* (New
Haven: Yale University Press, 1990), and, most
recently, Nick Land's *Thirst for Annihilation: Georges
Bataille and Virulent Nihilism* (London: Routledge,
1992).

62 *Philosophy and Truth: Selections from Nietzsche's Note-
books of the early 1870's*, trans. and ed. by Daniel
Breazeale (Atlantic Highlands, NJ: Humanities Press;
Hassocks: Harvester, 1979).

63 'Nietzsche's Lecture Notes on Rhetoric: A Translation',
Philosophy and Rhetoric, 16/2 (1983), 94–129.

64 *Friedrich Nietzsche on Rhetoric and Language*, ed. and trans. by Sander L. Gilman, Carole Blair, and David J. Parent (Oxford and New York: Oxford University Press, 1989).

65 *Nietzsche*, trans. by David Farrell Krell, 4 vols (New York: Harper and Row, 1979–87).

66 *Nietzsche News*, 7 (Spring 1991), p.1.

67 *Nietzsche News*, 10 (Spring 1992), p.1.

68 Sebastian Barker's epic poem *The Dream of Intelligence* (Todmorden: Littlewood Arc, 1992), Irvin D. Yalom's *When Nietzsche Wept: A Novel of Obsession* (New York: Basic Books, 1992), and Daniel Weissbort's *Nietzsche's Attaché Case* (Manchester: Carcanet, 1993).

69 *Philosophy Now*, 5 (Spring 1993).

Translator's Note

To translate, to open up a path through a language by using its resources, to decide upon *one* meaning, is to escape the agonizing, aporetic impasses of any translation, to make the philosophical gesture *par excellence*: the gesture of betrayal. ('Beyond Aporia?')

The text on which this translation is based is that of the second edition of *Nietzsche et la métaphore* (Paris: Galilée ('Débats'), 1983). The six extra endnotes which Sarah Kofman had added to that edition have now been incorporated into the main text at the appropriate places, as have the eighteen further notes which the author has added for this new translated edition. The majority of the works to which Kofman refers are now available in English (with the notable exception of the Jean Granier book which is discussed in the Appendix), and references have thus been given to these English translations.

Where possible, all Nietzsche passages have been quoted from the most standard English translations, with occasional modifications in the interest of consistency. The origins of the second and third sections of *Nietzsche and Metaphor* lie in a review by Kofman of French translations of Nietzsche's early works *The Birth of Tragedy* and *Philosophy in the Tragic Age of the Greeks*, and although these works have been translated, in each case the French edition contained other early essays and fragments which Kofman uses, and which have been traced back to and translated from the original German. The same applies to the other main group of unpublished and untranslated notes, those published in French translation as *La volonté de puissance*, in the two-volume Friedrich Würzbach selection (1935 and

1937) from volumes XI–XVI of the 'Grossoktavausgabe' of Nietzsche's works. Volumes XV and XVI correspond to *The Will to Power*, and have been quoted from Hollingdale and Kaufmann's edition; the rest have been translated from the German. The 'Grossoktavausgabe' has been used because the Colli-Montinari 'Kritische Gesamtausgabe' is still incomplete, although the latter has been used and translated from in the few places where Kofman refers to it. As a result, the only Nietzsche passages which have unfortunately had to be translated from the French are the notes on 'Rhetoric and Language', and the passages in the Appendix from Henri-Jean Bolle's edition of *Œuvres Posthumes*, which are for all practical purposes untraceable.

I have felt obliged to retain Kofman's (and Nietzsche's) use of masculine pronouns in referring throughout to 'the philosopher', 'the author', 'the reader', and so on. I have added translator's notes in order both to account for the translation of any words which are particularly intractable, and to cross-reference either within the present work, or to other more recent works of Kofman's (beyond those to which she herself refers in her additional notes), or to works by other critics. Foremost among the latter is Jacques Derrida – the question of Kofman's relation to Derrida is addressed in the Translator's Introduction.

I should like to thank the author for her invaluable help in the preparation of this translation, and particularly in the compilation of the bibliography. Thanks are also due to René Bosch, Brigid Haines, Christina Howells, Jim Reed, Sheila Watts, and especially Steve Giles, in response to whose invitation a first version of the Translator's Introduction was presented as a paper to the Nottingham Critical Theory Seminar.

Abbreviations

1 EDITIONS OF NIETZSCHE'S WORKS

AC: *The Antichrist*, in *Twilight of the Idols and The Antichrist*, trans. by R.J. Hollingdale (Harmondsworth: Penguin, 1968)

APO: 'Additional Plans and Outlines', in *Philosophy and Truth: Selections from Nietzsche's Notebooks of the early 1870's*, trans. and ed. by Daniel Breazeale (Atlantic Highlands, NJ: Humanities Press; Hassocks: Harvester, 1979), pp.149–65

BGE: *Beyond Good and Evil*, trans. by R.J. Hollingdale (Harmondsworth: Penguin, 1973)

BT: *The Birth of Tragedy*, in *The Birth of Tragedy and the Case of Wagner*, trans. by Walter Kaufmann (New York: Vintage, 1967)

CP: 'Einleitung in das Studium der classischen Philologie', in GOA XVII, 327–52

CW: *The Case of Wagner*, in *The Birth of Tragedy and the Case of Wagner*; see BT

DAR: 'Description of Ancient Rhetoric', in *Friedrich Nietzsche on Rhetoric and Language*, ed. and trans. by Sander L. Gilman, Carole Blair, and David J. Parent (Oxford and New York: Oxford University Press, 1989)

DW: 'Die dionysische Weltanschauung', in GOA IX, 85–99

EH: *Ecce Homo*, trans. by R.J. Hollingdale (Harmondsworth: Penguin, 1979)

GM: *On the Genealogy of Morals*, in *On the Genealogy of Morals and Ecce Homo*, trans. by Walter Kaufmann (New York: Vintage, 1969)

GMD: 'Das griechische Musikdrama', in GOA IX, 33–52

GOA: *Nietzsche's Werke* ('Grossoktavausgabe'), 19 vols (Leipzig: Naumann; Kröner, 1901–13)

GS: *The Gay Science, With a Prelude in Rhymes and Appendix of Songs*, trans. by Walter Kaufmann (New York: Vintage, 1974)

HH: *Human, All Too Human*, trans. by R.J. Hollingdale (Cambridge: Cambridge University Press, 1986)

KGB: *Nietzsche: Briefwechsel Kritische Gesamtausgabe*, ed. by Giorgio Colli and Mazzino Montinari, 16 vols (Berlin and New York: De Gruyter, 1975–84)

KGW: *Nietzsche: Werke Kritische Gesamtausgabe*, ed. by Giorgio Colli and Mazzino Montinari, 30 vols (Berlin and New York: De Gruyter, 1967-   )

MW: 'Über Musik und Wort', in GOA IX, 212–29

NCW: *Nietzsche contra Wagner*, in *The Portable Nietzsche*, ed. and trans. by Walter Kaufmann (New York: Viking, 1954)

NF: 'Nachgelassene Fragmente' from the time of *Human, All Too Human* (1876–1878), Notebooks 16–26, in KGW IV$_2$, 381–582

OP: *Œuvres Posthumes*, trans. by Henri-Jean Bolle, 2nd edn (Paris: Mercure de France, 1934)

P: 'The Philosopher: Reflections on the Struggle between Art and Knowledge', in *Philosophy and Truth*, pp.3–58; see APO

PTG: *Philosophy in the Tragic Age of the Greeks*, trans. by Marianne Cowan (Chicago: Gateway, 1962)

SL: *Selected Letters of Friedrich Nietzsche*, trans. and ed. by Christopher Middleton (Chicago: University of Chicago Press, 1969)

ST: 'Sokrates und die Tragödie', in GOA IX, 53–59

SW: 'The Struggle between Science and Wisdom', in *Philosophy and Truth*, pp.127–46; see APO

TI: *Twilight of the Idols*, in *Twilight of the Idols and The Antichrist*; see AC

TL: 'On Truth and Lies in a Nonmoral Sense', in *Philosophy and Truth*, pp.79–97; see APO

UM: *Untimely Meditations*, trans. by R.J. Hollingdale (Cambridge: Cambridge University Press, 1983)

WP: *The Will to Power*, trans. by Walter Kaufmann and R.J. Hollingdale, ed. by Walter Kaufmann (London: Weidenfeld and Nicolson, 1968)

WS: *The Wanderer and his Shadow* (*Human, All Too Human*, part II, section 2); see HH

Z: *Thus Spoke Zarathustra*, trans. by R.J. Hollingdale (Harmondsworth: Penguin, 1961)

2 EDITIONS OF OTHER WORKS

SE: *The Standard Edition of the Complete Psychological Works of Sigmund Freud*, trans. and ed. by James Strachey, 24 vols (London: Hogarth Press and Institute of Psycho-Analysis, 1953–66)

VE: *Georges Bataille: Visions of Excess. Selected Writings, 1927–1939*, ed. by Allan Stoekl, trans. by Allan Stoekl, Carl R. Lovitt, and Donald M. Leslie, Jr (Minneapolis: University of Minnesota Press, 1983; Manchester: Manchester University Press ('Theory and History of Literature', 14), 1985)

Translator's
Acknowledgements

The translator would like to thank the following publishers for giving permission to quote from copyright
material: Cambridge University Press (*Human, All Too
Human*, by Friedrich Nietzsche, translated by R.J. Hollingdale, 1986); Humanities Press International, Inc.,
Atlantic Highlands, NJ (*Philosophy and Truth: Selections
from Nietzsche's Notebooks of the early 1870's*, translated
and edited by Daniel Breazeale, 1979); Penguin Books
Ltd (*Beyond Good and Evil*, by Friedrich Nietzsche,
translated by R.J. Hollingdale (Penguin Classics 1973,
revised edition 1990. Translation copyright © R.J.
Hollingdale, 1973, 1990. Reproduced by permission of
Penguin Books Ltd); Random House, Inc. (*The Gay
Science*, by Friedrich Nietzsche, translated by Walter
Kaufmann. Copyright © 1974 by Random House, Inc.
Reprinted by permission of Random House, Inc.; *On the
Genealogy of Morals*, by Friedrich Nietzsche, translated by
Walter Kaufmann. Copyright © 1974 by Random
House, Inc. Reprinted by permission of Random House,
Inc.).

I

An Unheard-of¹ and Insolent Philosophy

The speaker has already *vulgarized* himself by speaking. – From a moral code for deaf-mutes and other philosophers. (TI, 'Expeditions of an Untimely Man', 26)

Writing on Nietzsche presents a difficulty, made that much greater by writing on metaphor. If one speaks conceptually of Nietzsche's uncategorizable text, does that not mean reducing it to the most traditional of philosophical categories? Is it not paradoxical to make use of concepts in writing on a philosopher who privileges metaphor? But to be faithful to Nietzsche must one adopt a metaphorical 'style' which would signify that philosophy and poetry are not contradictory and that 'mathematical expression is not a part of the essence of philosophy' (P 53)? That would still be a betrayal of Nietzsche, for whom philosophy, if it is not science, is not poetry either. Philosophy is impossible to classify under any of the existing headings, and it calls for the invention of a new and original type of writing, one which is irreducible to any other: 'Great dilemma: is philosophy an art or a science? Both in its purposes and its results it is an art. But it uses the same means as science – conceptual representation. Philosophy is a form of artistic invention. There is no appropriate category for philosophy; consequently, we must make up and characterize a species for it' (P 53).

There is no *one* philosophical method, no *one* path to follow which has been marked out since time immemorial, or even by Nietzsche, and which we in turn are meant to take:

> I came to my truth by diverse paths and in diverse ways: it was not upon a single ladder that I climbed to the height where my eyes survey my distances.
>
> And I have asked the way only unwillingly – that has always offended my taste! I have rather questioned and attempted the ways themselves.
>
> All my progress has been an attempting and a questioning – and truly, one has to *learn* how to answer such questioning! That however – is to my taste:
>
> not good taste, not bad taste, but *my* taste, which I no longer conceal and of which I am no longer ashamed.
>
> 'This – is now *my* way: where is yours?' Thus I answered those who asked me 'the way'. For *the* way – does not exist!
>
> Thus spoke Zarathustra. (Z III, 'Of the Spirit of Gravity')

So being faithful to Nietzsche does not mean doing as he does, writing as he does. This would be an impossible task, one which would imply the existence of an absolute norm of 'good taste' and good style, an imperative which everyone would have to obey. Just as he multiplies perspectives, so Nietzsche intentionally diversifies his styles in order to save the reader from misunderstanding a single style as a 'style in itself': 'Good style *in itself* – a piece of pure folly, mere "idealism", on a par with the "beautiful *in itself*", the "good *in itself*", the "thing *in itself*" [...]. Considering that the multiplicity of inner states is in my case extraordinary, there exists in my case the possibility of many styles – altogether the most manifold art of style any man has ever had at his disposal' (EH, 'Why I Write Such Excellent Books', 4). A 'good' style is one which can communicate through signs a certain 'inner state' symptomatic of a certain taste (such a communication presupposing a listener or a reader with the same taste). All style

reiterates a primary writing, that of the 'drives'.[2] Thus it is
as vain to seek to impose a canonical model on writing as it
is futile to seek to legislate universally in morality: each *must*
do only what he *can*.

It seems to me more Nietzschean to write conceptually in
the knowledge that a concept has no greater value than a
metaphor and is itself a condensate of metaphors, to write
while opening up one's writing to a genealogical decipherment, than to write metaphorically while denigrating the
concept and proposing metaphor as the norm. Tyranny is
reprehensible in all its forms, including that of any
philosopher seeking to raise his spontaneous evaluation to
the status of an absolute value and his style to that of a
philosophical style 'in itself', opposed to poetic style 'in
itself' like truth opposed to untruth, good to evil. But the
tyranny of anyone seeking simply to invert the terms and
commend the value of metaphor alone is equally reprehensible: he remains ensnared in the same system of thought as
the metaphysician. Whether writing is conceptual or metaphorical (and since Nietzsche the opposition has hardly
applied any longer), the essential thing is to be able to laugh
at it, to be at enough of a distance from it to make fun of it.

To make fun of writing but also to make fun with it:[3] an
art which implies knowing 'what can be done with
language as such' (EH, 'Why I Write Such Excellent
Books', 4) by 'scattering to the four winds' means and
methods which are unheard-of and subversive. An art of
waste, an art of grand style which invites the philosopher to
abandon his reserve, and by means of which Nietzsche
imagines he 'flew a thousand miles beyond that which has
hitherto been called poesy' (ibid.). Yet despite this subversion of language one still runs the risk of being understood,
of being heard, misheard,[4] translated into another language: the game of writing, for Nietzsche, remains
subordinate to a new art of interpreting the world, the
communication of a new perspective. It is part of this new
philosophy which looks for followers (in this respect

Nietzsche remains a true philosopher), which wants to recruit enthusiasts by attracting them on to 'new secret paths and dancing places' (BT, 'Attempt at a Self-Criticism', 3). But how is it possible to communicate 'personal' views using a language which, despite the displacements to which it is subjected, remains common and vulgarizing? Without 'speaking badly', how can one express a Dionysus who speaks a language totally different to that of Schopenhauer or Kant?

If being a philosopher implies wanting to be understood, even by just a small number who are related 'on the basis of common and rare aesthetic experiences' (BT, 'Attempt at a Self-Criticism', 3); if, moreover, common language can only divulge and disfigure an original perspective, then one can understand Nietzsche's thinking that he should have sung and not spoken when writing *The Birth of Tragedy*, or at least that he should have expressed as a poet what he had to say (ibid.)! The 'Attempt at a Self-Criticism' recalls how at that time he was the first to try to translate the 'Dionysian pathos' into a 'philosophical pathos':[5] a translation which was at the same time a transfiguration, a transposition of the 'music of the world' into the imperfect language of the word:

> What found expression here was anyway [...] a *strange* voice, the disciple of a still 'unknown God', one who concealed himself for the time being under the scholar's hood, under the gravity and dialectical ill humour of the German, even under the bad manners of the Wagnerian. Here was a spirit with strange, still nameless needs, a memory bursting with questions, experiences, concealed things after which the name of Dionysus was added as one more question mark. What spoke here – as was admitted, not without suspicion – was something like a mystical, almost maenadic soul that stammered with difficulty, a feat of the will, as in a strange tongue, almost undecided

whether it should communicate or conceal itself. It should have *sung*, this 'new soul' - and not spoken! What I had to say then – too bad that I did not dare say it as a poet. (BT, 'Attempt at a Self-Criticism', 3)

Later Nietzsche writes *Zarathustra*, a few poems and dithyrambs; but the greatest part of his output is in 'prose', even if the prose is indeed unique: exclamatory, interrogative, filled with metaphors, with terms in italics or in inverted commas,[6] in such a way that it will be for ever distinct from any other philosophical text, unplaceable, atopic. Is it not a paradox, analogous to that which makes us write 'conceptually' on metaphor, to commend the privileged position of music or poetry and yet to write with a 'philosophical pathos'? Is it through powerlessness? Is it not rather a way of acknowledging the specificity of philosophy, its irreducibility to any other form of expression – even if this philosophy no longer has anything traditional about it, even if it is an unheard-of and insolent philosophy? A philosophy which, by combining all the 'genres'[7] in its writing, deletes all oppositions with one great burst of laughter.

II
Metaphor, Symbol,
Metamorphosis

In the Dionysian dithyramb man is incited to the greatest exaltation of all
his symbolic faculties; something never before experienced struggles
for utterance – the annihilation of the veil of *māyā*, oneness as the soul of
the race and of nature itself. The essence of nature is now to be expressed
symbolically; we need a new world of symbols; and the entire
symbolism of the body is called into play, not the mere symbolism of
the lips, face, and speech but the whole pantomime of dancing, forcing
every member into rhythmic movement. Then the other symbolic
powers suddenly press forward, particularly those of music, in rhyth-
mics, dynamics, and harmony. To grasp this collective release of all the
symbolic powers, man must have already attained that height of self-
abnegation which seeks to express itself symbolically through all these
powers – and so the dithyrambic votary of Dionysus is understood only
by his peers. With what astonishment must the Apollinian Greek have
beheld him! With an astonishment that was all the greater the more it was
mingled with the shuddering suspicion that all this was actually not so
very alien to him after all, in fact, that it was only his Apollinian
consciousness which, like a veil, hid this Dionysian world from his
vision. (BT 2)

1 MUSIC, THE PRIVILEGED ART

As early as *The Birth of Tragedy* Nietzsche judges the
conceptual language of philosophy the most inappropriate
to express the 'truth of the world', since it is at three
removes from it, simply a metaphor for a metaphor.[1] In
fact we can have only representations of the essence of
things, since we ourselves, and the universe along with us,
are only images of this completely 'indecipherable' innermost essence. Among the representations we can dis-

tinguish two categories to which distinct symbolic spheres correspond. Just as those representations which appear in the form of pleasure and pain and accompany 'with their *basso continuo* all the other representations' (Nietzsche retains the Schopenhauerian name 'will' for them) are the most important ones, on which man bases his understanding of all becoming and willing, so the symbolic sphere which corresponds to this most general form of phenomena is as 'fundamental to language as is this form of phenomena to the other representations': the degrees of pleasure and pain are symbolized by the tone of speech, whereas the other representations are expressed by symbolic gesturing.

Since pleasure and pain are manifestations of a unique 'substratum' which is the same for all, the language of sounds, beyond the diversity of languages, is a universal language. The plurality of languages must be seen as 'the strophic text of this primordial melody of pleasure and pain'. The consonant and vowel systems in language are part of the symbolism of the gesture, for, without the fundamental tone, vowels and consonants are just positions of the organs, i.e. gestures: it is tonality, the echo of pleasure and pain, that serves as a foundation for the symbolism of the gesture (cf. MW, p.215). Therefore written language is even more limited in its power of expression than language spoken aloud, where the 'intervals, the rhythms, the pace and the stress are symbolic of the emotional content which is to be expressed'. So music is a necessary 'supplement'[2] to words, which are 'the most defective signs there are', allowing them to express feelings.

In *The Birth of Tragedy* we thus see Nietzsche still drawing on a whole metaphysical tradition by establishing a hierarchy between the different symbolic languages, which are metaphorical transpositions of the 'music' of the world, itself the most appropriate representation of the innermost essence of things. And it is because music is the best language, the one which expresses best and most universally the general form of phenomena which is the will, that Nietzsche calls the will, metaphorically, the music or melody of the world.

Melody (and within it rhythm,[3] so that all true music calls for dance and is inseparable from it) is thus the 'basic general fact' which can be variously objectified in texts which will be like so many metaphors for it. In this way lyric poetry is an Apollinian metaphor for Dionysian music. The lyric poet strives to imitate music through rapidly changing, multi-coloured images caught up in a mad whirl. To express music through images in this way he requires all the movements of passion, which serve as metaphors for him to interpret the music with. Thus the lyric poet, who can perceive himself only through the prism of music, can express nothing which was not already there in the music to an extraordinary degree, and lyric poetry is therefore a metaphorical expression of Dionysian music, through visions full of imagery and through feelings. Metaphor must be understood here not as a rhetorical figure, but as 'a substitutive image which the poet really perceives in place of the idea', a live spectacle at which he is present. The lyric genius expresses in his way what the Dionysian musician, by identifying himself with the primitive echo of the world, is able to make resonate without having to resort to images.

However, even if lyric emotion can symbolize music, it could never replace it. The world of the sound and the world of the image are two languages with no necessary interrelation. All images and feelings suggested analogically by music are merely crude expressions of the sound and must efface themselves before it, before the presence of Dionysus himself and his most authentic symbolization. Therefore when a musician sets a lyric poem to music he takes his inspiration neither from the images nor from the representations nor from the feelings it contains. Musical emotion, issuing from a wholly different sphere, can express itself only metaphorically in a text which is just a symbol and has the same relation to music as has the Egyptian hieroglyph of valour[4] to the valiant warrior [...]. In the presence of the supreme God and his authentic revelation, the symbol loses all meaning; indeed it now appears as an insulting accessory. (MW, p.220)

Far from making music 'intelligible', images can only obscure it. For the votary of Dionysus – for him and his peers – music is intelligible by itself: thus it is 'an essential feature of Dionysian art that it takes no account of the listener'. Equally it is not for the benefit of the listener but for his own benefit that the poet explicates music to himself with the aid of the symbolism of images and emotions. Conversely, though, sound could not be used as a metaphor for the image without inverting the legitimate hierarchical order: and the different symbolic spheres, all of them inappropriate transpositions of the essence of things, are not equivalent. Anyone claiming to illustrate a poem musically by subordinating the music to the text is wrongly privileging a crude metaphor, privileging metaphor in relation to the proper;[5] they want to substitute the son for the father,[6] man for god. They want the impossible, for the Apollinian world cannot produce the sound to symbolize the Dionysian sphere, which this Apollinian vision itself conquers and excludes:

We shall have to maintain that the lyric poem's relationship to its musical composition must at any rate be different from that of a father to his child. (MW, p.217)

What a topsy-turvy world! An undertaking which strikes me as similar to a son wanting to beget his father! Music can engender images which will only ever be schemata, instances of its authentic and universal content, so to speak. But how could the image, the representation – let alone the concept, 'the

poetic idea', as it is called – engender music! Just as
surely as the musician's mysterious castle is linked to
the open space of images by a bridge, which the lyric
poet steps out over, so it is impossible to go in the
opposite direction, even if there are those who are said
to believe they have done so. (MW, p.216)

To bring about this inversion in the hierarchy between the
different symbolic spheres, making the sound a metaphor
for the image, is to make bad music, like in opera: it is a
downright abuse of power, 'as if one were trying to raise
oneself by one's own bootstraps'. The symbolism of
music, then, is purely conventional; music becomes transformed into rhetoric, into a 'system of mnemonic signs', as
it is now intended merely to stimulate deadened or
slackened nerves. This is what Nietzsche will later condemn in the music of Wagner: as a musician he was a
rhetorician, making the music serve the text and seeking
above all to be 'expressive', to give a commentary on an
idea using a thousand symbols, to stimulate the senses like a
veritable Circe. Whereas 'good' music – Dionysian music –
must make one dance, Wagner's music seeks to make one
swim and hover, shattering all unity of time and force (cf.
CW 8; NCW, 'Wagner as Danger', 1). This musical
rhetoric is no more than a caricature of Dionysianism, a
counterfeit, a piece of play-acting.
    Operatic culture is the most well-known name for
'Socratic culture': the need which gave birth to the modern
genre of the opera is not aesthetic but moral and theoretical
in nature, as recitative and *stilo rappresentativo* bear out. The
subjection of the music to the libretto springs from
nostalgia for an idyllic life, from the belief in 'primitive
man as the man naturally good and artistic' (BT 19). Opera
is a remedy for pessimism. Whereas Dionysian music takes
no account of the listener, here it is the listeners who usurp
control and demand that the music be subordinated to the
text: 'It was the demand of thoroughly unmusical hearers

that before everything else the words must be understood, so that according to them a rebirth of music is to be expected only when some mode of singing has been discovered in which text-word lords it over counterpoint like master over servant. For the words, it is argued, are as much nobler than the accompanying harmonic system as the soul is nobler than the body' (BT 19). 'According to the clearest evidence, *opera* now begins, with the *listeners' demand to understand the words*. What? The listeners have *demands?* The words should be understood?' (MW, p.224).[7] Thus opera, deciphered by a reading which can already be termed genealogical, marks the triumph of Socrates or Christ over Dionysus, of nihilism over the affirmation of life, of the slave over the master.[8]

Music is the most appropriate symbolic sphere only because it is suited to affirm the manifold diversity of life. It is, in fact, the mother of all the arts, for it breaks up into a thousand metaphors itself; it is a language 'capable of infinite interpretations'. Whereas Apollinian intoxication arouses above all the eye, in the Dionysian state the entire emotional system is aroused and intensified

> so that it discharges all its powers of representation (*Darstellung*), imitation, transfiguration, transmutation, every kind of mimicry and play-acting, conjointly. [...] Dionysian man [...] enters into every skin, into every emotion; he is continually transforming himself. (TI, 'Expeditions of an Untimely Man', 10)

As a special art, music is a belated specialization favouring the sense of hearing to the detriment of the other senses, in particular the muscular: a specialization that puts an end to the symbolism of the body, which is always present in the true Dionysian state. So all the arts are related: they form a whole whose parts have gradually specialized, and such specialization is a sign of the poverty of taste, the

powerlessness to enjoy with all the senses, which is
characteristic of modern aesthetics:

> it is generally accepted as axiomatic in aesthetics that
> the union of two or more arts, far from intensifying
> aesthetic pleasure, is a barbarous aberration of taste.
> But this axiom at most betrays our modern bad habit
> of never enjoying anything with all our human
> faculties any more: we find ourselves torn apart, so to
> speak, by absolute artistic experience, and indeed we
> can no longer enjoy anything except as parts of
> ourselves, now as the ear, now as the eyes, etc. Let us
> contrast that with the image of ancient drama as total
> art form [*Gesammtkunst*]. (GMD, p.36f.)

So it is only the full panoply of the arts, in their
hierarchized diversity subordinated to music, that symbolizes Dionysus: this god who is dismembered into a
thousand pieces and who revives every year, reunified. The
Bacchic masquerades represent the metamorphoses of the
god, mythical metaphors for the multiple languages in
which Dionysus is indirectly expressed.

However, for the artist to be able to symbolize Dionysus
in this way he must first have been metamorphosed and
stripped of his individuality himself. He must have
identified himself with the human race, with the very being
of nature. In this state the artist expresses himself in unity
with the whole; his 'ego' symbolizes the full panoply. The
artist becomes a metaphor for the world and, as such, he is a
medium which reflects eternal being. All authentic art
involves intoxication, and with it the loss of the 'proper', as
one is transported out of oneself in a way which alone gives
the power to symbolize. Expressing oneself metaphorically and undergoing a metamorphosis can thus be
assimilated. It is this ecstasy outside of the self which is at
the origin of Greek music drama, the total art form *par
excellence* (cf. GMD, p.40f. and DW, 96f.). The author of

the ancient music drama can be compared to the pentathlete, the virtuoso in five types of sport,[9] and the drama
can be symbolized by the floating drapery introduced by
Aeschylus: the drama triumphs over all that remained
forced and isolated in the different arts; it reconciles
discipline and grace, diversity and unity, Apollo and
Dionysus (cf. GMD, pp.43 and 52). In the drama, each art
can serve another as its metaphorical expression: the
movements of the chorists, who draw arabesques on the
stage, make the music, as it were, visible,[10] just as the music
reinforces the daring metaphors and the leaps of thought
which are given in the poem. But it was music alone that
gave birth to tragic myth, which expresses in symbols the
Dionysian truths, just as only the full panoply of the arts
expresses Dionysus.

2   THE STRATEGIC STATUS OF METAPHOR

From this, one can understand why Nietzsche should have
sung and not spoken when writing *The Birth of Tragedy*, or
should have expressed himself as a poet: philosophical
language is the most unsatisfactory there is, for it petrifies
the 'music of the world' into concepts. Scientific dialectics
and reflection play the same role for the philosopher as does
verse for the poet, and they are just as inadequate in
expressing philosophical intuition as is verse in translating
the metamorphosis of the poet:

> And just as for the dramatist words and verse are but
> the stammering of an alien tongue, needed to tell what
> he has seen and lived, what he could utter directly only
> through music or gesture, just so every profound
> philosophical intuition expressed through dialectics
> and through scientific reflection is the only means for
> the philosopher to communicate what he has seen. But
> it is a sad means; basically a metaphorical and entirely
> unfaithful translation into a totally different sphere
> and specch. Thus Thales had seen the unity of all that

is, but when he went to communicate it, he found himself talking about water! (PTG, p.44f.)[11]

So right from *The Birth of Tragedy* we can find in Nietzsche a generalized 'theory' of metaphor, based on the loss of the 'proper' in two senses. On the one hand there is no metaphor without a stripping away of individuality, without masquerade and metamorphosis. To be able to transpose, one must be able to transpose oneself and one must have conquered the limits of individuality: the same must partake in the other, must be the other. At this level metaphor is founded on the ontological unity of life represented by Dionysus. But if there is metaphor it is because this unity is always already in pieces and can only be reconstituted when symbolically transposed into art. Beyond individual separation, symbolized by the dismemberment of Dionysus, metaphor allows for the reconstitution of the originary unity of all beings, symbolized by the resurrection of the god.

On the other hand metaphor is linked to the loss of the 'proper' understood as the 'essence' of the world, which is indecipherable and of which man can have only representations which are quite 'improper'. Corresponding to these representations are more or less appropriate symbolic spheres. Neither the 'representations' nor the symbolic languages are equivalent to one another. Since musical language is the best metaphor, all other expressions are in turn more or less crude metaphors for it: the most appropriate metaphor assumes the status of 'proper' in relation to all the others. Conceptual language is the poorest, for its symbolic meaning is the weakest and it can recover its strength only through music or poetic images (cf. in particular DW, p.97).

Thus as early as this youthful work, which still draws on Schopenhauer, Nietzsche brings about a highly symptomatic reversal in the relationship which he establishes between metaphor and concept: metaphor is no longer referred to the concept, as in the metaphysical tradition inherited from Aristotle, but rather the concept is referred to metaphor. For Aristotle the concept is primary in relation to metaphor, metaphor being defined as carrying one concept over on to another, or as the transition from one logical place to another, from a 'proper' place to a figurative one.[12] Aristotle's definition of metaphor could not be retained as such by Nietzsche since it is based on a division of the world into well-defined genera and species corresponding to essences, whereas for Nietzsche the essence of things is enigmatic, so genera and species are themselves but human, all-too-human metaphors. 'Carrying over' must not be understood here as a transition from one place to another: it must itself be taken as a metaphor which, in *The Birth of Tragedy*, condenses several meanings: transfiguration, transformation, ecstasy, self-dispossession and metamorphosis (which is possible only if the distinction into well-demarcated genera and species is erased); as well as: transposition of the truth of Being into symbolic languages.[13] In this last sense the traditional relationship between the 'proper' and the figurative re-emerges, simply displaced, since these symbolic languages are such only when referred to the essence of the world or the most appropriate symbolic sphere.

Nietzsche gives a metaphor for metaphor which reveals this youthful text as adhering to the metaphysical tradition, and which continues to draw on Aristotle's definition: the proper is likened to a father, with metaphors as his sons or grandsons. The secondary metaphorical languages derive from the most appropriate symbolic language, which could not be made to derive from them, just as the sons could not engender the father, nor the grandsons the sons. In relation to the father or the god – the presence of the essence itself – the son is just a useless accessory, to be done away with.

This metaphor for metaphor implies a devalorization of metaphor, for it is considered to be inferior if not to the concept, which is itself metaphorical, then at least to the essence, the authentic proper – Dionysus. The hierarchical distinction between a 'good' rhetoric, a natural symbolic system, and a 'bad', purely conventional rhetoric, must not lead us to forget that 'good rhetoric' itself is just a stopgap, and that it is inappropriate to express the proper. If one thinks of the essence of language as rhetoric (even if we must wait for the *Philosophenbuch*[14] for Nietzsche to draw out all the consequences), then immediately this means referring it to an 'accurate'[15] language and subordinating it to it. So the generalization of metaphor, as it occurs in *The Birth of Tragedy*, remains caught up in the 'closure of metaphysics'. But is it possible to escape this closure so long as one continues to refer the metaphor to the proper? And could one arrive at a generalized theory of metaphor by eliminating all reference to the proper? As Nietzsche has taught us, two opposites belong to the same system, and if one cannot deconstruct the one without generalizing the other, the deconstruction remains trapped within the territory it seeks to go beyond.

It is thus remarkable that it should be above all in his first works (*The Birth of Tragedy*, *Philosophy in the Tragic Age of the Greeks*, the *Philosophenbuch* and the notes from the same period)[16] that Nietzsche should make 'metaphor' a fundamental operator, in those works where he seems precisely to be still accepting an innermost essence of things, independent of the metaphor which symbolizes it. In the later texts the notion of metaphor will lose its strategic importance, once it has served to deconstruct the 'proper' by its generalization. Nietzsche will substitute for it the notions of 'text' and 'interpretation' which, while they still have a metaphysical 'smell' about them, at least have the advantage of no longer being the direct opposites of the 'proper'. In these works, where metaphor is effaced as a strategic notion, the 'proper' itself has the status of a simple interpretation, whereas metaphor, in the light of these new operative notions, is thought of as a metaphorical notion, symbolic of the artistic force of interpretation which constitutes the 'proper', the concept, as well as the metaphor. This artistic force will then be designated 'will to power'. But equally the notion of metaphor becomes totally 'improper' since it is henceforth no longer referred to a proper but to an interpretation. To continue using this notion as a key concept might have been dangerous because of its metaphysical implications, and it is understandable that Nietzsche should have abandoned it after making strategic use of it.

3 THE REHABILITATION OF METAPHOR

However, despite everything which still connects Nietzsche's first works to the tradition, their innovativeness, as far as the status of metaphor is concerned, reveals an original conception of philosophy and of philosophical 'style'. They introduce new relations between philosophy, art, and science. Previously philosophy and science, in the desire to speak 'properly' and demonstrate without using images or similes in order to be convincing,[17] repressed metaphor and confined it to the poetic sphere. The philosopher resorted to metaphor only for didactic reasons or as a stopgap, and with great caution. By bestowing highly precise limits on the metaphorical he was able to hide the fact that the conceptual is itself metaphorical. By effacing the opposition of kind between metaphor and concept and substituting merely a difference of degree (with metaphor being the less metaphorical), Nietzsche inaugurates a type of philosophy which deliberately uses metaphors, at the risk of being confused with poetry. Such a confusion would not be regrettable in Nietzsche's eyes: for the opposition between philosophy and poetry derives from metaphysical thinking; it is based on the fictitious separation of the real and the imaginary, on the no less fictitious separation of the 'faculties'. Philosophy is a form of poetry: speaking in metaphors makes language find its most natural form of expression once more, 'the most accurate, the truest, the simplest' (EH, 'Why I Write Such Excellent Books', Z, 3) means of figurative expression.

It is merely a form of poetry, for the new philosopher does not put metaphor to rhetorical use but subordinates it to the prospect of an accurate language, or to the strategic objective of using non-stereotyped metaphors in order to unmask the metaphors which constitute every concept. The philosopher does not just 'play' with metaphors: his play is of a 'formidable seriousness', for it is designed to oppose modernity's hatred for art, to obliterate precisely the opposition between play and seriousness, dream and reality, to show that

> mathematical expression is not a part of the essence of philosophy. (P 53)
> We want to so rearrange the world for you with images that you will shudder. […] Even if you stop up your ears, your eyes will see our myths. Our curses will fall upon you. (P 56)

The 'imagination' plays as important a role in philosophy as it does in poetry. '[The philosopher] knows in that he invents, and he invents in that he knows' (P 53). The imagination allows one to grasp analogies; reflection intervenes only after the event to replace them with equivalences, to replace successions with causal relations, and to bring the measure of the concept to bear. Philosophy is a 'continuation of the *mythical drive*' (P 53).

4 THE PRE-SOCRATIC MODEL

If Nietzsche can thus venture a new type of philosophy, it is because this type has always already existed; such a philosophy is possible because it already saw life with the Pre-Socratics. It is a case of *bringing back* the originary Greek philosophy, rescuing it from the forgotten state into which the triumph of the forces of nihilism forced it, repeating it by taking it as a model. In *Philosophy in the*

Tragic Age of the Greeks, Nietzsche subjects the Greek philosophers to a genealogical reading, taking as his touchstone the 'style' of the philosopher. 'What does a philosopher who writes metaphorically *want*? What does someone who writes "abstractly" want? Of what is the transition from one type of writing to another symptomatic?' Such are the questions which are implicit in the work, and they are substituted for the usual questions about the truth or falsehood of systems.[18] Nietzsche is looking neither to approve of them nor to refute them, for one cannot refute conditions of existence: each system is like a plant, and just as one can trace back from the plant to the ground which produced it, so one can trace back from the system to the author of whom it is the image.[19] A system must be evaluated not according to its truth, but according to its force and beauty: it is a question of knowing whether what made the system possible was a superabundant or a needy form of life, whether the philosopher was affirming or denying life by it. Metaphorical style is the sign of a plenitude of life, just as 'demonstrative' style indicates a poverty of life. The deliberate use of metaphors affirms life, just as the privileging of concepts reveals a will to nothingness, an adherence to the ascetic ideal.

The opposition between the two 'styles' is expressed by that between two types of philosopher, one type linked to Heraclitus and the other to Aristotle. The opposition is also conveyed by that of two antithetical figures: Dionysus and Socrates. The transition from the one to the other is marked by the death of tragedy, with Euripides succeeding Aeschylus, language replacing song; and so the affirmation of life in its multiple diversity gives way to the triumph of the individual, consciousness prevails over the unconscious, self-knowledge and reflection prevail over naïvety.[20] Thus Anaxagoras and Euripides appear as 'the first calm men of sense among drunken people'.

The reason why *indemonstrable* philosophizing retains some value, and for the most part a higher value than a

scientific proposition, lies in the *aesthetic* value of such
philosophizing, in its beauty and sublimity. Even
when it cannot prove itself as a scientific construction,
it continues to exist as a *work of art*. [...] The poorly
demonstrated philosophy of Heraclitus possesses far
more artistic value than do all the propositions of
Aristotle. (P 61; cf. ST, p.55f.)

They [the Hellenes] only rarely translate the pro-
fundities of their wisdom and knowledge into words:
between the greatest man of the concept, Aristotle,
and the customs and art of the Hellenes, the greatest
abyss still yawns. (CP, p.352)

The metaphor of the *abyss* not only indicates a historical
separation between two periods; it is also the metaphor for
the 'pathos of distance' which separates two types of life
that have always already been in existence: the one flourishing and superabundant, projecting its own excess into
things and embellishing them; the other degenerate, able
only to impoverish the world by reducing it to the narrow
and ugly measure of the concept, in order to spite itself and
out of *ressentiment*[21] towards life. The abyss separates, but
it also engulfs; which makes it a metaphor for forgetting:
forgetting the import of pre-Socratic philosophy, forgetting metaphor, and forgetting the full panoply of the
drives in favour of one alone (that of knowledge).

Forgetting was made possible not 'because of time', but
by the triumph of the ascetic ideal, which deliberately
maintained the abyss that had been opened up. After the
pre-Socratic Greeks, philosophers are no more than 'gri-
macing figures, pale and depressed, theological counterfei-
ters': logic and reason prevail over intuition, Aristotle
prevails over Heraclitus and the artistic drive.

It is consequently no surprise to see Aristotle accuse
Heraclitus of violating the principle of non-contradiction
with that enigmatic formulation that 'everything forever
has its opposite along with it' (PTG, p.52).[22] Now by using

conceptual language Heraclitus was bound to fail his intuition whilst at the same time laying himself open to the reproach of illogicality. However, by defying logical contradiction he hits on the most incredible of all cosmic metaphors – that of the world as Zeus's game – to suggest that which reason finds incredible: that the one is at the same time multiple. Zeus's game is like that of the artist and the child who innocently construct and destroy. Life's artistic drive is constantly calling new worlds into being, with as much freedom and necessity as there is in play (PTG, p.62).[23]

Aristotle's accusation that the Pre-Socratics committed a 'crime against reason' betrays his reductive reading of the philosophers who preceded him – they possessed a truth in potential which he had the privilege of bringing out. In potential, in other words confusedly, obscurely, without knowing. Mythical philosophy conceals a hidden, unarticulated λόγος; it is philosophy in its infancy. For Aristotle, metaphorical writing is the sign not of an affirmative and flourishing type of life but of a lack of maturity, a state of incompletion. By this reading, by subjecting the Pre-Socratics to his authority, Aristotle robs them of their impregnable qualities – their originality, their personality.[24] This reading of Aristotle's, by which the individuality of each philosopher is absorbed into the identity of philosophy and its ἀρχή, is opposed to Nietzsche's. For Nietzsche resumes the dialogue with the pre-Socratic 'giants' which the deafness of metaphysics had interrupted in the interest of listening to noisy 'dwarves' (PTG, p.32).

Beyond western philosophy with its Aristotelian heritage, as a disciple of Heraclitus, from whom he borrows the metaphor of the world as a game, Nietzsche bridges the abyss that was opened up and goes back in order to repeat pre-Socratic philosophy; in the very picture which he paints of the Greeks, he expresses in miniature[25] the opposition between metaphor and concept and the effacement, by and in the concept, of metaphor. Since each philosopher is an expression of the soil which gave birth to him, anyone tracing a philosopher's life must not do so with the aid of abstract general concepts; he must not summarize it by giving a synopsis, as handbooks do, and thus transform the philosopher into a ghost. On the contrary he must use expressive and vivid metaphors to resurrect a personality in its most typical attributes.

> The complete enumeration of all the transmitted doctrines, as it is the custom of the ordinary hand-books to give, has but one sure result: the complete silencing of personality. That is why those reports are so dull. (PTG, p.25)
>
> I am going to emphasize only that point of each of their systems which constitutes a slice of *personality* and hence belongs to that incontrovertible, non-debatable evidence which it is the task of history to preserve. It is meant to be a beginning, by means of a comparative approach, toward the recovery and re-creation of certain ancient names, so that the poly-phony of Greek nature at long last may resound once more. (PTG, p.24)[26]

Far from following Aristotle in considering pre-Socratic philosophy to be a simple 'babbling' which was surpassed by later Greek philosophy, Nietzsche establishes a veritable hiatus between the dawn of philosophy and its evolution: the Pre-Socratics are a rare type, irreducible to any other. So their image needs to be reconstituted 'by painting them on the walls a thousand times'. In place of an 'evolutionary' history Nietzsche substitutes a typological reading.

The Pre-Socratics are to be painted, not caricatured or 'reduced'. The summary effaces the personality just as the concept effaces the metaphor. Between the two 'efface-ments' there is not just a simple analogical relationship: the forgetting of metaphor is an effacement of the personality.[27]

III

The Forgetting of Metaphor

In the case of everything perfect we are accustomed to abstain from asking how it became: we rejoice in the present fact as though it came out of the ground by magic. Here we are probably still standing under the after-effect of a primeval mythological invention. We still *almost* feel (for example, in a Greek temple such as that at Paestum) that a god must one morning have playfully constructed his dwelling out of these tremendous weights; at other times that a stone suddenly acquired by magic a soul that is now trying to speak out of it. The artist knows that his work produces its full effect when it excites a belief in an improvisation, a belief that it came into being with a miraculous suddenness; and so he may assist this illusion and introduce those elements of rapturous restlessness, of blindly groping disorder, of attentive reverie that attend the beginning of creation into his art as a means of deceiving the soul of the spectator or listener into a mood in which he believes that the complete and perfect has suddenly emerged instantaneously. – The science of art has, it goes without saying, most definitely to counter this illusion and to display the bad habits and false conclusions of the intellect by virtue of which it allows the artist to ensnare it. (HH I, 145)

1 THE ORIGINARY METAPHORICAL ACTIVITY

What, then, are we to make of this forgetting, this effacement? Is Nietzsche merely giving an empirical genesis of the concept, with the concept as metaphor becoming 'forgotten' through simple use and wearing away?[1] The metaphor of money becoming worn and losing its originary effigy[2] to express the effacement of metaphor conceals a forgetting which is more profound.[3] It implies the belief in a linear historical time which

Nietzsche shattered right from his earliest works. Both the metaphor of the abyss and the typological conception of history already mark a break with the traditional conception of time: return in the difference of the same, beyond 'historical' periods, is one of the forms taken by the eternal return. The abyss can be bridged in the other direction; time is not an irreversible progress beginning with an origin and orientated towards a specific goal: it is a rhythmic play between opposing forces which prevail by turns, innocently constructing and deconstructing worlds. A rhythmic play which implies repression and a return of the repressed forces. The *Untimely Meditations* thus see the whole history of civilization as a play between Hellenism and Orientalism, each winning out by turns:

> the old question whether a culture can be transplanted to a foreign soil at all is still the problem over which the moderns weary themselves. The rhythmic play against one another of these two factors [Hellenization and Orientalization] is what has especially determined the course of history hitherto. Here Christianity, for example, appears as a piece of oriental antiquity, thought and worked through by men with excessive thoroughness. As its influence has waned, the power of the Hellenic cultural world has again increased [...]. Thus there are between Kant and the Eleatics, Schopenhauer and Empedocles, Aeschylus and Richard Wagner such approximations and affinities that one is reminded almost palpably of the very relative nature of all concepts of time: it almost seems as though many things belong together and time is only a cloud which makes it hard for our eyes to perceive the fact. (UM IV, 4)[4]

If 'time' is just an illusion, then it is essential to work out a new concept for forgetting and to erase the monetary metaphor.

Thus the forgetting of metaphor does not occur at a specific point in time – after a certain time – and it does not simply apply with respect to and because of the concept. It is originary, the necessary correlate of metaphorical activity itself: man has always already forgotten that he is an 'artist from the beginning', and that he remains one in all his activities.

When Nietzsche sets intuition against the concept, the illogical against the logical – as if a sphere existed from which the metaphorical might be excluded – he does so as a result of the 'forgetting', the 'abyss' opened up by the metaphysicians, who create two antithetical worlds which they claim to be irreducible. This moment corresponds to a strategy designed to fill the abyss, to delete the opposition between concept and metaphor, to show that 'reason' and 'logic' are the products of what man, because of 'forgetting', calls an 'illogical' activity. But if everything is 'illogical', the 'logical' and 'illogical' are two terms which are both equally 'improper'. Thus from the *Philosophenbuch* onwards Nietzsche speaks of an originary *instinctive* activity, an artistic force creating fictions.[5] This allows man to remake the world in his image so as to master it: an anthropomorphic transposition which, in order to be effective, must necessarily be performed self-effacingly. Metaphorical activity is termed instinctive because it is unconscious, and because like all drives it seeks sole mastery of the world. It is not just a drive like any other; it could be called the general form of all drives. It is instinctive also because it is hereditary and specific.[6]

By defining man as 'a metaphorical animal', the *Philosophenbuch* thus pours scorn on Aristotle's definition: 'the rational animal' is just a product of the metaphorical activity which is common to all living things. Consciousness can speak only in metaphors of this instinctive metaphorical activity, taking as a model its own activities – a model which is deficient since conscious phenomena are merely a superficial simplification of instinctive activity. It is a model which is nevertheless not falsely analogous since conscious activity is an extension of instinctive activity, a simple, indirect or sublimated[7] means of expression. Thus in order to indicate that conscious and unconscious activities, despite their differences, have the same objective, Nietzsche makes conscious activities into metaphors for bodily activities and vice-versa. But the two sorts of metaphor are not equivalent. Just as *The Birth of Tragedy* judged the image a good metaphor for sound but sound a poor metaphor for the image, so one must consider the metaphors which take consciousness as their model as inferior to those which take as their model the body. To privilege conscious activity as a model is to want to invert the hierarchy once more, to try to pass off consciousness as the proper. If both types of metaphor are indeed 'improper', good rhetoric must take the body as a guiding thread: 'The multiplicity of the drives: – we must assume there is a *master*; but it is *not* in consciousness, for consciousness is an organ, like the stomach' (GOA XIII, 618).

Though it is true that the body is described as a 'collectivity of numerous souls', and digestion is described as 'the interaction [*Zusammenspiel*] of *a very great number of intellects*' (GOA XIII, 588), nevertheless one must not imagine that organic actions are carried out with the aid of the intellect, for that would make them incomprehensible; instead one should imagine the intellect as the ultimate consequence of organic life and speak of it as one would of a stomach.[8] By means of this reciprocal (yet not equivalent) metaphorical expression of the body by consciousness and of consciousness by the body, Nietzsche deletes the metaphysical opposition between the soul and the body and establishes between the two an original relationship of symbolic expressivity. The body and consciousness are two systems of signs which signify each other reciprocally, the language of the one expressing the writing of the other in 'abridged' form, and at the same time deforming it. But because man had to begin by conquering the world for conscious thought he considers conscious thought essential, and, forgetting that it is just a transposition of unconscious activity, he uses it as a point of departure to describe this activity metaphorically.

Admitting to oneself the metaphorical character of this description hides the fact that conscious thought is itself merely an extension of unconscious activity, and that it is just restoring to it what it began by borrowing from it:

> In short: everything had first to be conquered for *consciousness* – a temporal sense, a spatial sense, a causal sense – when for a long time already it had all existed much more richly without consciousness. We gave them the plainest, simplest, most reduced form: our *conscious* will, sensibility, and thought are in the service of a much more extensive will, sensibility, and thought. – Really? (GOA XIV, i, 83. Cf. GOA XIII, 565; XIV, i, 516)

Speaking of a 'metaphorical' activity or an unconscious artistic force therefore means taking as a model conscious rhetorical and artistic activities which are nevertheless merely circumlocutions and simplifications of unconscious activity and cannot be understood without it.

How can art and rhetoric serve as models for unconscious activity, and why does Nietzsche use these two models? Does he make use of them simultaneously or successively and, if the latter, is the transition from one model to the other decisive?

2 THE ARTISTIC PARADIGM

The artistic model is in operation as early as *The Birth of Tragedy* and is the more constant. Artistic activity gives everything a surface; it creates forms that do not exist in nature, which has neither inside nor outside, neither top nor bottom:

Art belongs not to nature, but to man alone. – In nature
there is no *sound*, it is mute; no colour. No form either,
for form is the result of a reflection of the surface in
the eye, but essentially there is neither high nor low,
neither inside nor outside. If we could see by any other
means than this reflection, we would not speak of
forms but we would perhaps see into the interior, so
that our eyes would gradually cut through a thing.
Nature, if we subtract our subjectivity, is a matter of
great indifference, most uninteresting, neither the
mysterious original ground, nor the enigma of the
world disclosed; [...] the more we dehumanize nature,
the emptier and more meaningless it becomes for us. –
Art is based entirely on humanized nature, on nature
enveloped in and interwoven with errors and illusions
which no art can disregard. (NF 23 [150], KGW IV$_2$,
554)

In other words artistic activity is only made possible by an
effort of transposition, and because we have always
already instinctively transposed 'the world' into a set of
forms. Art extends the work of the unconscious artistic
force. Both our eye and our thinking are mirrors which
reflect forms: the world of which we can become conscious
is just a world of surfaces. Each of our senses is one of the
mirrors which creates a specific world by reflection: 'at
every instant we need art in order to live. Our eyes detain us
at the *forms*. But if we have gradually acquired such eyes for
ourselves, then there is an *artistic power* which holds sway
within us' (P 51; cf. P 54; P 107; TL, p.80; GS 354).

So 'images', in other words the surfaces of things
concentrated in the mirror of our senses, are the original
thoughts. Thus space and time are not real; they exist only
for a sentient being who sees everything through these two
fundamental metaphorical forms, each a metaphor for the
other. So the unconscious artistic force is the creator of
images in the eye and in thinking, just as art is the creator of
new forms.

Moreover, as a result of the intoxication, in one form or another, which gives the artist a feeling of enhanced force and plenitude, art 'idealizes' the world – which does not mean to say that it impoverishes it, but that it highlights some of its principal features and makes others disappear. The artist transforms things until they reflect his power, a process which gives him a feeling of perfection and beauty: things are never beautiful by themselves but appear so to anyone who projects on to them his superabundance of life. But just as unconscious activity is unaware of itself as such, so man 'forgets himself' as the cause of these 'beauties' and imagines that the world itself is laden with them (cf. TI, 'Expeditions of an Untimely Man', 19).

Without an effort of transposition which makes one perceive things with greater intensity by refusing to want to see or hear everything – the artist eliminating certain details and adding others, arranging certain parts so as to mask others – there could be no art:

> *What one should learn from artists.* – How can we make things beautiful, attractive, and desirable for us when they are not? And I rather think that in themselves they never are. Here we could learn something from physicians, when, for example, they dilute what is bitter or add wine and sugar to a mixture – but even more from artists who are really continually trying to bring off such inventions and feats. Moving away from things until there is a good deal that one no longer sees and there is much that our eye has to add if we are still to see them at all; or seeing things around a corner and as cut out and framed; or placing them so that they partially conceal each other and grant us only glimpses of architectural perspectives; or looking at them through tinted glass or in the light of the sunset; or giving them a surface and skin that is not fully transparent – all this we should learn from artists while being wiser than they are in other matters. For

with them this subtle power usually comes to an end
where art ends and life begins; but we want to be the
poets of our life – first of all in the smallest, most
everyday matters. (GS 299. Cf. P 55)

Realism, which claims to 'see what is' and to work from
nature, is an artistic nonsense and an impossibility. Each
artist, like any man, has his *'camera obscura'* which tames the
real (TI, 'Expeditions of an Untimely Man', 7).[9] 'Realism',
far from being faithful to the real, merely turns everything
in its grasp anaemic. It is symptomatic of an impoverish-
ment of life, an anti-artistic drive – both signs of an artistic
decadence.

Art's effort of idealization corresponds to a second
moment in the activity of the unconscious, which not only
produces a profusion of images but chooses between them,
accentuating some and eliminating the others, choosing the
similar by hiding differences.[10] This is what consciousness
calls 'memory', 'imagination' or 'analogical reasoning'.
The image chosen by resemblance produces in its turn a
profusion of similar images.

> Like recalls like and compares itself to it. That is what
> knowing consists in: the rapid classification of things
> that are similar to each other. Only like perceives like:
> a physiological process. The perception of something
> new is also the same as memory. (P 131. Cf. P 55, 117–
> 44)

Finally, artistic activity is again a good model because its
apparently free play of forms is actually dictated by an
internal necessity, just as the production of images and their
selection by unconscious activity is not arbitrary but
depends on a specific nerve stimulus, even though on the
'surface' thought is considered free. The physiological
process is absolutely necessary: the same nervous activity
produces the same image, and all the forms which have

once been produced by the nervous system are repeated eternally.

However, if art is a legitimate paradigm of unconscious activity, that is because it is just a specific instance of it, the one which can present itself as what it is: a cult of the surface. It is an instance which man needs in order to bear the severe 'reality' he has constructed for himself, the fictional nature of which he conceals from himself; it is an instance which he needs, when life has grown strong enough to allow it, in order to accept truth as absence of truth and to will illusion as such. Art thus educates us to play games with ourselves and become 'noble'; it teaches us to distance ourselves from our own evaluations:

> *What should win our gratitude.* – Only artists, and especially those of the theatre, have given men eyes and ears to see and hear with some pleasure what each man *is* himself, experiences himself, desires himself; only they have taught us to esteem the hero that is concealed in everyday characters; only they have taught us the art of viewing ourselves as heroes – from a distance and, as it were, simplified and transfigured – the art of staging and watching ourselves. Only in this way can we deal with some base details in ourselves. Without this art we would be nothing but foreground and live entirely in the spell of that perspective which makes what is closest at hand and most vulgar appear as if it were vast, and reality itself. (GS 78)
>
> *Our ultimate gratitude to art.* – If we had not welcomed the arts and invented this kind of cult of the untrue, then the realization of general untruth and mendaciousness that now comes to us through science – the realization that delusion and error are conditions of human knowledge and sensation – would be utterly unbearable. *Honesty* would lead to nausea and suicide. But now there is a counterforce against our honesty

that helps us to avoid such consequences: art as the *good* will to appearance. [...] As an aesthetic phenomenon existence is still *bearable* for us, and art furnishes us with eyes and hands and above all the good conscience to be *able* to turn ourselves into such a phenomenon. At times we need a rest from ourselves by looking upon, by looking *down* upon, ourselves and, from an artistic distance. laughing *over* ourselves or weeping *over* ourselves. We must discover the *hero* no less than the *fool* in our passion for knowledge; we must occasionally find pleasure in our folly, or we cannot continue to find pleasure in our wisdom. (GS 107)

The artistic paradigm allows the metaphysical oppositions between reality and appearance, the speculative and the artistic, the man of action and the contemplative to be erased. The world which man 'contemplates' is merely a product of himself, as are artistic forms. And just as an artist has a feeling of enhanced power on contemplating his work, so men feel a greater sense of security in a world which is merely the 'reflection' of their power:

> Only we have created the world *that concerns man*! – But precisely this knowledge we lack [...]: we fail to recognize our best power and underestimate ourselves, the contemplatives, just a little. (GS 301)

3 THE RHETORICAL PARADIGM

So artistic activity is a good model for unconscious activity. That being the case, why does Nietzsche add a second model, that of rhetoric? This latter does not just reduplicate the former; it relates to a strategic moment clearly delimited in Nietzsche's *œuvre*. The artistic model allows the opposition between reality and appearance to be unequivocally effaced; it allows us to understand that without man the 'world' would not exist and would have no meaning: artistic activity, at the same time as it invents forms, posits values and meanings which, in its absence, the world would find itself lacking. To call this artistic construction 'metaphor' is to carry on referring 'our' world to another which would be the world *proper*, the thing 'in itself'. Thus it is no surprise to see the artistic model stealing a lead over the rhetorical model and being substituted for it, just as the 'proper' finds itself replaced by appropriation.

It is primarily the *Philosophenbuch* which constitutes the moment of detour via the rhetorical model,[11] a necessary stage in the generalization of metaphor. Here the rhetorical model is used to describe unconscious activity insofar as it transposes into the world explanatory schemata which man fashions after himself. Metaphorical activity does not just mean anthropomorphism by another name: explanatory schemata express the world improperly, but they are no more appropriate to express man. When he uses them to understand himself he is still practising rhetoric, for if man indeed takes what is 'given' to him in order to transpose it elsewhere (which is what constitutes metaphor), what is given to him has always already been tamed by the '*camera obscura*' or sifted through consciousness: the conscious world is a language which symbolizes a text written originally by unconscious activity, and which consciousness knows only in a masked and transposed form. The transposition is achieved by carrying over the 'known' on to the unknown. It presupposes an activity of assimilation, of digestion, of reducing differences, which is a fundamentally 'unjust' will to mastery (Nietzsche later calls it 'will to power'). Operating already at the organic level, it is still present in intellectual activity, which is supposedly disinterested and at the highest level: the will of the 'mind',[12] too, is to achieve unity out of diversity, to restrict and subjugate the unfamiliar. Its needs and its qualities are the same as those of everything that lives, grows, and multiplies; it seeks to incorporate new 'experiences' within

old frameworks (cf. BGE 230). Every event is from its
inception a moral event, in the sense that already in the
simplest processes the 'passions' dominate. On hearing a
foreign language one transposes into the words that one
hears familiar sounds which are intimate to the ears; when
reading, one guesses more than one reads. One does not see
a tree, one imagines it lazily without looking at the original
details.

The familiar, which by its repetition passes for necessary, assumes the status of the proper and is metaphorically
and metonymically transported everywhere – from one
sphere to another, ·from the conscious to the unconscious,
from man to the world, from one specific sphere of
activity to another – through assimilation and generalization which are 'illegitimate', treacherous, and unjust:
metaphoricity, by its exercise of sole mastery, implies the
loss of individuality and the reduction of differences. It is
again to this same unconscious metaphorical activity that
man owes his 'truth drive', which is the product of an
unjust transposition by metastasis (displacement) and generalization, from the moral to the intellectual sphere. Not
to live in untruth and to believe in the truth of everything
then become an essential inclination. But for this generalization to stabilize itself the concept 'true' must intervene: to
be true must mean always to be true.

Man does not by nature exist in order to know:
truthfulness (and *metaphor*) have produced the inclination for truth. Thus the intellectual drive is produced
by an aesthetically generalized moral phenomenon. (P
130)
    Thus he [man] transfers his own inclination to the
world and believes that the world *must* also be true to
him. (P 134)

4 THE CONCEPT

In other words the concept, itself a product of metaphorical activity, plays a privileged role in the forgetting of metaphor, in that it hides the metaphorical character of the process of generalization by founding it on an essential generality: the concept vouches for the 'untruth' and 'treacherousness' of metaphor, ensuring their stability whilst at the same time maintaining a forgetfulness of the genesis of the process, along with every other genesis. One might say, to speak with Freud,[13] that the concept plays the role of the force of anticathexis which sustains repression. It entails, along with the originary 'forgetting', a secondary repression. It allows a system of secondary rationalizations to be set up after the event, effacing the fact that metaphorical activity is originary, at the origin of all knowledge and all activity. Thus it is at the level of the concept that metaphorical activity, because it is at its most concealed, for that reason becomes most dangerous: thanks to the concept, man arranges the whole universe into well-ordered logical categories without realizing that he is thus continuing the most archaic metaphorical activity. In fact the concept is neither an *a priori* idea nor a model, as it claims to be. It is a lasting impression which became

> retained and solidified in the memory. It is compatible with very many appearances and is for this reason very rough and inadequate to each particular appearance. (P 144)

The fixation and generalization have been achieved by a series of metaphors. The starting-point, 'the impression', is itself a metaphor, a transposition of a nerve stimulus which varies from one individual to the next, producing individual sensation-images in the symbolic language of one of the five senses. Then each new and unfamiliar impression is, by means of 'unconscious analogical reasoning', metaphorically linked to the first by an '*imitative*' carrying-over

(P 146–49). Imitation is the repetition of the perceived image in a thousand metaphors which are like so many analogues of it. Imitation discovers and revitalizes resemblances, appropriating the unfamiliar. It brings flooding in all the images which are akin to the first.

The third moment, marked by the imposition of the word, is the transition to the concept; a transition from the analogous to the identical, from the similar to unity, implying both the intervention of language and society and an 'unjust' application of the principle of reason and of substance.

a) Concept and Language

Because there is no concept without language, every concept is general – not only in the sense that it preserves what is similar and results from the identification of the non–identical,[14] but also because it designates impressions which are common to a group of individuals with the same preoccupations and the same experiences.[15] Language and consciousness go hand in hand, and individual life does not require them. Consciousness developed under the pressure of the need to communicate: it is linked to action, its urgency and dangers: the origin of conceptual language lies in neediness;[16] it presupposes the need to appropriate the world and to act quickly, for men to understand each other by avoiding 'misunderstandings'. Men can no more respect the differences which exist between themselves than they have the time to be interested in the differences between things: language consigns to concepts average impressions and the evaluations of the greatest number; it imposes as a norm the perspective of the herd. Metaphorical – to be more precise metonymical – activity consists in setting up as an absolute value a language which is valid only for the 'average' man, i.e. for no one, repressing individual metaphor as dangerous to the life of the group: a repression which hides the metaphorical nature of the concept itself. Admitting that to oneself would mean recognizing that the 'agreement' between men is as precarious and artificial as the agreement between things. Inasmuch as it is metaphorical, language is supremely 'unjust', even if it is this injustice alone, as a state of equilibrium[17] between differences, that permits justice and the social order.

b) Concept and Principle of Reason

Because the concept is a transition from the analogous to the identical, from diversity to unity, it implies the transposition of the metaphorical and metonymical schemata of causality and substance.

These two schemata are modelled on a bad interpretation of the activity of willing. Any talk of 'will', or of a self-willed ego or of willing as cause, already brings in metaphorical and metonymical activity.

Such talk is metaphorical because it involves transposing the unconscious activity of the drives on to the level of consciousness; it is metonymical, because the single name of 'will' represents only the most powerful drive, the one which has succeeded in subordinating all the others and making them serve it; a single name which reveals how the multiplicity of the drives – and their effective work, which is necessary to the operation of *willing* – gets forgotten. *The* will in fact designates a system of unconscious hierarchized forces. And yet this system is explained by a model from the province of consciousness: at the level of unconscious forces the situation is like a neatly hierarchized society where the dominant class identifies itself with the state as a whole and claims the profit from the work of the dominated classes. An analogy which is legitimated by the fact that the hierarchical relations within a society are themselves merely the result of the struggles between forces seeking power.[18]

Thus *the* will is just a rhetorical figure: if one tries to break down the process one will never arrive at something simple, for the final element is still a relation. Willing is something 'complicated', which consciousness and language simplified illusorily.[19]

Nevertheless it is this 'unity' of willing that serves as a metaphorical schema to constitute the unity of every concept – a false unity concealing a multiplicity (cf. WS 33) – just as the unity of the concept guarantees the permanence and substantiality of the subject.

Again it is willing, interpreted as cause of an act, that allows the schema of causality to be constituted. This schema is but a generalization of the relation which is experienced between willing and the act, the transposition through habit of a simple relation of succession.

> The only causal relation of which we are conscious is the one between willing and acting. We transfer this on to all things and explain to ourselves the relationship between two alterations which are always found together. The intention or willing yields the *nomina*; the acting, the *verba*. (P 139)[20]

So the noun, as the cause of the action expressed by the verb, derives from misinterpreted experience; it is action that comes first, and from this we reach conclusions about qualities:

> 'Seeing' comes first, and then 'vision'. 'The one who sees' is taken to be the cause of 'seeing'. Between the sense and its function we feel that there is a regular relationship. Causality is the transfer of this relationship [...] to all things. [...] The first causal sensation occurs when *a stimulus is felt as an activity* [...]. We explain the world to ourselves in terms of our sensory functions, i.e. we presuppose causality everywhere, because we ourselves *continually experience* alterations of this sort. (P 139)[21]

The schema of causality is used to constitute the concept as a cause that explains the diversity it encloses in its unity. The schemata of substance and causality are akin. Just as the diversity of acts seems inessential in the light of the final explanatory cause – the permanent subject – so individual differences end up disappearing in favour of conceptual unity alone. Eventually the differences are interpreted as a degraded product of the concept, the status of which becomes paradigmatic.

So explaining simply means naming, including within a category; it means reducing differences and differends[22] by harmonizing a certain number of acts considered to be the innumerable actions of one and the same quality: 'We have here a transposition: an abstraction encompasses innumerable actions and assumes the value of a cause.'

Thus Thales explains the genesis of everything with one single concept: water. One simple predicate, 'the wet', is transformed into a totality and mistaken for a sum of predicates. Man is operating here by metonymy: 'The whole world is wet, so being wet is the whole world.' In a general sense, the rhetorical figures which constitute language are the product of false syllogisms. 'Reason' and 'logic' are based on an 'originary confusion' (cf. P 142–43), and science is built on unconscious and 'illogical' tropes. So human knowledge, with such arbitrary foundations, cannot arrive at the 'thing' itself, as it claims: 'The sculptor of language was not so modest as to believe that he was only giving things designations, he conceived rather that with words he was expressing supreme knowledge of things' (HH I, 11; cf. I, 14; I, 28 and P 150).

So the classificatory categories within which we contain the universe in the belief that we are explaining it are anthropomorphic metaphors. But the work of transposition does not stop there. We subdivide the concepts into genders, masculine and feminine:[23] a new metaphor; we designate a being by one of its characteristics or one of its properties: metonymy. For example, the designation 'snake' connotes merely a twisting movement and could equally well suit a worm. Each language introduces artificial categories and divisions which make it distinctive; none arrives at the 'originary entities'.

Thus the concept, a rigid and general abstraction, is a condensate of multiple metaphors and metonymies. At each moment in its genesis there is a transition from one sphere of signs to another, each able to serve as a metaphor for the other; but these spheres do not communicate between each other.[24] Each in its own way, and all of them 'improperly', to a greater or lesser degree of abstraction, they express what Nietzsche in the *Philosophenbuch* is still calling 'original entity', 'thing in itself', essence. The artist of language, by means of his 'bold metaphors', has been able to express only man's relations to things, not the things themselves:

> we believe that we know something about the things themselves when we speak of trees, colours, snow, and flowers; and yet we possess nothing but metaphors for things – metaphors which correspond in no way to the original entities. (TL, p.83)

5 THE METAPHORS FOR METAPHOR

However, 'transposition', 'carrying over', 'sphere', and 'thing in itself' are still metaphors. In fact all these notions imply space, the fundamental metaphorical schema: the notion of metaphor is itself just a metaphor. Thus in order to describe metaphorical activity Nietzsche gives several metaphors which are mutually complementary, each emphasizing a particular aspect of metaphor, none in itself sufficient to describe it 'properly'. But in their very inadequacy the metaphors are better at describing metaphorical activity than a 'pure' concept which claimed to define it would be.

Initially Nietzsche uses the metaphor of *Chladni's sound figures*, a metaphorical model designed to represent sound vibrations visually.[25]

> In the same way that the sound appears as a sand figure, so the mysterious X of the thing in itself first

appears as a nerve stimulus, then as an image, and finally as a sound. (TL, p.83)

Sound, a simple metaphor, represents the thing in itself; the sand figures represent the metaphors. At the level of the scientific model, sound is the 'original entity' which is to be represented metaphorically in the visual sphere. Now for Nietzsche the sphere of sound is the most suited to symbolize the 'music of the world', so it is no surprise to see that he should choose sound as a metaphor for the essence, just as metaphors could not be better represented than by the figures in the sand. But a deaf person would look on these figures in vain, for he would not gain a knowledge of sound from them – at best he would be able to imagine it. Thus with the aid of his metaphors – which are of his own making, just as the Chladni figures are made by the scientist – man cannot arrive at the thing in itself.

The metaphor of the Chladni figures highlights the impossibility of adequately expressing the proper by any kind of transposition, even though it gives the illusion of allowing one to arrive at the essence; deaf to the 'music' of the world, man confuses image and sound.

There follows a second metaphor, that of the painter without hands expressing in song the picture he has before his eyes:

> For it is not true that the essence of things 'appears' in the empirical world. A painter without hands who wished to express in song the picture before his mind would, by means of this substitution of spheres, still reveal more about the essence of things than does the empirical world. (TL, p.86f.)

This second metaphor is not a simple repetition of the previous one in a different form. Passing from one to the other takes one from a symbolic language in which the hierarchy is respected, to a language which inverts the 'correct' relationship between the sound and the image; it introduces a subversive order into the symbolic spheres. However, despite all the deficiencies of such a symbolization, sound is better at representing the image than the empirical world is at expressing the essence of things: the painter, in wanting to express through song the picture he has before his eyes, is leaping illegitimately from one metaphorical sphere to another, whereas man in his activity of 'transposition' is making a much more important leap – he wants to express the 'proper itself' by the metaphorical.

The second metaphor for metaphor represents the impossibility of comparing 'measures with one another'; the various symbolic languages are like so many incommunicable spheres which are analogical but non-equivalent. To transpose 'the world of the subject' into the 'world of the object' is much more illegitimate than the other way around, for it means taking the son or the grandson for the father:

> For between two absolutely different spheres, as between subject and object, there is no causality, no correctness, and no expression; there is, at most, an *aesthetic* relation: I mean, a suggestive transference, a stammering translation into a completely foreign tongue. (TL, p.86)[26]

6 GENESIS OF THE CONCEPT AND GENESIS OF JUSTICE

Moreover, giving several metaphors for metaphor also has a strategic purpose: that of avoiding the exclusivity of one single metaphor, which would 'harden and stiffen' and risk being taken for a 'proper'. For it was indeed the 'stiffening and hardening' of metaphors in the concept which effaced its genesis and led in the end to its metaphoricity being forgotten. This sclerosis did not result from a natural evolution, a simple passage of time which ended up wearing away the metaphors and making them lose their sensory force. The metamorphosis of the metaphor into a 'proper' implies relations of violence, and transformations in the relations of force:

> The impression is petrified [...]; it is captured and stamped by means of concepts. Then it is killed, skinned, mummified, and preserved as a concept. (P 149)

Metaphorical activity, always already 'forgotten', is secondarily repressed by being deliberately abandoned in favour of the concept, of logic and science. It is as if there is an anticathexis of the originary forgetting by the creation of a 'social memory' which goes hand in hand with the creation of responsibility, self-consciousness, and moral conscience. The 'injustice' of metaphorical activity is kept repressed and sublimated in the form of 'social justice'.

In fact, communications and verbal exchanges are similar to economic exchanges in that a non-contingent parallel exists between the genesis of the concept and that of justice: in both cases the same metamorphoses and the same forgettings take place. Indeed it is the same metaphorical activity, reducing differences and assimilating the similar, that is at the origin of the genesis both of 'justice' and of the concept: an activity which is characteristic of man, the metaphorical animal, who, because he is always merely establishing equivalences and measuring, has called himself '*Mensch*'. To think is to weigh:[27]

> Setting prices, determining [*abmessen*] values, contriving equivalences, exchanging – these preoccupied the earliest thinking of man to so great an extent that in a certain sense they constitute thinking *as such* [...]. Perhaps our word 'man' (*manas*) still expresses something of precisely *this* feeling of self-satisfaction: man designated himself as the creature that measures values, evaluates and measures, as the 'valuating

animal as such'. Buying and selling, together with their psychological appurtenances, are older even than the beginnings of any kind of social forms of organization and alliances. (GM II, 8; cf. WS 21: '*Man as the measurer*')

The metaphorical equivalence between 'think' and 'weigh' represents the metaphorical character of every equivalence: man invents equivalences as he does analogies. In both cases – and for the same reasons – he seeks to establish an equilibrium between more or less equal powers, and to force everyone else to accept. There are relations of violence preceding any social organization, constituting the social order and the 'highest' moral values.

The equilibrium is established by dint of an evaluation which is arbitrarily set up as an absolute norm: 'price', like the concept, is a measure fixed by man, imposed on all things and all people. Because of this fetishization of value, the fact that value is the product of evaluation gets forgotten, and the latter is now measured against the former; the fact that the concept results from a metaphorical activity gets forgotten, and it is taken for a transcendent model, with all specific things and actions being simply degraded copies or simulacra of it. The phantasmatic construction of a transcendent world means that the genesis of the measuring standard gets forgotten.

Personal law, in its rudimentary form, along with the feelings which accompanied it – those of exchange, contract, debt, obligation, and compensation – were then *carried over* into the relations of the primitive social configurations with their peers, as well as the habit of *measuring* powers one against the other. A whole series of metaphorical transferrals thus takes one from the most primitive form of justice to the other forms, from barter to the sphere of moral obligation.

Thanks to the notions of weight, measurement, equilibrium, and counterweight (punishment and opprobrium), men climbed into realms that are quite unmeasurable and unweighable but originally did not seem to be. (WS 21; cf. GM II *passim*)

Principle of equilibrium [...]. The community is originally the organization of the weak for the production of an *equilibrium* with powers that threaten it with danger. An organization to produce preponderance would be more advisable if the community could thereby become strong enough to *destroy* the threatening power once and for all: and if it were a matter of a single powerful depredator this would certainly be *attempted* [...]. *Equilibrium* is thus a very important concept for the oldest theory of law and morality; equilibrium is the basis of justice. When in ruder ages justice says: 'An eye for an eye, a tooth for a tooth', it presupposes that equilibrium has been attained and seeks through this redistribution to *preserve* it [...]. On the contrary, by virtue of the *jus talionis*[28] the equilibrium of the disturbed power relationship is *restored*: for in such primeval conditions one eye, one arm *more* is one piece of power more, one weight more in the scales. – Within a community in which all regard themselves as equivalent there exist *disgrace* and *punishment* as measures against transgressions, that is to say against disruptions of the principle of equilibrium: disgrace as a weight placed in the scales against the encroaching individual who has procured advantages for himself through his encroachment and now through the disgrace he incurs experiences disadvantages which abolish these earlier advantages and *outweigh* them. The same applies to punishment: against the preponderance which every criminal promises himself it imposes a far greater counterweight, enforced imprisonment for acts of violence, restitution and punitive fines for theft. (WS 22; cf. WS 32, *'Fairness'*)

Just as man's forgetting of metaphor allows him to believe

that the concept is an *a priori* idea, pure and cut off from anything sensory or violent, so he has the illusion that a 'just' action is disinterested because he forgets its genesis, and because a violent process intervenes. Like the over-valuation of the concept, the high value granted to justice, which is continually increased by the zeal, effort, and sacrifices which individuals devote to it, derives from an illusion. And just as those who transgress justice are punished, with punishment playing the role of counter-weight designed to re-establish the equilibrium, so those who misuse the concept – the liar, the artist, the dreamer – are excluded from the city: both sets jeopardize the equilibrium of society and might reveal the illusion in which justice and the concept have their roots. All 'great' things, all 'values' are 'a *sign language of the emotions*' (BGE 187); they have 'grown up out of the same roots as those we believe evilly poisoned [...]. Good actions are sublimated evil ones' (HH I, 107). These roots are those of the will to power, but owing to the beautiful names with which man adorns his fictions (cf. GM II, 10) he forgets their origin: 'How little moral would the world appear without forget-fulness! A poet could say that God has placed forgetfulness as a doorkeeper on the threshold of the temple of human dignity' (HH I, 92; cf. P 84).[29] This capacity to forget transforms every exchange into a counterfeiting: 'It is only by means of forgetfulness that man can ever reach the point of fancying himself to possess a "truth" of the grade just indicated. If he will not be satisfied with truth in the form of tautology, that is to say, if he will not be content with empty husks, then he will always exchange truths for illusions' (TL, p.81).

It is as if, in the transition from justice as barter to justice as obligation and in the transition from the metaphor to the concept, a volatilization of the constitutive elements takes place, a 'sublimation'; only the result is preserved, while the process of genesis is hidden. So we have a new, chemical metaphor to describe the forgetting of metaphor and of the barbaric origin of justice.

Chemistry of concepts and sensations. [...] there exists, strictly speaking, neither an unegoistic action nor a completely disinterested contemplation; both are only sublimations, in which the basic element seems almost to have dispersed and reveals itself only under the most painstaking observation. All we require, and what can be given us only now the individual sciences have attained their present level, is a *chemistry* of the moral, religious, and aesthetic conceptions and sensations [...] what if this chemistry ended up by revealing that in this domain too the most glorious colours are derived from base, indeed from despised materials? (HH I, 1)

[Man] universalizes all these impressions into less colourful, cooler concepts, so that he can entrust the guidance of his life and conduct to them. Everything which distinguishes man from the animals depends upon this ability to volatilize perceptual metaphors in a schema, and thus to dissolve an image into a concept. (TL, p.84)

But volatilization, in turn, only occurs as the result of a violent and painful operation by which man acquires a social memory. One cannot learn to be just (i.e. unjust) without differences being sacrificed. To make up for the forgetting of origins which it conceals, memory struggles against forgetting as an active life-force – against self-forgetting, forgetting the other and the past. It gives us the opportunity to take on the future and to make promises; it gives us conscience, responsibility, personal identity. But these gratifications are merely a deception, for this violent process culminates in the triumph of the collective over the individual. The 'proper' is subjected to the social norm just as impressions and images are branded by the concept, subjected and subdued by it. The fundamental objective of memory is to make one forget difference and genesis as such at all costs: for to society each presents the risk of

change, instability, and insecurity. The triumph of justice
and of the concept go hand in hand with the abandonment
of individual perspectives. The objective of 'memory' is to
make us forget life; the order of concepts seeks to give the
illusion that becoming and difference are degradations of
an *a priori* world, a 'real and true' world.

> Everything finished and complete is regarded with
> admiration, everything still becoming is under-valued
> [...] wherever one can see the act of becoming one
> grows somewhat cool. (HH I, 162; cf. I, 145 and I,
> 252)

Anything that cannot have its genesis mapped out is called
'a product of genius', a designation which effaces the
effort that went into producing the work. For the same
reasons the metaphorical process at work in the genesis of
the concept is concealed. What masks metaphor in this case
is the nakedness of the concept, which is more seductive
than the brilliant colours of metaphor: forgetting is due to a
stripping–away, a mummification, a preservation in a
concept labelled with a branding mark.[30] Abstraction,
allied to danger and fear, operates as a veritable Circe.

A parallel genesis, then, for the concept and for justice,
which is hardly surprising since the concept of justice is
merely a particular instance of the concept. It is a privileged
instance, though, because it belongs to the moral sphere –
which is precisely where man has the greatest interest in
hiding from himself the fact that his concepts are subject to
becoming and that they have a cruel origin, the fact that the
same violent and unjust forces against which morality is
opposed presided at their birth. The effacement of genesis
is here necessary to prevent the whole edifice of morality
from crumbling.

Equally, the forgetting of metaphor and the concealment of the genesis of the concept could be sustained only
with the help of 'moral' and religious forces which were

particularly interested in repressing differences and becoming. They are what opened up the 'abyss' between metaphor and concept, turned them into two radically separate worlds and, by the perspectival inversion which they introduced, allowed a retroactive falsification of the history of concepts to take place.

7 FORGETTING, THE PRODUCT OF A PERSPECTIVAL SHIFT

So Nietzsche embarks on a genealogical rather than a linear history of the concept/s. It is deceptive to represent the effacement of metaphor by the metaphor of money becoming worn, for this makes forgetting into a passive phenomenon. Now *On the Genealogy of Morals* distinguishes forgetting as an inert force from an active forgetting: 'forgetting is no mere *vis inertiae* as the superficial imagine; it is rather an active and in the strictest sense a positive faculty of repression' (GM II, 1). It is a sort of 'doorkeeper, a preserver of psychical order, repose, and etiquette' (ibid.).[31]

Unaware of forgetting as an active force, the empiricists with their 'superficial minds' came up with a linear history of the concept and gave it as a motor three phenomena which they judged to be passive: 'utility', 'forgetting', and 'habit'. Nietzsche summarizes their genesis of moral concepts thus:

> 'Originally [...] one approved unegoistic actions and called them good from the point of view of those to whom they were done, that is to say, those to whom they were *useful*; later one forgot how this approval originated and, simply because unegoistic actions were always *habitually* praised as good, one also felt them to be good – as if they were something good in themselves.' (GM I, 2)

A 'perverse' genesis, a genealogy against the grain which puts the reactive forces of *ressentiment* at the origin of concepts. This empiricist genesis obliterates the fact that moral evaluations are an appropriation of the world by one type of will in combat with another. Forgetting is in fact not an effacement by time, but the product of a perspectival shift which sifts through the evaluations made from the former perspective so as to keep only what can be reconciled with the new point of view.

The genealogical reading (which Nietzsche is merely sketching out in the *Philosophenbuch* because he does not yet have the hypothesis of the will to power to work with and his operative concepts (forgetting, utility, habit) are thus precisely those of the empiricists) discovers that the 'selfish–disinterested' antithesis arises only when aristocratic evaluations are in decline. The opposition of concepts is symptomatic of the herd instinct which imposes its evaluations in reaction against noble evaluations. If time is indeed a necessary condition for the forgetting of the first evaluations, it is not a sufficient one: forgetting only *has* to occur because new forces have prevailed and been able to make other evaluations triumph: 'we can destroy only as creators' (GS 58). The new evaluations, through a distinctive violence, serve as an anticathexis of the earlier ones, which are revaluated retroactively:

> it was a long time before that instinct attained such dominion that moral evaluation was actually stuck and halted at this antithesis. (GM I, 2)

It is the halting at antithesis, the absence of a change of perspective for a fairly long period, that produces the illusion of equivalence between 'moral' and 'unselfish'. It is this halting which 'hypnotizes' and produces '*idées fixes*' by transforming a metaphor that expresses a certain specific type of life, a unique perspective, into an absolute concept, an essence. Once the relations between the forces change, once the centre of perspective is displaced, then 'moral' and 'unselfish' can cease to be equivalent and the former evaluations can be resurrected. The inversion of values was effected by Jewish hatred which, through the revaluation of all concepts which it proposes, violently *dis-figures*[32] the adversary. Such a disfigurement in effigy, a condemnation solely on the spiritual level which consists in stripping away individual impressions and mummifying them as a concept, is a falsification of history, the negation of an origin and the transfer of the concept into a metaphysical, divine world. The weak 'castrate' concepts and take their life from them; they conceal the will to power by sublimating it (GM I, 10).

The result of this castration is that the new concepts are nothing but a sinister caricature of the old ones. So forgetting is the product of a deformation, of a transvaluation of all values. It implies the transition from the affirmation of life in its diversified plurality to the will to nothingness, the ascetic ideal.

8   THE ROLE OF THE PRIEST

These evaluative contrasts 'finally tore chasms between man and man that a very Achilles of a free spirit would not venture to leap without a shudder' (GM I, 6).[33] We must note here the fundamental role of the Jewish priest, seizing on the spontaneous evaluations of the weak in his favour, systematizing them, and deliberately setting them up as an absolute. In the priesthood the Jewish priest belongs to the highest caste: originally the priesthood and royalty were not distinguished from one another. It is at the time of the specialization of functions that the political concept of pre-eminence is transformed into a psychological concept; it is because the priests at that stage insisted on a precise demarcation of caste distinctions that they transformed the aristocratic distinction 'good/bad' ('*gut/schlecht*') into 'pure/impure' ('*rein/unrein*'). Such a prizing of purity exaggerates the 'pathos of distance' and pushes it to its extreme consequences, to the point where the evaluator is no longer free with respect to this same pathos, his feeling of distance and his own evaluations. The true noble, the free spirit, the man in good health, is able to laugh at his own perspectives.[34] Purity is the *illness* of the nobility. The priest is an obsessional kind of invalid who retreats into his caste for fear of being contaminated. The 'pure one' is initially 'a man who washes himself, who forbids himself certain foods that produce skin ailments, who does not sleep with the dirty women of the lower strata, who has an aversion to blood' (GM I, 6). The system of prohibitions to which he conforms is a collection of defences in order to remain 'clean' ['*propre*'].[35] Because they derived from an *idée fixe*, from an obsession,[36] the practices peculiar to the priests allowed the contrasts between evaluations to be accentuated and the sensory to be *isolated* from the intelligible until they could be turned into two worlds with nothing in common. The priest's ruse was to transform what had a non-symbolic meaning into a spiritual meaning, to pass off the requirement to be 'materially' clean as a moral and intellectual requirement: to have a pure heart or contemplate pure ideas. To be effective, the priests' remedy needed to be generalized. The only way they could triumph over the healthy aristocracy was to affirm the omnipotence of thought: 'Mankind itself is still ill with the effects of this priestly naïvety in medicine!' (GM I, 6). But at the same time it is by means of this priestly therapeutics that man began to become an interesting animal, 'acquire *depth* and become *evil*' (ibid.).

Thus, for the halting at antithesis to become definitive, it was necessary to pass by way of illness. It is because the 'intelligible world' had a therapeutic value, because it was the only way the weak could still affirm their power, that it was able to be imposed. But it is not insignificant that it should have been an illness of the nobility. Only nobles – even when ill – could introduce values which accentuated the *differences* between man and man, to the extent of radically opposing men. Illness is not a negation of health, it is not its other, it does not result from the operation of an opposing death force which inhibits life.[37] It is still life which, going too far in its own [*propre*] direction, ends up like all excellent things by 'sublating' itself [*se 'relever' elle-même*] ('sie endet wie jedes gute Ding auf Erden, *sich selbst aufhebend*' (GM II, 10)).[38] Illness is a 'relief'[39] for health: though it is true that in order to be strong a will must exercise itself in the same direction for a long time, yet to stay so it must be able to play games with itself: the centres of perspective must 'relieve' each other or else be relieved by illness. Life means playing, at the risk of being had.[40] Illness is health's 'stubbornness' in a particular direction, its spirit of seriousness which ultimately separates man from all his powers, save one.

But how could part of the aristocratic caste fall ill? Nietzsche explains himself very little on this subject. *On the Genealogy of Morals* indicates merely that in the priestly aristocracies the dominant customs, being hostile to action, privileged fantasy and the discharge of affect. Hence the illness was initially psychical, an internalization of the drives with, as a physiological consequence, 'that intestinal morbidity and neurasthenia which have afflicted priests at all times' (GM I, 6). Hostility to action seems to be a consequence of the specialization of functions. One may suppose that it was military defeat which prompted the schism inside the aristocratic caste and the concomitant transformation of noble evaluations. In fact, in the different examples which Nietzsche gives of transition from the political sense of a concept to a psychological one, a deterioration in the conditions of existence always occurs at the same time: thus the Greek nobility, in the *Elegies* of Theognis, designates itself as 'truthful' the moment it loses its power in the Megarian city and a democratic, demagogic government replaces it.[41] The nobles then called themselves the 'Truthful Ones', because the lower strata had passed themselves off for what they were not by calling themselves 'the good'. Whereas previously the lower strata had been 'simple, unequivocal men' to the nobles, they

became the men of the lie, and the nobles, who had been
simply '*those who have reality*', became by contrast the
'*Truthful Ones*'.[42]

In *The Antichrist* (24–26) Nietzsche shows how the Jewish
priests transformed their conception of the divinity under
pressure of historical circumstances. Originally their god is
symptomatic of a highly tenacious vital force: he is a
warrior god who fights with the Jewish people against its
enemies; he is generous and gives an abundance of goods,
herds, children, rain; in short, he is the god of a chosen
people. Through such a representation the Jews glorify
themselves by projecting their own power as a god; their
god is just a way of showing their gratitude towards life
for a superabundance of life. But after the period of the
Kings, internal anarchy and, externally, the triumph of the
Assyrians made the Jews lose the confidence they had put in
their god: was he really *their* god if he could change camps
like that? It became essential to abandon such a changeable
god: but the Jews preferred to change the conception they
had of him. They turned him into a god who was good and
peaceful and forbade war, embodying the power of their
enemies at the same time in the devil. The devil and the
good Lord were born simultaneously, the one symbolizing
a harmful power, the other the powerlessness of a power.
They explained after the event why God had abandoned
them: their God remained so only on condition that
morality was observed. In such a way the inversion of
values was effected: the natural order received a moral
interpretation. The natural principle of causality was
replaced by the moral principle of sin. Everything natural
was devalued, just as everything which went against life
was declared good.

So the Jews were not decadents but, faced with a new
historical situation in which they risked disappearing as a
people and losing their autonomy, they preferred to
continue existing at any cost, even that of inverting values.
In their intelligence, which was strengthened by the

perilous situation, they realized that they could turn the evaluations of the decadents to good account. The priestly caste, the most powerful, systematized the evaluations of the weak, giving them a divine authority so as to make them a tool of its power. It understood that, in the face of the danger which the Gentiles represented, the only hope lay in preserving the autonomy of the Jewish people: this was achieved by sustaining the hierarchy in its favour and by transforming values. The priestly caste triumphed over the world by devaluing it. The deliberate nature of the enterprise was what distinguished the priests from the decadents who experience the spontaneously anti-natural evaluation of their weakened drives. In order to stay alive, Nietzsche argues, the priests donned the mask of decadence: 'The Jews are the counterparts of *décadents*: they have been compelled to *act* as *décadents* to the point of illusion, they have known [...] how to place themselves at the head of all *décadence* movements [...] so as to make of them something stronger than any party *affirmative* of life' (AC 24). In order to safeguard its hierarchical superiority and to continue dominating the masses, the priestly caste set up as supreme values those evaluations which were suited to consolidate the weakness of the invalids; it falsified the past of the Jewish people by giving a moral interpretation of its whole history; the great victorious period of the Kings, where the priests played merely a secondary role, was declared impious and the events which followed were declared punishments for the sins of the period of greatness. Everything that was useful for preserving or developing the power of the priest was considered divine, and his will became 'the will of God'.[43]

There is no real contradiction between the readings in the *Genealogy* and *The Antichrist*, despite the fact that the former describes the priest as having in principle 'something morbid' about him. Each is situated in a slightly different perspective, for in the one case Nietzsche is describing typologically, in the other he insists on the

historical conditions which necessitated a transvaluation of
values. The significance of this double reading is to
highlight the fact that the inversion of values was possible
only because of the conjunction of different sociological,
psychological, and physiological factors.

9 MORALITY, THE ALLY OF LOGIC

The detour we have just completed helps us to understand
that the forgetting of metaphor and the illusion of the
'proper' cannot be produced by a simple effacement. If use
results in a disfigurement, it is because there is a force which
has an interest in disfiguring the money. For one to see the
metal and no longer the effigy, a perspectival shift is
required, this halting in antithesis between two opposing
worlds. By giving the strong a conscience – a bad conscience to the extent that they disregard their unique
perspectives – the weak bring on the forgetting of the
former evaluations:

> Only by forgetting this primitive world of metaphor
> can one live with any repose, security, and consis-
> tency: only by means of the petrifaction and coagula-
> tion of a mass of images which originally streamed
> from the primal faculty of human imagination like a
> fiery liquid, only in the invincible faith that *this* sun,
> *this* window, *this* table is a truth in itself, in short, only
> by forgetting that he himself is an *artistically creating*
> subject, does man live with any repose, security, and
> consistency. If but for an instant he could escape from
> the prison walls of this faith, his 'self consciousness'
> would be immediately destroyed. (TL, p.86)[44]

What the monetary metaphor does not explain is the fact
that a single coin should have been in use and set up as an
absolute value. It is in fact the exclusivity of a single
metaphor, its fixation by hypnotic procedures, that
imposes the habit of using it; a habit which becomes a

necessity, with the result that the metaphor is taken for a 'proper', a norm of thought and action. Thanks to the convention of lying established as truth, man learns to think and act as a 'herd animal', a 'reasonable being'; he confers an essence on himself at the same time as he confers it on things; and he no longer puts up with being led by 'sudden impressions' and by metaphors, for only the habitual produces satisfaction and security:

> there is no 'real' expression and *no real knowing apart from metaphor*. But deception on this point remains, i.e. the *belief* in a *truth* of sense impressions. The most accustomed metaphors, the usual ones, now pass for truths and as standards for measuring the rare ones. The only intrinsic difference here is the difference between custom and novelty, frequency and rarity. (P 149)

The triumph of a unique perspective marks the victory of death over life, of the ascetic ideal over the artistic ideal, of Christ over Dionysus, of mediocre man over the aristocrat. It was the same forces which repressed metaphor in favour of the concept and imposed the morality of the herd, for the same reasons: the neediness of a certain type of life, that of the greatest number, which was not strong enough, not 'bad' enough to will its perspective as such.

These forces work to promote the preservation of the 'species': their aim is peace, the anaesthetization and domestication of the animal, man. They cannot achieve their goal without fighting against all the forces of metaphor: Plato expels the poets from the city because 'misology is misanthropy'; society excludes the liar who uses designations suited to make the unreal seem real – by misusing strict conventions, he becomes dangerous because man wants truth only in order to escape the regrettable consequences of lying:

> The pathos of the truth drive presupposes the obser-vation that the various metaphorical worlds are at

variance and struggle with one another. E.g. the
world of dreams, lies, etc., and the ordinary usual
view of things: the first type of metaphorical world is
rarer; the other is more frequent. Thus the rule
struggles against the exception, the regular against the
unaccustomed: hence the higher esteem for everyday
reality than for the dream world.

Now however, what is rare and unaccustomed is
more attractive: the lie is felt as a stimulus. Poetry. (P
149)

So 'morality' and the concept are natural allies: morality
uses the generality of the concept to guarantee its universality; the concept uses morality to impose itself as a norm
of truth. Both are symptomatic of a will to nothingness
and a decadent taste. The ultimate objective they share is
'moral': the triumph of one type of life over another,
within specific conditions of existence. Owing to this
alliance, a collection of metaphors and metonymies passes
as truth and is respected as such:

What then is truth? A mobile army of metaphors,
metonymies, and anthropomorphisms: in short, a
sum of human relations which have been poetically
and rhetorically intensified, transferred, and embellished, and which, after long usage, seem to a people
to be fixed, canonical, and binding. (TL, p.84)

To express it morally, this is the duty to lie
according to a fixed convention, to lie with the herd
and in a manner binding upon everyone. Now man of
course forgets that this is the way things stand for
him. Thus he lies in the manner indicated, uncon-
sciously and in accordance with habits which are
centuries old; and precisely *by means of this unconscious-
ness* and forgetfulness he arrives at his sense of truth.
(TL, p.84)

IV
Metaphorical Architectures

Genoa. – For a long while now I have been looking at this city, at its villas and pleasure-gardens and the far-flung periphery of its inhabited heights and slopes. In the end I must say: I see faces that belong to past generations; this region is studded with the images of bold and autocratic human beings. They have *lived* and wished to live on: that is what they are telling me with their houses, built and adorned to last for centuries and not for a fleeting hour; they were well disposed toward life, however ill disposed they often may have been toward themselves. I keep seeing the builders, their eyes resting on everything near and far that they have built, and also on the city, the sea, and the contours of the mountains, and there is violence and conquest in their eyes. All this they want to fit into *their* plan and ultimately make their *possession* [*Eigentume*] by making it part of their plan. This whole region is overgrown with this magnificent, insatiable selfishness of the lust for possessions and spoils; and even as these people refused to recognize any boundaries in distant lands and, thirsting for what was new, placed a new world beside the old one, each rebelled against each at home, too, and found a way to express his superiority and to lay between himself and his neighbour his personal infinity. Each once more conquered his homeland for himself by overwhelming it with his architectural ideas and refashioning it into a house that was a feast for his eyes. In the north one is impressed by the law and the general delight in lawfulness and obedience as one contemplates the way cities are built. One is led to guess at the ways in which, deep down, people posited themselves as equal and subordinated themselves; that must have been what was dominant in the souls of all builders. But what you find *here* upon turning any corner is a human being apart who knows the sea, adventure, and the Orient; a human being who abhors the law and the neighbour as a kind of boredom, and who measures everything old and established with envious eyes. With the marvellous cunning of his imagination he would like to establish all of this anew at least in thought, and put his hand to it and his meaning into it – if only for the moments of a sunny afternoon when his insatiable and melancholy soul does feel sated for once, and only what is his and nothing alien may appear to his eyes. (GS 291)

1 ARCHITECTS' GOOD AND BAD TASTE

In the *Philosophenbuch*, so as to describe the world of set concepts and to unmask the metaphorical character of supposed 'propers', Nietzsche reiterates metaphors so stereotyped that they were unrecognizable as such. Nietzsche's repetition, by which he attaches novel and unheard-of metaphors to habitual ones, enables the latter to be enlivened and revaluated, their inadequacies to be highlighted. At the same time, by this new use of metaphor, Nietzsche revitalizes language and does the work of a poet: he transmutes the norms of thought and action, transforms the slave into a free man, 'reality' into a dream. Through this metaphorical play he himself becomes a metaphor for life and its artistic power:

> With creative pleasure [the intellect released from its former slavery] throws metaphors into confusion and displaces the boundary stones of abstractions, [...] [man] speaks only in forbidden metaphors and in unheard-of combinations of concepts. He does this so that by shattering and mocking the old conceptual barriers he may at least correspond creatively to the impression of the powerful present intuition. (TL, p.90)

To describe the hierarchized system of concepts to be found in ordinary language and in science – the 'well-made' language above all – Nietzsche uses architectural metaphors, and in doing so he seemingly follows tradition. But Nietzsche's originality lies in his accumulating metaphors and substituting them for each other, attaching a totally new figure to a stereotyped image, thus provoking a revaluation of traditional metaphors at the same time as ridiculing them. From the architecture of the beehive to that of the dungeon, via the Egyptian pyramid, the Roman columbarium, the Tower (of Babel), the stronghold, as well as the spider's web, a simple assemblage of beams, and scaffolding – such is Nietzsche's metaphorical itinerary. The genealogical reading deciphers each of these fantastic architectures as symptoms of the health or sickness of their constructors: every construction is actually the expression of an internal architecture, in other words of a certain hierarchization of the drives, a subordination of the multiplicity of drives to the strongest drive which then serves as a provisional centre of perspective. The 'strength' or 'weakness' of the will is the expression of the greater or lesser mastery by one drive over the others. Only the hypothesis of the will to power allows architects' 'good' or 'bad' taste, the weakness or strength of their will, to be deciphered behind the different architectural metaphors:

> Pride, victory over weight and gravity, the will to power, seek to render themselves visible in a building; architecture is a kind of rhetoric of power, now persuasive, even cajoling in form, now bluntly imperious. The highest feeling of power and security finds expression in that which possesses *grand style*. Power which no longer requires proving; which disdains to please; which is slow to answer; which is conscious of no witnesses around it; which lives oblivious of the existence of any opposition; which reposes in *itself*, fatalistic, a law among laws: *that* is what speaks of itself in the form of grand style. (TI, 'Expeditions of an Untimely Man', 11. Cf. GS 280, 283, 290)

What taste, then, is revealed by these architectures, metaphors for the system of concepts?

a) The Beehive

The *beehive* is the first construction which represents the conceptual edifice. It is a metaphor traditionally used to describe a serious, bustling, engrossing piece of work: a metaphor which also frequently crops up when the perfection of instinctive work is opposed to the intelligent but defective work of man.[1] Nietzsche, on the contrary, intends it to inscribe scientific work directly in life, to delete the opposition between the speculative and the practical,[2] mind and instinct: concepts are the product of an instinctive metaphorical activity as is the construction of honey cells by the bee. The beehive, as a geometrical architectural ensemble, is the symbol for the systematic ordering of concepts. The perfection of the architecture itself reveals that it is the work of instinct. The 'beauty' of the edifice is not disinterested but is symptomatic of the initial neediness, the motor for the whole construction, at the same time as it masks it. This neediness accounts for the bustling nature of the work, its necessity: just as the bee constructs cells in order to survive and fills them with the honey which it has been to get outside, so science constructs an empty formal architecture and makes the whole world fit inside.

The scientific edifice, full of splendour, is compared to that of a miserable insect, with such small cells, in order to ridicule science's claim to cut the world down to its size, a presumption which takes metaphors for essences (TL, p.83f.). Science can never explain the world; it can only describe it in terms of metaphorical schemata which are human, all too human. It is a pure 'system of signs' (a semiology), a mythology (a world of fictions). It is of the same nature as ordinary language, which it simply extends. It originates in the same metaphorical activity and is constructed on the basis of concepts which it just multiplies and renovates, using the same materials:

> It is always building new, higher storeys and shoring up, cleaning, and renovating the old cells. (TL, p.88)
> 'Interpretation', the introduction of meaning – not 'explanation' (in most cases a new interpretation over an old interpretation that has become incomprehensible, that is now itself only a sign). (WP 604)

Science's only advance on ordinary language is that it

describes the 'world' 'better', in other words it describes us better, in a more systematic, refined, and masked manner. It eliminates any anthropomorphisms which were too apparent, so as better to hide its metaphorical nature and pass off its interpretations as truths.

> [Man's] picture of the world thus becomes ever more true and complete. Naturally it is only a clearer and clearer *mirroring*. But the mirror itself is nothing entirely foreign and apart from the nature of things. On the contrary, it too slowly arose as [part of] the nature of things. We observe an effort to make the mirror more and more adequate. The natural process is carried on by science. Thus the things mirror themselves ever more clearly, gradually liberating themselves from what is all too anthropomorphic. For the plant, the whole world is a plant; for us, it is human. (P 102)[3]

Science's need to conceal its metaphorical character is symptomatic of its weakness, since it cannot admit that its perspective is a perspective lest it should perish as a consequence. Its systematic character allows it both to master the world, by enclosing it within the narrowness of its concepts, and to protect itself from it by concealing it. Just as the bee makes honey from the flowers whose nectar it gathers ceaselessly, so science diverts the individual from himself and his own metaphorical power, forcing him to go and gather nectar outside, to go and find the truth in its beehive:

> *our* treasure is where the beehives of our knowledge are. We are constantly making for them, being by nature winged creatures and honey-gatherers of the spirit; there is one thing alone we really care about from the heart – 'bringing something home'. (GM, 'Preface', 1)

However, if the 'individual' is susceptible to the injunctions of science, it is perhaps because he is no longer 'strong' enough to be able to affirm his own perspectives. Science's neediness correlates with that of the scholar, who is 'objective' because he has no drive within him strong enough to prevail over the others and impose its evaluations. The poverty of his internal architecture leads him to take refuge in a 'hut' not far from the tower of science which protects and feeds him. So the metaphor of the beehive has a meaning which is overdetermined, richer and more revealing than it might have seemed at first sight. The implications which it contains become more explicit in the other metaphors which complement and modify it.

b) The Tower, the Bastion, the Stronghold

For the beehive is also a tower, a protective bastion, a stronghold. The beehive, because of its size, is unsuited to symbolize the protection which science offers. Thus Nietzsche attaches to it the metaphors of the tower and the stronghold, metaphors which are less habitual than that of the bulwark.

Not only does this slight displacement bring the former, more or less stereotyped metaphor to life, but it also indicates that it is more than just external dangers which need to be guarded against: the supreme danger is life itself; and one must defend oneself against everything which affirms life, whether within or outside of oneself. Man needs to put up the barricades and isolate himself, to protect his constructions from the violence which other powers 'with the most varied colours' might direct against them. Defences need to be put up against lying, myth, and art, against all those who openly proclaim the cult of appearance, of surface, of fiction, who dare to admit their perspective as such: they might draw attention to the fact that scientific truths are also the expression of a human, all-too-human measure, that 'reality', the 'real world' is simply a dream and a fiction. The tower and the stronghold are shields against the enemy as well as ways of cutting oneself off from life. These metaphors reveal that artistic creativity, which creates forms and constructs a world in the image of man, is also will to power (although in the *Philosophenbuch* Nietzsche has not yet formulated the hypothesis): they express a conflict between opposing powers, with the one seeking to affirm life and the other to deny it.

Thus the 'greatness' of science is merely an impoverished greatness, a poor man's greatness; purely fictional, it is a mask designed to scare and deceive. The stronghold, the tower, the bastion – deconstructed by rigorous philology – are transformed into a mass of planks, frames, and beams to which the weak cling in order to survive. That science has a vital function is evident also from its 'bad taste', from its 'shamelessness': no gap remains in this strange architecture which man constructs from himself; there is no space for the slightest fancy:

> above all, [science] takes pains to fill up this monstrously towering framework and to arrange therein the entire empirical world, which is to say, the anthropomorphic world. (TL, p.88)

This filling-up reaches monstrous proportions and suggests that the tower of science is more akin to a tower of Babel than that of a stronghold. Sharing an origin with ordinary language, the language of science distances itself further and further from the 'music of the world', from a 'natural language' which might name things 'properly' as God did on the day of creation. Science has an artificial language, made up of abstract signs and numbers, veritable enigmas which represent the passions of men and their conflicts more than they do the essence of things: 'The compass and tower-building of the sciences has grown enormous' (BGE 205).[4]

So the preservation of the human species is achieved by building a 'new, regular, and rigid world', at the cost of

dividing men from each other and separating them from
the world and from life; for the rigidity of the construction mimics that of a skeleton: it is only by being
always already dead in life that man can survive.

c) The Egyptian Pyramid and the Roman Columbarium

Thus the beehive, the tower, and the stronghold turn into a
construction the shape of a geometrical pyramid, analogous in its order to Spinoza's deductions. This new architecture signifies that, thanks to the concept, it was possible to
build a hierarchized world, classify everything within its
categories, assign a specific place to everything, and
constitute a legal order, that of the rational and the
reasonable. The pyramidal order is imposed as the 'true'
order and opposed to the fluctuating world of impressions,
the false world of appearances. The pyramidal order is the
metaphor for the intelligible world of essences serving as
models and norms.

> For something is possible in the realm of these
> schemata which could never be achieved with the
> vivid first impressions: the construction of a pyrami-
> dal order according to castes and degrees, the creation
> of a new world of laws, privileges, subordinations,
> and clearly marked boundaries – a new world, one
> which now confronts that other vivid world of first
> impressions as more solid, more universal, better
> known, and more human than the immediately per-
> ceived world, and thus as the regulative and impera-
> tive world. (TL, p.84)

The pyramidal order is the rigid order of a skeleton, four-
square like a die; it is the order of the *Egyptian pyramid*
containing within itself the *mummified* impressions which it
entombs.[5] But from this metaphor, Nietzsche slides to that
of the *Roman columbarium*, for mummification[6] implies that
the face of the dead person still remains perceptible: the

pyramid is a noble tomb, and life, even if in an impoverished form, is still present there. The *Roman columbarium* preserves no more than the ashes of the deceased, just as the concept is simply a 'residue' of metaphors. Ashes mean that any effigy has been completely effaced, any singularity volatilized; preserving nothing but the ashes of life is an extreme reduction of differences: it is supreme equality, supreme injustice.[7] Thus science is a 'sepulchre of the intuitions', but it is also the tomb of the scientist, even of all the affirmative powers of life. For this remedy for neediness is in fact a poison: it gives the strong a bad conscience, seducing them with the honey of abstractions distilled in the beehives of knowledge. The deified idea is a formidable Circe who castrates and operates by cunning: dressed in old rags and tatters, stripped of all sensory clothing, she could be found repulsive. But man is attracted precisely by 'nakedness', purity, the appeal of the great void, nothingness, God, Being – the hollowest concepts of all, which he places at the summit or the base of his architecture. For, by an effect of inversion proper to the optic of the weak, the high becomes the low and the low, the high: what is the culmination of a whole process, coming at the end, is put at the beginning. By putting God at the beginning and at the end, these anti-artistic spirits depreciate life and make it ugly: the world which they create is the reflection of their own neediness.

Thus the columbarium ends up burying its constructor and destroying itself: if God is the foundation of the edifice then it is destined for demolition. The magnificence of the architecture masks the fact that it rests on metaphors, on sensory becoming, which fluctuates like running water:

Just as the Romans and the Etruscans cut up the heavens with rigid mathematical lines and confined a god within each of the spaces thereby delimited, as within a *templum*, so every people has a similarly

mathematically divided conceptual heaven above
themselves and henceforth thinks that truth demands
that each conceptual god be sought only within *his own*
sphere. Here one may certainly admire man as a
mighty genius of construction, who succeeds in piling
up an infinitely complicated dome of concepts upon
an unstable foundation, and, as it were, on running
water. (TL, p.85)

So the stability of the edifice is illusory. It floats without
support, subject to the whim of chance: the bases of the
pyramid are dice. Produced in order to deny becoming, the
conceptual system rests upon it, and like becoming it is a
game of chance. The pieces in the construction are not
irremovable: it is sufficient to change one's perspective, to
throw the dice again, transforming the initial metaphors
and, with them, the face of the architecture. The conceptual norm, which is imposed as necessary, is a pure
convention linked to a unique perspective, that of a life
which can preserve itself only by hiding its perspectivism
from itself:

Whereas each perceptual metaphor is individual and
without equals and is therefore able to elude all
classification, the great edifice of concepts displays the
rigid regularity of a Roman columbarium and exhales
in logic that strength and coolness which is characteristic of mathematics. Anyone who has felt this cool
breath [of logic] will hardly believe that even the
concept – which is as bony, four-square, and trans-
posable as a die – is nevertheless merely the *residue of a
metaphor*, and that the illusion which is involved in the
artistic transferral of a nerve stimulus into images is,
if not the mother, then the grandmother of every
single concept. (TL, p.84f.)

So the whole edifice is a 'game', a 'plaything', but one

which cannot be broken with impunity. The rule of the game is that one must take it seriously or be ruled out.[8]

The game of concepts, like the political game which it makes possible, camouflages the relations between forces which constitute it.

> In this conceptual game of dice 'truth' means using every die in the designated manner, counting its spots accurately, fashioning the right categories, and never violating the order of caste and class rank. (TL, p.85)

d) The Spider

Because this splendid and cold architecture rests on an illusory plinth, because it is made out of the very material of those it has to shelter and protect, because it conceals their death and the death of all life, it is metamorphosed from a columbarium into a spider's web: Spinoza's geometrical order is in the last resort an arachnidan one. (Nietzsche is playing here on the phonetic analogy between *Spinne* and Spinoza.)[9] The architecture of the concepts is assimilated to the network of a spider's web, for it has to be at the same time fine enough to be transported with the streams on which it rests and solid enough not to be dispersed by the lightest wind. Furthermore the analogy highlights the fact that the concepts are constructed from man himself just as the spider creates its web from its own substance.

Thus – how ridiculous! – the beehive is just a spider's web, the bee's useful work can be assimilated to the harmfulness of the spider, a 'harmfulness' which does not arise from an ill will but is rooted in necessity.

The metaphor of the spider is at the origin of a whole series of images – the text as tissue, mask or clothing; it is also the symbol for castration.[10] A veritable vampire, the spider sucks the blood of the midges it has attracted into its nets, just as the concept disfigures life, makes it pale, sad, and ugly because it is ravenous for it and feeds off it. Feeding off life does not, however, bring it to life itself: it is but the simulacrum and the ghost of life; the rags in which it decks itself, with holes in them like the spider's web, are symptomatic of its neediness. The concept has only the appearance of life because it feeds off a life already anthropomorphized: man takes from the world only what he has already given it; he feeds off his own substance, which he then unwinds in concepts like the spider unwinding its web (cf. UM IV, 5).

Thus the joy of cognition is that which recognition brings; it is that of regaining security by narcissistically assimilating the world to oneself. But the regularity of the web man has woven gives him the illusory assurance that the world he has created for himself is objective:

> it is only by means of the rigid and regular web of concepts that the waking man clearly sees that he is awake. (TL, p.89)
>
> As a genius of construction man raises himself far above the bee in the following way: whereas the bee builds with wax that she gathers from nature, man builds with the far more delicate conceptual material which he first has to manufacture from himself. (TL, p.85)

The metaphor of the spider also allows the teleological proof of the existence of God to be demystified through ridicule: if God is the architect of the world, he is simply its supreme spider. Man-spider transposes his workman-like causality metaphorically into Nature, and he solemnly calls God the workman who produced the world.[11] God, a product of the spider, is himself metamorphosed into a spider weaving intelligible models of which the sensory is a painted copy – and a badly painted one at that:

> [...] This awakens the idea that, in addition to the leaves, there exists in nature the 'leaf': the original

model [*Urform*] according to which all the leaves were perhaps woven, sketched, measured, coloured, curled, and painted – but by incompetent hands, so that no specimen has turned out to be a correct, trustworthy, and faithful likeness of the original model. (TL, p.83)

The inversion which turns the effect into a cause and the cause into an effect, the end into a beginning and the beginning into an end, is one of man's fundamental errors:

They put [...] the 'highest concepts', that is to say the most general, the emptiest concepts, the last fumes of evaporating reality, at the beginning *as* the beginning. [...] Thus they acquired their stupendous concept 'God'. ... The last, thinnest, emptiest is placed as the first, as cause in itself, as *ens realissimum*. (TI, '"Reason" in Philosophy', 4)
    And he himself [the God of the Christians] so pale, so weak, so *décadent*. ... Even the palest of the pale have still been able to master him, *messieurs* the metaphysicians, the conceptual albinos. These have spun their web around him so long that, hypnotized by their movements, he himself became a spider [*Spinne*], a metaphysician. Thenceforward he span the world again out of himself – *sub specie Spinozae* – thenceforward he transformed himself into something ever paler and less substantial, became an 'ideal', became 'pure spirit', became '*absolutum*', became 'thing in itself'. ... *Decay of a God*: God became 'thing in itself'. (AC 17)

In a general way, the metaphor of the spider is attached to the metaphors of the rag, the ghost, and sickly pallor to indicate that the concept is hatred of life and the death of desire, to signify also that castration is not caused by an 'ill will' but by necessity: the creation of a 'world of the ideal' is the unique trick which certain of the living, whose life is impoverished in the extreme, play in order to keep themselves alive.

> Insects sting, not out of malice, but because they too want to live. (HH II, 164; cf. II, 153 and 194)
>
> In the last resort, we achieve nothing more by cognition than the spider achieves by weaving its web, hunting, and sucking the blood of its prey: it wants to live and satisfy itself by means of these arts and activities – and this is precisely what we, too, are after when, in the process of cognition, we grasp suns or atoms, retain [*festhalten*] them and establish [*feststellen*] them, so to speak – it is a detour which brings us back to *ourselves* and our needs. (GOA XII, i, 79)

Transforming the world into set metaphors means deciphering behind the mask of metaphysical tatters a nihilistic will, a life which is afraid of life, which fears being seduced by sensuality because it would not be strong enough to bear its intoxication, and which preaches renunciation to the senses because, despite its desire, it would be incapable of satisfying them. Metaphor set up as a proper is this fear of the senses interpreted as an ideal. In its name philosophers, like Ulysses' companions, stop up their ears so as no longer to hear the sirens, [12] for all music is to them a seduction, a detour from the straight and narrow. But once the ears are stopped up and deaf, they no longer hear the musicality of the world and they deny it. However, the world of the ideal is more seductive than that of the senses, and that is its danger. The new philosopher must reveal the poison which is hidden there and bring to light the system of desires to which it corresponds:

> *ideas* are worse seductresses than our senses, for all their cold and anaemic appearance, and not even in spite of this appearance: they have always lived on the

'blood' of the philosopher, they always consumed his senses and even, if you will believe us, his 'heart'. These old philosophers were heartless; philosophizing was always a kind of vampirism. [...] Don't you sense a long concealed vampire in the background who begins with the senses and in the end is left with, and leaves, mere bones, mere clatter? I mean categories, formulas, *words* (for, forgive me, what was left of Spinoza, *amor intellectualis dei*, is mere clatter and no more than that: What is *amor*, what *deus*, if there is not a drop of blood in them?). In sum: all philosophical idealism to date was something like a disease, unless it was, as it was in Plato's case, the caution of an over-rich and dangerous health, the fear of *over-powerful* senses, the prudence of a prudent Socratic. – Perhaps we moderns are merely not healthy enough *to be in need of* Plato's idealism? (GS 372)[13]

But Spinoza, the prime example of the philosopher-spider, is simply continuing in the tradition inaugurated by Parmenides and perpetuated from Plato onwards: the Parmenides who rejected the multicoloured world of becoming in favour of Being, the hollowest and emptiest idea of them all, a metaphor emptied of all its meaning, all its blood.[14]

2 SATURNALIA

> I will say now that poetry is, I think, the sacrifice
> where the words are victims. We use words and make
> them the instruments of useful acts, but we would
> have no humanity if the language in us had to be
> entirely servile. Nor can we do without the efficient
> relations which words set up between men and things.
> But we wrench them from these relations in a
> delirium.
>
> (G. Bataille)

Thus the most symptomatic – and the richest – of the
metaphors for metaphor is that of the castle made of
spider's web, an architecture in 'bad taste' necessary to a
type of living things which are incapable of building
themselves a residence in 'grand style' but are nevertheless
incapable of doing without a habitat in which to feel
secure. So they must expel from their workers' city,
governed by the spirit of seriousness, any power which
wants to play with their architecture, to dismantle and
deconstruct it in order to substitute another in an original
style which defies the measure of habitual concepts. A new
construction which in turn deconstructs itself for the
benefit of another, just as Nietzsche deletes each of the
metaphors he proposes by attaching it to other, more or less
'unheard-of' ones – like the Heraclitean Zeus, constructing
and deconstructing everything in his innocent play; like any
artistic force.[15]

The metaphorical drive – which is repressed in conceptual and scientific activity, where it shows itself only in
sublimated and masked form – gives itself free rein in
other areas, in lying, dreaming, myth, art: in these it dares
to admit its perspective and recognize the mask as mask,
thanks to a superabundance of life which allows it to *will*
illusion. The drive which urges man to make metaphors,
repressed in one area, is displaced and manifests itself

elsewhere: it is indestructible, for it coincides with life itself. But whereas at times life reveals itself for what it is – evaluative, lying, artistic – at others it veils itself because it is not strong enough to go as far as it can. In this latter case it aims simply to tame power, to domesticate the strong man and reduce him to a 'sublime abortion'. The living who are truly alive can proclaim their truths 'with the most varied colours':

> This drive is not truly vanquished and scarcely subdued [...]. It seeks a new realm and another channel for its activity, and it finds this in *myth* and in *art* generally. (TL, p.89)[16]

They therefore *want* confusion, they want to return to the archaic life of dream and childhood, to be freed from the slavery to which they are subjected by the rigid web of concepts; they *want* to play with what is 'serious':

> This drive continually confuses the conceptual categories and cells by bringing forward new transferrals, metaphors, and metonymies. It continually manifests an ardent desire to refashion the world which presents itself to waking man, so that it will be as colourful, irregular, lacking in results and coherence, charming, and eternally new as the world of dreams. (TL, p.89)[17]

Such a will puts science in jeopardy, for it betrays the fact that without the conceptual fictions which imprison us behind rigid bars, we would not be able to distinguish waking from dreaming: 'reality' is based on a regular coherence[18] which deceptively passes for necessity. 'Reality' and 'appearance', waking and dreaming, seriousness and play are so many oppositions deleted by the strategic generalization of one of the two opposites: 'Heraclitus will always be right in this, that being is an empty fiction. The "apparent" world is the only one: the "real" world has only

been *lyingly added*' (TI, '"Reason" in Philosophy', 2; cf.
BGE 34). Metaphysical fictions are 'supplements'[19] added
to life, as if it lacked something, as if it were not an
affirmative power devoid of negativity. So they are
necessarily produced by a type of life which is
impoverished and deficient, which projects its own
powerlessness outside of itself at the same time as it
transforms the nature of desire, which is pure affirmative
force, into a lack, a void to be filled. At which point it needs
to fill this void by creating a fictional world, 'the other
world', conceived – to suit the needs of the cause – as
'purely' positive: a world of the absolute, the real, the true,
analogous to the neo-reality produced by psychotics.
Measured against this imaginary world, the 'real' world
becomes an 'apparent' world – relative, fluctuating, and full
of negativities. A split thus arises between the two worlds –
the delirious product of the ascetic ideal, its meaning: 'the
ascetic ideal means: that something was *lacking*, that man
was surrounded by a fearful *void* – he did not know how to
justify, to account for, to affirm himself; he *suffered* from
the problem of his meaning' (GM III, 28).[20] The meaning
provided by the ascetic ideal is a veritable nonsense. But it
was accepted by men, who consented to treat 'fictions' as
'realities' because it benefited them (in the sense in which
Freud speaks of benefiting from an illness):[21] it enabled
them to *will*, even if only to will nothingness.

Pascal's *pensée*: 'If a workman were sure to dream for
twelve straight hours every night that he was a king, I
believe that he would be almost as happy as a king who
dreamt for twelve hours every night that he was a
workman' (quoted TL, p.89)[22] is an aphorism which, as
Nietzsche interprets it, metaphorically sums up and
expresses as if in miniature [*en abîme*] the relationship which
Nietzsche establishes between concept and metaphor in the
Philosophenbuch. This *pensée* erases the opposition between
dream and waking, which are distinguished solely by their
length. The continuity of waking is introduced by the

conceptual coherence which transforms habit into necessity. Furthermore, the dream is a wish-fulfilment; i.e.
waking, itself simply a coherent dream, is a fictional
response to human needs: the workman who thinks of
himself as a king when dreaming corresponds to man in
waking life who, thanks to his unconscious metaphorical
activity and the work of science, becomes king of the
universe.

Being king is a happy dream which gives pleasure to the
man who hides from himself the metaphorical nature of
the concept. The king having the bad dream of being just a
workman corresponds to the disillusionment man feels
when he recognizes that his kingdom is just one of the
products of his fantasy but, unable to bear the truth,
remains as happy as if he were in fact the king of the
universe: for him, truth is just a 'bad dream'.

The workman's dream is comparable to the waking day
of a people stimulated by myth which, as a continuous
waking dream, works a continuous miracle. Thanks to
myth, man is king of the world: he projects himself into it
in the form of a divinity; the world is for him a masquerade
of the gods.

The king's dream is comparable to the daytime of the
thinker disenchanted with science. Through dream – and
myth and art – the workman transforms himself into a
king, and the king transforms himself into a workman: the
end of the reign of concepts brings with it veritable
Saturnalia:[23] the end of the order of castes and prohibitions, the mixing of the categories; and for a certain time
the slave takes the place of the master. The 'natural' and
'social' orders are transgressed, and it then comes to light
that they are not necessary but rest on simple conventions
and on metaphors.

When a poet makes a tree speak like a nymph, by thus
transgressing the natural order he indicates the possibility
of speaking according to a different order than the one
created by our habits. Letting vegetation speak when it

'ought' not to be able to[24] signifies that the absence of
words conceals another system of metaphors, 'proper' to
the plant, and unmasks our language, too, as metaphorical.

To represent a god in the guise of a bull making off with
a mortal is both to transgress a sexual prohibition and to
will an illicit confusion of the species. The guise indicates
both that sexuality can only be satisfied if it disguises itself,
and that the divinity is a metamorphosis of the bull, a
simple metaphor...[25]

Representing a goddess on a chariot next to a man
(Pisistratus) wilfully confuses the human and the divine
orders.[26]

Thanks to art and myth, which lift prohibitions, everything becomes possible. Nature, far from being reduced to
ashes, is glorified: it is art, and plays games with itself,
constructing and deconstructing worlds; using metaphors
constantly, it plays at deceiving man. To play this game, it
needs to be strong enough to will illusion, mask,
appearance, surface. This taste for mystification is inherent
in the metaphorical drive, and it is revealed wherever man is
sure enough of himself or whenever he has nothing to fear
from transgression, as in the theatre:

> that master of deception, the intellect, is free; it is
> released from its former slavery and celebrates its
> Saturnalia. [...] That immense framework and plank-
> ing of concepts to which the needy man clings his
> whole life long in order to preserve himself is nothing
> but a scaffolding and plaything for the most
> audacious feats of the liberated intellect. And when it
> smashes this framework to pieces, throws it into
> confusion, and puts it back together in an ironic
> fashion, pairing the most alien things and separating
> the closest, it is demonstrating that it has no need of
> these makeshifts of neediness and that it will now be
> guided by intuitions rather than by concepts. (TL,
> p. 90)

The more the drive has been subjected, the greater the debauchery will be. The licence which is given hides the fact that everyday life, too, is a dream and a fantasmagoria, since it allows the false world of habit to be endured in its normative rigidity. However, though there is a path leading from waking life to dream, no bridge leads from dream to the world of concepts: the concept can serve as a metaphor for intuition, but intuition cannot be a metaphor for the concept. Hence the necessity of multiplying metaphors, if one wants to speak of the concept, though silence would be a better language yet.

> There is no regular path which leads from these intuitions into the land of ghostly schemata, the land of abstractions. There exists no word for these intuitions; when man sees them he grows dumb, or else he speaks only in forbidden metaphors and in unheard-of combinations of concepts. He does this so that by shattering and mocking the old conceptual barriers he may at least correspond creatively to the impression of the powerful present intuition. (TL, p.90)

Thus, already in the *Philosophenbuch* Nietzsche distinguishes and opposes two types of man:

1) Rational man, who is insensitive to art and masters life through foresight, prudence, regularity; led by the abstractions which protect him from unhappiness without procuring him any happiness, he basically aspires to be freed from suffering. Prime examples of this idiosyncrasy: Spinoza and the Stoic. The latter, in his unhappiness, is a masterpiece of concealment. His nobility of soul is merely play-acting.

2) Irrational man, the joyous hero, freed from neediness since he considers only a life disguised as appearance and beauty to be real. This human type, thanks to art, is happy, lives more than the other in the acceptance of joy and

suffering, through love of life. He also suffers more because he lacks 'memory' and does not learn any lessons from experience. The prototype of this kind is the pre-Socratic Greek who conceals the ugliness of the world by projecting on to things a superabundance of life, which beautifies them:

> All the manifestations of such a life will be accompanied by this dissimulation, this disavowal of neediness, this glitter of metaphorical intuitions, and, in general, this immediacy of deception: neither the house, nor the gait, nor the clothes, nor the clay jugs give evidence of having been invented because of a pressing need. It seems as if they were all intended to express an exalted happiness, an Olympian cloudlessness, and, as it were, a playing with seriousness. (TL, p.90f.)[27]

V
Nakedness, Dress

OF THE LAND OF CULTURE

I flew too far into the future: a horror assailed me.

And when I looked around, behold! time was my only contemporary.

Then I flew back, homeward – and faster and faster I flew: and so I came to you, you men of the present, and to the land of culture. [...]

But how did I fare? Although I was so afraid – I had to laugh! My eye had never seen anything so motley-spotted!

I laughed and laughed, while my foot still trembled and my heart as well: 'Here must be the home of all the paint-pots!' I said.

Painted with fifty blotches on face and limbs: thus you sat there to my astonishment, you men of the present!

And with fifty mirrors around you, flattering and repeating your opalescence!

Truly, you could wear no better masks than your own faces, you men of the present! Who could – *recognize* you!

Written over with the signs of the past and these signs overdaubed with new signs: thus you have hidden yourselves well from all interpreters of signs!

And if one tests your virility, one finds only sterility! You seem to be baked from colours and scraps of paper glued together.

All ages and all peoples gaze motley out of your veils; all customs and all beliefs speak motley out of your gestures.

He who tore away from you your veils and wraps and paint and gestures would have just enough left over to frighten the birds.

Truly, I myself am the frightened bird who once saw you naked and without paint; and I flew away when the skeleton made advances to me.

I would rather be a day-labourer in the underworld and among the shades of the bygone! – Even the inhabitants of the underworld are fatter and fuller than you!

This, yes this is bitterness to my stomach, that I can endure you neither naked nor clothed, you men of the present!

(Thus Spoke Zarathustra)[1]

1 PROPER, APPROPRIATION, PROPERTY

However, the reading of the two types of men distinguished in the *Philosophenbuch* can only be completed with the hypothesis of the will to power. Then the 'rational' man, subjected to the test of the genealogical hammer, is deciphered as a nihilist; 'irrational' man, as an affirmative will.

But equally the will to power is then substituted for the operative and strategic concept of metaphor, of which it is the ultimate signification: metaphorical activity coincides with that of the will to power. Metaphor becomes a text, the product of a unique perspective, an interpretation which posits an affirmative or negative meaning. If Nietzsche substitutes 'perspective' for 'metaphor', then, it is because the meaning which is posited and transposed in things is no longer referred to an essence of the world, a proper. The 'world', the 'essence' are themselves texts written by a specific type of will. The idea of an originary music of the world – a sort of original text making human texts into mere metaphors – disappears: every text becomes the correlate of an interpretation which constitutes a specific, provisional meaning symptomatic of a certain type of life's mastery over the world and over other types of life.

The hypothesis of the will to power, an evaluative artistic force which posits forms but seeks also to master by means of them, accounts for the generalization of metaphor, or of text, as well as for the illusion which passes them off as 'proper': every desire tends to impose its evaluations as absolute, tends to master, is 'philosophical'. The 'proper' is such only because it is the fruit of a unique perspective (which implies that 'individuality' is a hierarchization of forces by a provisional centre of perspective and not a departure from oneself, a metamorphosis, as in *The Birth of Tragedy*). The 'proper' is such only in the sense of an appropriation of the world by a specific will, which constitutes the 'properties' of the object grasped so as to

make it its 'property'. In attributing a proper metaphorically, one confers on oneself, by the same token, the
ownership [*propriété*] of the thing.[2]

> Whereas in fact thought, in perceiving a thing, goes
> through a series of signs which memory offers it,
> searching for similarities; and man, by means of a
> similar sign, posits a thing as 'known', apprehends it,
> *grasps* [*ergreift*] it, for a long time thinking he thereby
> *grasped its meaning* [*begreifen*]. The act of grasping and
> apprehending, of appropriating, already meant for
> him a way of recognizing, of knowing in depth; the
> very words of human language seemed for a long
> time – and still seem so today to the people – to be not
> signs but truths in relation to the things they desig-
> nated. (GOA XIII, 46)[3]

Presenting one's proper as 'proper in itself' - wanting to
impose it on others as a concept – means making a show of
authority and usurping power: it means being a tyrant. It
means wanting to prescribe to nature the canon of one's
own [*propres*] laws whilst still claiming to find them there.[4]
To name is to be the master and to make oneself master of
all and everyone:

> The lordly right of giving names extends so far that
> one should allow oneself to conceive the origin of
> language itself as an expression of power on the part
> of the rulers: they say 'this *is* this and this', they seal
> every thing and event with a sound and, as it were,
> take possession of it. (GM I, 2)[5]

From this it follows that imposing a name is enough to
make one believe one possesses a thing in its essentiality, or
to change its meaning: thus, thanks to a simple change of
name, the priests were able to perform the veritable
conjuring trick of making what had until then been hated
appear beneficial (GM III, 18).[6]

Originality lies in what no one has yet named or can name, or else in the namer: '*Originality*. – What is originality? To *see* something that has no name as yet and hence cannot be mentioned although it stares us all in the face. The way men usually are, it takes a name to make something visible for them. – Those with originality have for the most part also assigned names' (GS 261).

Conversely, even if they keep the same name, 'things' change meanings with a change of 'masters'. In the Third Essay of the *Genealogy*, Nietzsche shows that the ascetic ideal has not one essence but a multiplicity of meanings which vary according to whether an artist, a scientist, a philosopher, or a priest is pursuing it. These different meanings do not have the same importance, even if collectively they all at bottom reflect the same will to nothingness. Only the priest pushes this ideal to its ultimate consequences. Thus it is the meaning for the priest which allows the other meanings to be deciphered, and to be read as a mask when it is a philosopher who appropriates them, or as a simple borrowing in the case of the artist. So there is a typological unity being expressed through an irreducible diversity, but there is no essential unity. The question of essence, 'What is it?', is itself already an imposition of meaning, an interpretation:

'Essence', the 'essential nature', is something perspective and already presupposes a multiplicity. At the bottom of it there always lies 'What is that for *me*?' (for us, for all that lives, etc.).

A thing would be defined once all creatures had asked 'What is that?' and had answered their question. Supposing one single creature, with its own relationships and perspectives for all things, were missing, then the thing would not yet be 'defined'.

In short: the essence of a thing is only an *opinion* about the 'thing'. Or rather: 'it is considered' is the real 'it is', the sole 'this is'.

One may not ask: 'Who then interprets?' for the interpretation itself is a form of the will to power, and exists (but not as a 'being' but as a process, a becoming) as an affect. (WP 556)

The Second Essay establishes that punishment has not just one but several meanings – as many as there are forces appropriating it. Thus one must not confuse the origin of an institution with its goal, for that would amount to the belief that its meaning is unchanging and independent of those who are its masters: whereas each mastering is equivalent to a new interpretation which, by imposing itself, effaces the previous meaning and ultimately forces it to be forgotten. Grasping the goal of an institution simply means comprehending that a will to power succeeded in mastering something less powerful than itself; it does not mean grasping its origin:

all subduing and becoming master involves a fresh interpretation, an adaptation through which any previous 'meaning' and 'purpose' are necessarily obscured or even obliterated. [...] The entire history of a 'thing', an organ, a custom can in this way be a continuous sign-chain of ever new interpretations and adaptations whose causes do not even have to be related to one another but, on the contrary, in some cases succeed and alternate with one another in a purely chance fashion. (GM II, 12)[7]

So there is no purposiveness in the evolution of a concept, just as in a general way one must not interpret history dialectically. Meaning 'evolves' at the whim of the displacements in mastery and follows the chance developments in the struggle for power:

The 'evolution' of a thing, a custom, an organ is thus by no means its *progressus* toward a goal, even less a

logical *progressus* by the shortest route and with the
smallest expenditure of force – but a succession of
more or less profound, more or less mutually independent processes of subduing, plus the resistances
they encounter, the attempts at transformation for
the purpose of defence and reaction, and the results of
successful counteractions. The form is fluid, but the
'meaning' is even more so. (GM II, 12)

So it is impossible to 'define' a term: every concept is a
synthesis of undialectizable meanings. A definition can be
produced for that which has no history, i.e. nothing, or for
'metaphysical' concepts, pure fictions which are void of
'meaning', but in the synthesis of the concept now one
element, now another prevails: a predominance symptomatic of the type of will which was dominant at one
moment and provisionally imposed its perspective on
history.

2 HISTORY, ETYMOLOGY, GENEALOGY

Because every concept has a history, the new philosophy
which Nietzsche inaugurates is essentially 'historical'. It
reveals the 'becoming' inherent in each concept, and
unmasks behind the abstraction, generality, and unity of
each term the multiplicity of metaphors which it contains
and their transformation over the course of time. This
historical method is also *genealogical* because it reads each
metaphor (or each 'proper') as the symptom of a type of
will, whether noble or base. Similarly it calls itself a
philology for it deciphers every concept like a text, in order
to read the meaning and the direction of the meaning which
is being expressed, whether affirmative or negative. Thus
etymology, because it highlights the becoming of the
concept, is used by Nietzsche as a weapon against metaphysical dogmatism, and it plays a strategic role in the
genealogical deciphering of concepts:

What separates us most radically from all Platonic and
Leibnizian ways of thinking is this: we believe in no

eternal concepts, eternal values, eternal forms, or eternal souls; and philosophy, to the extent that it is scientific and not dogmatic, is for us merely the broadest extension of the concept of 'history'. On the basis of etymology and the history of language we consider all concepts as *having become*, and many of them as still becoming, so that the most general concepts, being the *falsest*, must also be the oldest. (GOA XIII, 46)

Genealogical etymology does not aim to find the originary, true, and accurate meaning,[8] but to discover multiple origins and to hierarchize them: it establishes 'distinctions between ages, peoples, degrees of rank among individuals' (GM, 'Preface', 3). Genealogy reveals the pre-eminence of a group of spontaneous, aggressive, and conquering forces which are usurpatory and which never cease to give new exegeses and new directions. Etymology teaches that weak wills can impose their meanings only by reaction, by inverting, disfiguring, and displacing the meaning attributed by the strong.

Nietzsche, for whom moralities are a 'long hieroglyphic record' (GM, 'Preface', 7), a semiotics and a symptomatology,[9] 'a *sign language of the emotions*' (BGE 187) – which are themselves a '*sign language of the functions of every organism*' (GOA XIII, 362) – traces the genealogy of moral concepts. Taking them 'literally' would produce 'misconstructions', for they are not facts but interpretations relative to the conditions and surroundings which gave birth to them: 'one word [morality] can conceal the most divergent tendencies' (TI, 'The "Improvers" of Mankind', 2).

A genealogical reading teaches that the language of morality is a falsifying interpretation, a metaphor for the bodily text transposed into the superficial language of consciousness. Working against the grain, Nietzsche reinstates the 'true' text of morality by inverting the metaphor and re-establishing the natural hierarchy between the different symbolic languages:

Both the *taming* [*Zähmung*] of the beast man and the breeding [*Züchtung*] of a certain species of man has been called 'improvement': only these zoological *termini* express realities – realities, to be sure, of which the typical 'improver', the priest, knows nothing – *wants* to know nothing. ... To call the taming of an animal its 'improvement' is in our ears almost a joke. (TI, 'The "Improvers" of Mankind', 2)

One language is deconstructed and replaced by another, more 'accurate' one, which shatters the first. The trickery of those who take seriously the 'improvement' of man meets with the mocking laugh of the 'gay science'.[10]

The etymology of moral concepts shows that the concepts 'good' and 'evil' vary in meaning according to whether they are born to the realm of the masters or of the slaves: moral concepts derive from the aristocratic meaning, by transformation and metaphorical displacement. By dint of the inversion in the evaluation of values performed by the priestly caste, the weak man sets up his 'proper' as an absolute. But the weak man has no 'proper', is not 'proper', since he has no drive strong enough to impose itself: he is what he is only through his opposition to the others. The originary meaning of a concept is always a *strong* meaning; the one which is posited by the weak is born of *ressentiment*, it is the refusal of the different and of differences.

Slave morality from the outset says No to what is 'outside', what is 'different', what is 'not itself'. (GM I, 10)

The signpost to the *right* road was for me the question: what was the real etymological significance of the designations for 'good' coined in the various languages? I found they all led back to the *same conceptual transformation* – that everywhere 'noble', 'aristocratic' in the social sense, is the basic concept [*Grundbegriff*] from which 'good' in the sense of 'with aristocratic soul', 'noble', 'with a soul of a high order', 'with a privileged soul' necessarily developed: a development which always runs parallel with that other in which 'common', 'plebeian', 'low' are finally transformed into the concept 'bad'. [...] About the time of the Thirty Years' War, late enough therefore, this meaning changed into the one now customary [*verschiebt sich dieser Sinn in den jetzt Gebräuchlichen*]. (GM I, 4)

The meaning given by the weak indeed *comes from* the one imposed by the strong, the mother idea: it derives from it but it also departs from it. The moral meaning expresses the strong meaning only metaphorically, just as the daughter cannot give birth to the mother. The 'strong' or 'proper' meaning expresses a system of forces, and the meaning is derived by displacing – repressing – the originary forces and their evaluations, resulting in their disfigurement. Metaphor is here a caricature, a parody, an aping, a distorted echo, a flattening-out of the first meaning, which goes hand in hand with the annihilation and domestication of the strong; only by setting up a whole system of suffering and hypnotization aimed at hiding the genesis of the concept can the weak guarantee that the inversion they have performed will last. Thanks to the retarding influence of the 'herd animal's democratic prejudice, the weak stand in the way of any investigation into the question of origins.

Etymology in fact reveals that, showing through the words and the roots which signify 'good', there is always a principal nuance of 'the noble' feeling themselves to be men of a superior rank. Sometimes they take their name from the superiority of their power (the Powerful, the Masters, the chiefs), at other times from the external signs of this superiority or from a typical feature of their character. If one studies the transformations in meaning of the term ἐσθλος in Theognis, it emerges that according to its root it means 'one who is, who is real'; then it becomes

'the truthful' – at which point it is the rallying sign for the
nobility and allows them to be distinguished from the
deceitful men, the common run. Finally, after the decline
of the nobility, it designates nobility of soul and takes on
the sense of 'something ripe and sweet'. The comparative
method reveals that the same displacement of meaning has
occurred in the various languages, and it allows one to
deduce a general law for the transformation of a pre-
eminent political concept into a psychological one (GM I,
5–6). The psychological concept is a metaphor for the
political concept, itself a metaphor for a pretext written by
the drives, a metaphor for the pre-eminence of one drive
exerting its tyranny over the others: the political hierarchy
is just the metaphorical expression of a hierarchy established within the 'soul'. Social distance can be desired only
if one can take one's distance from 'oneself' and one's
evaluations, only if one can change one's centre of
perspective, and with it one's 'proper'.

But conversely distance from oneself is possible only if
one has served one's apprenticeship in social distance.
Under certain conditions of existence nobility of soul can
be found only in a specific class which, alone, can use its
energies without reserve, play games with itself and
distance itself. Primarily the term 'good' is an absolute
description for a certain quality of the act – but one must
still be able to act:

> Without the *pathos of distance* such as develops from the
> incarnate differences of classes, from the ruling
> caste's constant looking out and looking down on
> subjects and instruments and from its equally constant
> exercise of obedience and command [...] that other,
> more mysterious pathos could not have developed
> either, that longing for an ever-increasing widening
> of distance within the soul itself, the formation of
> ever higher, rarer, more remote, tenser, more com-
> prehensive states, in short precisely the elevation of

the type 'man', the continual 'self-overcoming of man', to take a moral formula in a supra-moral sense. (BGE 257)

The moral formulation of the pathos of distance reinscribes in the metaphorical language of consciousness a text which has always already been written by instinctive evaluation, and which is always already effaced; it is this text which rigorous philology and etymology are aiming to arrive at. But though it is possible to pass from the surface to the depths, beneath the depths one will find more depths, and so on indefinitely. Surface, depths – two opposites to be deleted as such, whether it be the one or the other which is generalized. One could say of any text what Nietzsche says about the philosophical text: 'Does one not write books precisely to conceal what lies within us?'

> The hermit [...] will doubt whether a philosopher *could* have 'final and real' opinions at all, whether behind each of his caves there does not and must not lie another, deeper cave – a stranger, more comprehensive world beyond the surface, an abyss behind all depths, beneath every 'foundation'. Every philosophy is a foreground philosophy [...]. Every philosophy also *conceals* a philosophy; every opinion is also a hiding-place, every word also a mask. (BGE 289)

Rigorous philology does not aim to reconstitute the 'true' meaning of nature, for 'nature', 'truth', 'signification' are already interpretations by certain living things:

> That the value of the world lies in our interpretation (– that other interpretations than merely human ones are perhaps somewhere possible –); that previous interpretations have been perspective valuations by virtue of which we can survive in life, i.e. in the will to power, for the growth of power; that every elevation

of man brings with it the overcoming of narrower
interpretations; that every strengthening and increase
of power opens up new perspectives and means
believing in new horizons – this idea permeates my
writings. The world with which we are concerned is
false, i.e. is not a fact but a fable, an approximation on
the basis of a meagre sum of observations; it is 'in
flux', as something in a state of becoming, as a
falsehood always changing but never getting near the
truth: for – there is no 'truth'. (WP 616; cf. WP 552
(p.298f.))

3 THE ORIGINAL TEXT, *HOMO NATURA*[11]

When Nietzsche writes that one must reconstitute behind
every text the original text *homo natura*, that does not mean
finding a text cut off from all interpretation, a 'being in
itself', an ontological truth. On the contrary, it means he is
going against a metaphysical reading which conceals the
text as interpretation behind the rags it has woven.
Unmasking the metaphysical illusion does not mean
removing from the text a cloak veiling the truth;[12] on the
contrary it means showing the clothing which an apparent
'nakedness' conceals, it means doing away with the rags and
replacing them with clothes of flesh and blood. It means no
longer reading the 'letter' of the text but its 'spirit', i.e. its
'body', seeing it as a falsified and distorted reinscription of
the instinctive writing of the will to power. It means
making the figure[13] reappear beneath the disfigurement.

To arrive at the original text *homo natura* one must not let
oneself be seduced by metaphysical 'purity', by the make-
up of words: one must stop up one's ears to their charms.
One must bring about a displacement which is the reverse
of that brought about by history, changing one's perspective so that a new reading of the text, guided by a new art of
interpretation, makes the perspective appear as such (and so
that it is recognized as the expression of a hierarchical

relationship between forces). The instinctive text, the natural text, coincides with interpretation, with an evaluation which aims at power; this is the text of life, which at times presents itself as such, in the case of the strong, and at other times finds itself concealed by a secondary, deceptive interpretation which veils its character as interpretation, as a secondary writing on a pre-existent text, but is nevertheless just its disguised metaphorical expression, produced by a perspectival shift which conceals the genesis of the text. Arriving at the text of *homo natura* means risking the truth which the weak cannot admit, that there is no truth; it means revitalizing pale and emaciated ideas, reading every abstract text which has been sifted by consciousness as the disguised expression of unconscious desires, as a mask repressing the metaphorical meaning which constitutes it:

> In the meantime [...] we ourselves are likely to be least inclined to dress up in moralistic verbal tinsel [...]. They are beautiful, glittering, jingling, festive words: honesty, love of truth, love of wisdom, sacrifice for the sake of knowledge, heroism of the truthful [...]. But we hermits and marmots long ago became convinced that this worthy verbal pomp too belongs among the ancient false finery, lumber and gold-dust of unconscious human vanity, and that under such flattering colours and varnish too the terrible basic text [*Grundtext*] *homo natura* must again be discerned. For to translate man back into nature; to master the many vain and fanciful interpretations and secondary meanings which have been hitherto scribbled and daubed over that eternal basic text *homo natura* [...] that may be a strange and extravagant task but it is a *task*. (BGE 230)[14]

So the original text is that of *the will to power*. This will is not an ontological truth grasped by intuition, nor even the result of a deduction or an induction. It is an unhypothetical hypothesis posited in the name of 'the method's demand for economy',[15] a principle accepted by the philosophical tradition and which, revaluated genealogically, means a perspective should be pushed to its ultimate consequences so that one can see how far it can lead (an interpretation which therefore already presupposes the hypothesis it seeks to establish). It is the parodic repetition of a process which leads the logicians and the philosophers into self-contradiction: a logical principle is used in order to arrive at a hypothesis which deletes the opposition between the logical and the illogical – the ultimate mockery.

So the will to power is not the truth of being, but the correlate of a method, a pure name which designates the 'intelligible character' of being, the fundamental unity of the different forms of life in their diversity: a diversity which expresses the plurality and the greater or lesser differentiation in the relations between forces. Generalizing the hypothesis allows the oppositions between 'subject' and 'object', 'matter' and 'mind', 'life' and 'spirit' to be effaced. The will to power *designates* every force which acts. Posited in the name of a method, it is the correlate of a certain art of interpretation, the rigorous philological art of a 'strong will'. Every hypothesis is the expression of a previous 'thesis', a foreground thesis, a prejudice of the philosopher: 'will to power, as is *my* theory' (BGE 36),[16] says Nietzsche. The witticism which ends section 22 of *Beyond Good and Evil* suggests there is no interpretation without a certain art of reading. So the hypothesis of the will to power is also an interpretation, but one which presents itself as such. It accounts for every interpretation as interpretation at the same time as it allows each of them to be deciphered genealogically as so many symptoms of health or sickness. This hypothesis alone can justify the generalization of metaphor. But equally it authorizes us to do without this notion.

However, the 'will to power' is itself a metaphorical expression based on a political model. The 'will', as we have seen, can be reduced to a certain specific hierarchical relationship between unconscious forces, a relationship which in turn is only comprehensible by analogy with the hierarchical system of class relations within a society, whose principle of intelligibility is in the last resort the will to power. The political model proves illuminating only provided that it presupposes what it is meant to be illuminating. Otherwise the analogy is necessarily defective, 'human, all too human', inadequate to describe the 'intelligible character' of every thing:

> Someone could come along [...] – an interpreter who could bring before your eyes the universality and unconditionality of all 'will to power' in such a way that almost any word and even the word 'tyranny' would finally seem unsuitable or as a weakening and moderating metaphor – as too human. (BGE 22)

'Strong' and 'weak' wills are simply metaphors which can lead one into error if they are not recognized as such.

> There is no will, and consequently neither a strong nor a weak will. The multitude and disgregation of impulses and the lack of any systematic order among them result in a 'weak will'; their co-ordination under a single predominant impulse results in a 'strong will': in the first case it is the oscillation and the lack of gravity; in the latter, the precision and clarity of the direction. (WP 46)

Thus it was the forgetting of metaphor which produced the illusion of free will; an experience which men have in the political domain was illegitimately transposed into the metaphysical realm: in society the man who is subjugated and oppressed feels enslaved, whereas the privileged man who has all the rights feels 'free'. Each thinks that what makes him strong is also what makes him free: 'The theory of freedom of will is an invention of *ruling* classes' (WS 9).

Again, it is the forgetting of metaphor which makes one accept the will as the real essence of all things and makes one lapse into mysticism like Schopenhauer:

> Even the word 'will', which Schopenhauer remoulded as a common designation for many different human states and inserted into a gap in the language – greatly to his own advantage insofar as he was a moralist, since he was now at liberty to speak of the 'will' as Pascal had spoken of it – even Schopenhauer's 'will' has, in the hands of its originator, through the philosopher's rage for generalization turned out to be a disaster for science: for this will has been turned into a metaphor when it is asserted that all things in nature possess will; finally so that it can be pressed into the service of all kinds of mystical mischief it has been misemployed towards a false reification. (HH II, 5)

There are those who, by forgetting the metaphorical status of the will to power, have managed to see Nietzsche as the last metaphysician, who simply inverted Platonism.[17] This would then make Nietzsche's hypothesis itself just a fictional 'supplement' inserted into a gap in the language, an improper generalization, a reified metaphor: there would be nothing to distinguish Nietzsche from Schopenhauer.

However, Nietzsche's text hardly authorizes such an assimilation. The fact that the will to power is not an essence, nor even an explanatory concept, but a simple metaphorical name, is expressed by the multiple 'representatives' it has in the mythical figures of Dionysus, Apollo, Oedipus, etc.: metamorphoses of the will to power which repeat those of Dionysus and symbolize the protean character of life.

Dionysus and his avatars are a mythical figure for the 'original text of life', stripped of all metaphysical rags: Dionysus is naked, devoid of all shame:

> Indeed, if it were permitted to follow the human custom of applying to him beautiful, solemn titles of

pomp and virtue, I would have to extol his courage as investigator and discoverer, his daring honesty, truthfulness and love of wisdom. But such a God has nothing to do with all this venerable lumber and pomp. 'Keep that', he would say, 'for yourself and your like and for anyone else who needs it! I – have no reason to cover my nakedness!' – One will see that this species of divinity and philosopher is perhaps lacking in shame? (BGE 295)[18]

The nakedness of Dionysus does not symbolize the very presence of Being in its truth, but the innocence of a life which has nothing to reproach itself for, which is strong enough not to be ashamed of its perspective and its evaluations, beautiful enough to accept and love itself without having to put on a mask. Dionysus, who likes strong, handsome men, tells Ariadne that in order to resemble him even more, those who are already very ingenious, and clever enough to find their way through every labyrinth, must be stronger, wickeder, more profound and handsome in order to tolerate themselves without needing to disguise themselves in the shining dress of morality: borrowed dress, deceptive masks designed to veil the poverty and ugliness of their perspective, their inability to affirm themselves for what they are.[19] So the opposition between 'dress' and 'nakedness' is not that between 'error' and 'truth', but between two 'texts' of the world, one which makes it ugly, the other which metamorphoses it into a beauty.

> *How morality is scarcely dispensable.* – A naked human being is generally a shameful sight. [...] It seems that we Europeans simply cannot dispense with that masquerade which one calls clothes. Now consider the way 'moral man' is dressed up, how he is veiled behind moral formulas and concepts of decency – the way our actions are benevolently concealed by the concepts

of duty, virtue, sense of community, honourable-
ness, self-denial – should the reasons for all this not be
equally good? I am not suggesting that all this is meant
to mask human malice and villainy – the wild animal in
us; my idea is, on the contrary, that it is precisely as
tame animals that we are a shameful sight and in need
of the moral disguise, that the 'inner man' in Europe is
not by a long shot bad enough to show himself
without shame (or to be *beautiful*). The European
disguises himself *with morality* because he has become
a sick, sickly, crippled animal that has good reasons
for being 'tame' [...]. It is not the ferocity of the beast
of prey that requires a moral disguise but the herd
animal with its profound mediocrity, timidity, and
boredom with itself. With morality the European
dresses up – let us confess it! – to look nobler, more
important, more respectable, 'divine'. (GS 352)[20]

The opposition is not between nakedness and dress, but
between clothing woven by instinctive evaluations, which
forms a perfect marriage with the contours of the body it
clothes and thus reveals it, and a badly adapted clothing
which travesties the person it covers. The former corresponds to the original text *homo natura*, the latter to a text
corrupted by 'naïve humanitarian adjustment[s] and distortion[s] of meaning' (BGE 22), which has been sifted by
consciousness and translated into a 'feignedly exaggerated'
language (WS 5).[21]

As the 'last disciple of the philosopher Dionysus',[22] the
rigorous philologist, truthful and upright, must understand simply 'what the text intends to say but without
sensing, indeed presupposing, a *second* meaning' (HH I, 8);
he must get back to the 'literality' of the text of nature –
beyond its mystical and religious covering woven by
metaphysical exegesis, which gives a 'pneumatical' explanation for the book of nature, as the Church and its doctors
did in previous times for the Bible. The metaphysicians

perform a double inversion: they take the text of nature for a collection of symbols to be deciphered, whereas they read 'literally' the falsified text of consciousness, a secondary and metaphorical text, a symbolic and symptomatic mask. The writing of the drives thus passes for the divine word, and interpretation passes for 'fact'. By this double corruption every text is disfigured and caricatured, either because too many metaphors are read into it or not enough. So anyone who is not equipped with a rigorous art of interpretation finds that reading the text leads to multiple 'misconstructions'. Thus men were mistaken about the 'saint', for they falsely interpreted his moods as superhuman phenomena: the value he was granted did not derive from what he was but from what he had meant to others. He himself did not know himself:

> he himself deciphered the characters of his moods, inclinations, and actions by means of an art of interpretation that was as exaggerated and artificial as the pneumatical interpretation of the Bible. [...] He was not an especially good man, even less an especially wise one: but he *signified* something that exceeded the ordinary human portion of goodness and wisdom. (HH I, 143)

So one must learn to 'read well', to decipher the falsified secondary text in order to discover the literality of the writing of the 'drives', a system of differences symptomatic of the 'style' of one drive which provisionally masters the others and serves as a 'centre' of perspective, a centre which is displaced at the whim of chance in the relations between forces. Nietzsche invites us to a difficult task since

> it requires a great deal of understanding to apply to nature the same kind of rigorous art of elucidation that philologists have now fashioned for all books [...]. But as even with regard to books the bad art of

elucidation has by no means been entirely overcome and one still continually encounters in the best educated circles remnants of allegorical and mystical interpretations: so it is also in respect to nature – where, indeed, it is even far worse. (HH I, 8)[23]

VI
Writing, Reading

The book become almost human. – Every writer is surprised anew how, once a book has detached itself from him, it goes on to live a life of its own; it is to him as though a part of an insect had come free and was now going its own way. Perhaps he almost forgets it, perhaps he raises himself above the views he has set down in it, perhaps he no longer even understands it and has lost those wings upon which he flew when he thought out that book: during which time it seeks out its readers, enkindles life, makes happy, terrifies, engenders new works, becomes the soul of new designs and undertakings – in short, it lives like a being furnished with soul and spirit and is yet not human. – That author has drawn the happiest lot who as an old man can say that all of life-engendering, strengthening, elevating, enlightening thought and feeling that was in him lives on in his writings, and that he himself is now nothing but the grey ashes, while the fire has everywhere been rescued and borne forward. – If one now goes on to consider that, not only a book, but every action performed by a human being becomes in some way the cause of other actions, decisions, thoughts, that everything that happens is inextricably knotted to everything that will happen, one comes to recognize the existence of an actual *immortality*, that of motion: what has once moved is enclosed and eternalized in the total union of all being like an insect in amber. (HH I, 208)

Linguistic studies [...] are pursued more zealously than ever, but no one considers it necessary to educate himself in correct writing and speaking. (UM III, 8)

1 TO HAVE A THOUSAND EYES

The return to the text goes hand in hand with the need for a new philosophical writing. As a rigorous philologist, and in order to dispel the metaphysical seductions and the mis-constructions produced by deceptive interpretations,

Nietzsche, strategically, turns himself into a poet: he multiplies metaphors, repeating the traditional metaphors and attaching them to less usual ones, or pushing them to their ultimate consequences to see just where they can lead. The writing which results does away with the exclusive use of certain metaphors: privileging *one* metaphor would imply a reference to a 'proper' which it would represent better than any other. Diversifying metaphors, on the other hand, suggests that none is proper or more 'proper' than any other, that the 'proper' is simply the appropriation of the 'world' by a certain perspective which imposes its law on it. Knowledge and mastery are one and the same thing: one cannot aim at 'objectivity' by cutting oneself off from every 'point of view' but, on the contrary, one needs to multiply perspectives in order to see 'the world' with the greatest possible number of 'eyes', constructing and deconstructing worlds as an artist. The multiplication of metaphors symbolizes the plurality of the points of view with which the seeker after knowledge must play; it *is* this play, which coincides with '*amor fati*', the affirmation of life in all its forms. It is the *will* to a total art form. To make a systematic use of metaphor is to respect the 'justice' which wills perspective and difference, by arming oneself against the 'injustice' of the concept, the shield of the weak who set up as a norm their fixed perspective cut off from becoming.

Understood correctly, then, 'objectivity' coincides with 'subjectivity'. Metaphor foregrounds the 'personality' which is effaced by and in the concept. It deconstructs the concepts of 'subjectivity' and 'personality', which are reduced to a hierarchized system of forces. So metaphor indeed expresses a 'proper', but one which is provisional and multiple. Nevertheless, multiplying metaphors and the number of one's 'personalities' does not mean being a 'chameleon-man' and changing skins with time: metaphor is symptomatic of a strong will only if it has been pushed to its ultimate consequences. If 'chameleon-man' changes perspectives often it is merely because none of his desires is strong enough to impose itself on the others for any length of time. None of his perspectives really 'expresses' him. The deliberate use of multiple metaphors is on the contrary the sign of a noble will which, though capable of affirming one perspective for a long stretch of time, is nevertheless at enough of a distance from it to change it and see the world with 'other eyes'. Such a change implies an art of 'staging' and watching oneself, without which everyone would be simply 'foreground' and would be living enslaved to a single point of view, taking a crude perspective as 'proper' and as 'reality in itself' (cf. GS 78). Such a change of perspective gives an education in 'objectivity', displacement, and 'carrying over' from one 'ego' to another 'ego':

> To see differently [...], to *want* to see differently, is no small discipline and preparation of the intellect for its future 'objectivity' – the latter understood not as 'contemplation without interest' (which is a nonsensical absurdity), but as the ability *to control* one's Pro and Con and to dispose of them, so that one knows how to employ a *variety* of perspectives and affective interpretations in the service of knowledge. [...] There is *only* a perspective seeing, *only* a perspective 'knowing'; and the *more* affects we allow to speak about one thing, the *more* eyes, different eyes, we can use to observe one thing, the more complete will our 'concept' of this thing, our 'objectivity', be. (GM III, 12. Cf. BGE 211, 212, 231; GS 374; HH I, 513)[1]

Nevertheless, in this transition from one perspective to another, from one metaphor to another, a radical 'leap' would be impossible. One can become 'only what one is', and the different points of view 'express' the same soil; each of them is a stage in a ripening, the level reached by the dominant drive in its increasing affirmation. A retrospective reading can establish the systematic interrelation of the various perspectives; it can unify them and speak of *one* life, just as it can find the 'same taste', the same scent in the multiple metaphors and seek the law which governs the transition from one to the other or their transformation. A diversity, then, but a unity as well; a discontinuity within continuity. There is no play without repetition, without a certain probity: '*Nature never makes a leap*. – However vigorously a man may develop and seem to leap over from one thing into its opposite, closer observation will nonetheless discover the *dovetailing* where the new building grows out of the old. This is the task of the biographer: he always has to bear in mind the fundamental principle that nature never makes a leap' (WS 198).[2]

So expressing 'oneself' through multiple metaphors means being neither like the 'specialist', the prisoner of a unique point of view which he masters but which also masters him, nor like the 'polydexterous' man of letters 'with a thousand talents', 'the man of letters who really *is* [*eigentlich*] nothing but "*represents*" almost everything, playing and "substituting" for the expert' (GS 366). Scholars are still preferable to the man of letters, a real cultural parasite, for at least they 'represent' what they are, 'with uncompromising opposition to everything that is semblance, half-genuine, dressed up, virtuoso-like, demagogical, or histrionic in *litteris et artibus* – to everything that cannot prove […] its unconditional *probity* in discipline and prior training' (GS 366).[3]

This art of 'staging' and watching oneself is nevertheless not theatrical; it is play which is nevertheless not 'pure' play: the detour via morality is necessary in order for it to be overcome. But the overcoming is not a 'pure' inversion. The metaphorical play retains a certain sense of the seriousness of morality.

So the multiplication of metaphors is not purely rhetorical: attaching new metaphors to old ones or reiterating them implies a revaluation of their meaning according to the hypothesis of the will to power.

With the notion of 'perspective', Nietzsche takes up a Leibnizian metaphor[4] inscribed within the more general model of cognition which is vision. Metaphysics took this model because it considered sight the most 'speculative' of the senses, the one which delivered the object at a distance and allowed one to grasp it with the greatest clarity (without having to touch the object, to introduce a manipulating operation calling for the servile use of the hand). Paradoxically, vision was more especially representative of intuition, the most perfect kind of knowledge because it was the most immediate and closest to the object. The eye was also privileged because, situated at the top of the face, it is the most spiritual of the senses, the furthest from the earth, from the base, the sordid, the sex organs. The eye is a noble organ which does no work and does not involve itself in impure contact with matter. Conversely all the other senses, with the exception of hearing[5] – and in particular taste and smell – were excluded from the field of knowledge, repressed like the sex organs.[6]

With Nietzsche this hierarchy between the senses disappears.[7] For him, the eye is also a sense of smell and taste, of hearing and of touch; like the master of tragedy, it is a pentathlete, a virtuoso in five kinds of game. It is no more objective than the other senses, and like them it is will to power: there is no eye without a centre of perspective, with a 'view from nowhere'. The metaphysical reading simply betrays the lack of virility of one's drives: it fails to recognize the vital nature both of the eye and of cognition; it hides the work of the will to power and castrates the intellect.

> Henceforth, my dear philosophers, let us be on guard against the dangerous old conceptual fiction that posited a 'pure, will-less, painless, timeless knowing subject'; let us guard against the snares of such contradictory concepts as 'pure reason', 'absolute spirituality', 'knowledge in itself': these always

demand that we should think of an eye that is
completely unthinkable, an eye turned in no particular
direction, in which the active and interpreting forces,
through which alone seeing becomes seeing *something*,
are supposed to be lacking; these always demand of
the eye an absurdity and a nonsense. [...] But to
eliminate the will altogether, to suspend each and
every affect, supposing we were capable of this –
what would that mean but to *castrate* the intellect? (GM
III, 12)

Thus while he repeats the metaphor of the eye Nietzsche
makes fun of it in a thousand ways. He attaches all the
other senses to it. Once the opposition between contemplation and action has been deleted, once the philosopher has
been assimilated to the artist, it becomes impossible to
characterize him with *one* simple epithet. The 'contemplative' is also a 'taster' who, behind every affirmation, must
detect its good or bad taste.

The sense of taste has, as the true mediating sense,
often persuaded the other senses over to its own view
of things and imposed upon them its laws and habits.
One can obtain information about the subtlest myste-
ries of the arts at a meal-table: one has only to notice
what tastes good, when it tastes good, what it tastes
good after and for how long it tastes good. (WS 102)

As the etymology of *sapio* teaches us, the art of the
philosopher is that of the taster: he is characterized by an
acute ability to taste and know things, an aptitude for
discernment.[8] Taste alone allows one ultimately to appreciate whether the eye is a good or bad eye, whether it is suited
to discern particular differences or merely to grasp the
general qualities that things have in common.

But taste does not substitute for the eye so as to be a
tyrant in turn. The philosopher is also the one who can

smell the scent of things, the plebeian or aristocratic odour of words:

> *Odour of words.* – Every word has its odour: there exists a harmony and disharmony of odours and thus of words. (WS 119)

He is still a musician, in the sense that he listens in to the 'music' of life: 'The philosopher seeks to hear within himself the echoes of the world symphony and to re-project them in the form of concepts' (PTG, p.44). Finally the philosopher is also the one who wields the hammer, the axe, the scalpel: 'This proposition, hardened and sharpened beneath the hammer-blow of historical knowledge, may perhaps at some future time serve as the axe which is laid at the roots of the "metaphysical need" of man' (HH I, 37).

> However credit and debit balance may stand: at its present state as a specific individual science the awakening of moral observation has become neces-sary, and mankind can no longer be spared the cruel sight of the moral dissecting table and its knives and forceps. (ibid.)

Thus none of the senses is excluded from the new metaphorical order: all of them represent in their own way a form of the will to power of the philosopher. These metaphors, which erase each other, delete the opposition between passive and active, interested and disinterested in the realm of knowledge; they also efface the opposition between 'representative' senses and 'requirement'. Nietzsche plays with all the senses, in contrast to the weak, who always specialize in one sense or another. The plurality of metaphors for philosophy also indicates the diversity of the task of the philosopher – the philosopher being the one who has covered the whole range of all human values: 'we first had to experience the most manifold and contradictory states of joy and distress in soul and body,[9] as adventurers and circumnavigators of that inner world called "man", as surveyors and gaugers of that "higher" and "one upon the other" that is likewise called "man" – penetrating everywhere, almost without fear, disdaining nothing, losing nothing, tasting everything, cleansing everything of what is chance and accident in it and as it were thoroughly sifting it' (HH I, 'Preface', 7).[10]

The whole sensory register is used because there is no longer a 'proper' sense.[11]

2 VERTIGO

Thus the displacement to which Nietzsche subjects the metaphor of the eye is not exceptional. He proceeds in the same fashion with all the metaphors taken from the metaphysical tradition; after the 'death of God' all concepts change their meaning, lose their meaning: the madman who lights a lantern in broad daylight to look for God symbolizes the confusion of man when the traditional norms collapse, when meaning is removed. From that point on, all 'lunacy' becomes possible and all absurdity licit: day no longer means day, nor night, night, when the rigorous architecture of the concepts is dislocated and reduced to fragments of wreckage floating without direction on an enigmatic and infinite sea. The 'death of God', abolishing any proper, any absolute centre of reference, plunges man into Heraclitus' 'becoming-mad'.[12] Thus once sense (in both senses of the term)[13] has been abolished, all hierarchical oppositions based on an absolute distinction between 'high' and 'low' collapse. Metaphor can emerge from having been forgotten – there is no longer any foundation to order, nor any exclusivity; everything becomes possible:

> How could we drink up the sea? Who gave us the sponge to wipe away the entire horizon? What were we doing when we unchained this earth from its sun?

Whither is it moving now? Whither are we moving?
Away from all suns? Are we not plunging continually? Backward, sideward, forward, in all directions? Is there still any up or down? Are we not
straying as through an infinite nothing? Do we not
feel the breath of empty space? Has it not become
colder? Is not night continually closing in on us? Do
we not need to light lanterns in the morning? (GS 125)

With God dead, the philosophical axe attacks the roots of
the tree of metaphysics, which rises up to its full height on
the road not far from the sun.[14] The axe-blows produce a
veritable metamorphosis: first in the shape of a genealogical
revaluation of this metaphor, which is referred to the will
to power. The tree becomes the metaphor for a life or a
work, expressing this life as the tree expresses the ground
which produced it. Ideas ripen as the tree grows: they
undergo numerous transformations, but they are all related
through the identity of the same seed. So the tree signifies
first the relatedness of the different texts of the same life
or by the same author, the necessary link between the work
and the life, between the life and a system of forces which
constitutes it:

> Rather do our ideas, our values, our yeas and nays, our
> ifs and buts, grow out of us with the necessity with
> which a tree bears fruit – related and each with an
> affinity to each, and evidence of *one* will, *one* health,
> *one* soil, *one* sun. – Whether *you* like them, these fruits
> of ours? – But what is that to the trees! What is that to
> *us*, to us philosophers! (GM, 'Preface', 2)[15]

The metaphor of the tree also reveals the deep unity of all
living things in their aggressive efforts to conquer a soil for
themselves, adapt to it, and master it. The tree coincides
with the will to power:

> There undoubtedly comes for every man an hour
> when he stands before himself with wonder and asks:

'How does one manage to live at all? Yet nevertheless one does live!' - an hour when he begins to comprehend that he possesses an inventive faculty similar to the kind that he admires in plants, an inventiveness which twists and climbs until it finally forcibly gains a bit of light for itself and a small earthly kingdom as well, thus itself creating its portion of delight from barren soil. In one's own descriptions of one's own life there is always a point like this: a point where one is amazed that the plant can continue to live, and at the way it nevertheless sets to work with unflinching valour. (SW 200)

To the metaphor of the tree Nietzsche, like the whole tradition, attaches those of the sun and light. But he displaces things slightly: the sun is inseparable from half-light and fog, since the most 'elevated' and 'sublime' of human products have the same 'root' as 'evil'. This displacement 'highlights' everything that was concealing itself in the shade of the metaphysical sun and tree. The tree thus becomes the metaphor for the irresponsibility and innocence of a soul situated 'beyond good and evil': works are no longer judged by their merit but by their beauty:

as he [man] loves a fine work of art but does not praise it since it can do nothing for itself, as he stands before the plants, so must he stand before the actions of men and before his own. He can admire their strength, beauty, fullness, but he may not find any merit in them: the chemical process and the strife of the elements, the torment of the sick man who yearns for an end to his sickness, are as little merits as those states of distress and psychical convulsions which arise when we are torn back and forth by conflicting motives until we finally choose the most powerful of them – as we put it (in truth, however, until the most powerful motive chooses us). But all these motives, whatever exalted names we may give them, have grown up out of the same roots as those we believed evilly poisoned [...]. To perceive all this can be very painful, but then comes a consolation: such pains are birth-pangs. The butterfly wants to get out of its cocoon, it tears at it, it breaks it open: then it is blinded and confused by the unfamiliar light, the realm of freedom. It is in such men as are *capable* of that suffering [...] that the first attempt will be made to see whether mankind could *transform itself from a moral to a knowing mankind*. The sun of a new gospel is casting its first beam on the topmost summits in the soul of every individual: there the mists are gathering more thickly than ever, and the brightest glitter and the gloomiest twilight lie side by side. [...] If pleasure, egoism, vanity are *necessary* for the production of the moral phenomena and their finest flower, the sense for truth and justice in knowledge; if error and aberration of the imagination were the only means by which mankind was able gradually to raise itself to this degree of self-enlightenment and self-redemption – who could venture to denigrate those means? (HH I, 107)

Thus Nietzsche's tree is no longer really a tree: its soil is no longer secure, nor are its 'high' or its 'low'; it grows in all directions and at all times. A fantastic tree, it is the best paradigm of the new philosopher, who affirms life in all its forms, multiplying and displacing his perspectives, without referring to any absolute and definitive centre:

we ourselves keep growing, keep changing, we shed our old bark, we shed our skins every spring, we keep becoming younger, fuller of future, taller, stronger, we push our roots ever more powerfully into the depths – into evil – while at the same time we embrace the heavens ever more lovingly, more broadly, imbibing their light ever more thirstily with all our twigs and leaves. Like trees we grow – this is hard to understand, as is all of life – not in one place only but everywhere, not in one direction but equally upward and outward and inward and downward; our energy is at work simultaneously in the trunk, branches, and roots; we are no longer free to do only one particular thing, to *be* only one particular thing. ... This is our fate, as I have said; we grow in *height*; and even if this should be our fatality – for we dwell ever closer to the lightning – well, we do not on that account honour it less; it remains that which we do not wish to share, to make public – the fatality of the heights, *our* fatality. (GS 371)[16]

3 MISUNDERSTANDING[17]

However, to write while displacing the habitual meaning of metaphors, to write outside the norms of the concept, like a 'madman', is to risk not being understood – to *want* not to be understood – by the herd, by *common sense*. Dwelling ever closer to the lightning is a fatality no one envies, and which leaves anyone who chooses it isolated. Thus it is Nietzsche's fate to be 'misheard',[18] and perhaps not just until 1901, as he predicted.[19] The philosopher claims incomprehension as an honorary title, as *willed*: writing metaphorically means wanting to stay 'clean' [*'propre'*] and not mixing with the populace; it means addressing only those who have the same ears, those who possess the third ear, the disciples of Dionysus who can be convinced without the need for 'demonstration'. Writing metaphorically means not needing external ratification to feel one's power; it means addressing one's peers, who alone can hear and applaud one since they are one's relations – related, beyond differences, by a common taste. Metaphorical style is 'aristocratic'; it allows those of the same race to recognize each other and excludes the man of the herd as unclean, foul-smelling: to use common speech is to become vulgar. One must be able to keep one's distance for fear of contamination:

> That which divides two people most profoundly is a differing sense and degree of cleanliness. Of what good is all uprightness and mutual usefulness, of what good is mutual good will: the fact still remains – they 'cannot bear each other's odour!' The highest instinct of cleanliness places him who is affected with it in the strangest and most perilous isolation, as a saint: for precisely this is saintliness – the highest spiritualization of the said instinct. [...] Such an inclination is *distinguishing* – it is a noble inclination – but it also *separates*. – The saint's pity is pity for the *dirt* of the human, all too human. And there are degrees and heights at which he feels pity itself as defilement, as dirt. ... (BGE 271)
>
> Solitude is with us a virtue: it is a sublime urge and inclination for cleanliness which divines that all contact between man and man – 'in society' – must inevitably be unclean. All community makes somehow, somewhere, sometime – 'common'. (BGE 284)[20]

Hence metaphorical writing could be called 'obsessional'; the tendency to cleanliness [*propreté*], a noble tendency, is analogous to that of the saint, the ascetic priest, who pushes the pathos of distance to the point of sickness. The solitude of the saint is the solitude of the new philosopher: such is the dangerous fatality of the peaks or of the madman. However, the fatality of the philosopher is neither that of the madman nor that of the priest, even if the language in which Nietzsche expresses himself, in the texts we have just quoted, mimics that of the priest to the point of parody, to the point where they cannot be told apart, and where those who do not possess the third ear are led to misunderstand. Nietzsche's language is a parody of the obsession with purity which protects against the common and vulgarizing appropriation of one's 'own' [*'propre'*] thought. A parody which was so successful that a Prussian newspaper was able to see in *Beyond Good and Evil* a '"sign of the times" [...] the real genuine *Junker philosophy* for which the "Kreuzzeitung" merely lacked the courage' (EH, 'Why I Write Such Excellent Books', 1). Despite the precautions he took, the misconstructions and distortions were numerous: 'Ultimately, no one can extract from things, books included, more than he already knows' (EH, 'Why I Write Such Excellent Books',1).

Thus a 'noble' thinker fears being understood more than being misunderstood: 'style' is a way of removing, distancing unclean readers as well as of opening the ears of the well-bred:

> *On the question of being understandable.* – One does not only wish to be understood when one writes; one wishes just as surely *not* to be understood. It is not by any means necessarily an objection to a book when anyone finds it impossible to understand: perhaps that was part of the author's intention – he did not want to be understood by just 'anybody'. All the nobler spirits and tastes select their audience when they wish to communicate; and choosing that, one at the same time erects barriers against 'the others'. All the more subtle laws of any style have their origin at this point: they at the same time keep away, create a distance, forbid 'entrance', understanding, as said above – while they open the ears of those whose ears are related to ours. (GS 381. Cf. BGE 290 and TI, 'Expeditions of an Untimely Man', 26)

Like the use of metaphor, aphoristic writing also aims to discourage the *common* by requiring a reader to be equipped with a rigorous philological art. Aphoristic writing wants to make itself understood only by those who are linked by having the same refined impressions in common; it wants to banish the *profanum vulgus* and attract the free spirits 'on to new dance floors'.

> People find difficulty with the aphoristic form: this arises from the fact that today this form is *not taken seriously enough*. An aphorism, properly stamped and moulded, has not been 'deciphered' when it has simply been read; rather, one has then to begin its *exegesis*, for which is required an art of exegesis. (GM, 'Preface', 8)

The aphoristic form presents such difficulty because of its *brevity*. However, it is obscure only to those who read an aphorism in isolation and spare themselves the effort of a more complete reading, of decipherment: initially the aphorism seduces the light-minded and superficial who want to laugh too soon. Now the gay science is always a reward: it requires a detour via the grey of documents; it implies the – sorely neglected – art of rumination, which illuminates even the briefest of writings.[21] For want of the ability to laugh, the 'light-minded' reader – out of disappointment and *ressentiment* – takes the aphoristic form lightly and declares it superficial, void of all content. He illegitimately separates form and content, whereas aphoristic writing is only so because striking new ideas demand to be struck coldly, incisively – they must take the reader's breath away and not leave him time to recover and grow more weighty; for, if one must not want to laugh too soon, neither must one have a weighty and serious mind and look beneath the surface, seeking the deepest depths.

In its brevity and density, the aphorism is an invitation to dance: it is the actual writing of the will to power, affirmative, light, and innocent. It is a writing which deletes the opposition between play and seriousness, surface and depth, form and content, spontaneous and considered, amusement and work. If one reads an aphorism and takes note of only one of the two 'contraries' in each group of oppositions, one is doomed to incomprehension. One must be able to stay nimble as one reflects, and stay on the 'surface' whilst reading between the lines. A task which requires one to elevate 'reading to the level of an art': there is no reading without interpretation, without commentary – in other words without a new writing which slightly displaces the meaning of the first, pushes the perspective of the aphorism in new directions and makes it come into its own. Every reading gives birth to a different text, to the creation of a new form: that is indeed an artistic effect. At the same time the text, the expression of a system of forces, acts on the reader and 'cultivates' him, in other words again it makes him come into his own. One must first of all be 'deeply wounded' and then 'secretly delighted' in order to be able to boast of having understood an aphorism: we can discover in a text only what we ourselves are but were unaware of. So reading transforms the reader and the text at the same time. The aphoristic form is the actual writing of an artistic force positing and imposing forms which are as new and as numerous as there are readers to conquer and appropriate a text. A new reading/writing destroys the traditional categories of the book as a closed totality containing a definitive meaning, the author's; in such a way it deconstructs the idea of the author as master of the meaning of the work and immortalizing himself through it. The aphorism, by its discontinuous character, disseminates meaning and appeals to the pluralism of interpretations and their renewal: only movement is immortal.

So it is not the fault of the 'author' if his aphorisms fail to be understood. Or rather his only mistake is to have believed that his future reader would be strong enough to take up his writing once more and make it his own.

So the aphorism becomes a precaution against feeble minds, against the *profanum vulgus*; it allows one to express revolutionary ideas in the knowledge that one will be understood only by those who possess the third ear:

A maxim is a link in a chain of thoughts; it requires the reader to reconstitute this chain from his own resources: this is a lot to ask. A maxim is an act of presumption. – Or of circumspection, as Heraclitus knew. A maxim, to make acceptable fare, must first be stirred and mixed with other ingredients (an example, experiences, stories). Most fail to understand that, which is why one can express disturbing things quite safely in maxims. (NF 20 [3], KGW IV$_2$, 457)

Such dissatisfied people are also responsible for the numerous complaints about the obscurity of Heraclitus' style. The fact is that hardly anyone has ever written with as lucid and luminous a quality. Very tersely, to be sure, and for that reason obscure for readers who skim and race. [...] After all, even in matters of ordinary practical life one must, as Schopenhauer says, be most careful to make one's meaning plain in order to prevent misunderstanding, if possible; how could one then permit oneself to express unclearly or enigmatically those most difficult, abstruse, scarcely attainable goals of thinking that it is philosophy's task to express. So far as terseness is concerned, however, Jean Paul has a useful admonition: 'Generally speaking, it is quite right if great things – things of much sense for men of rare sense – are expressed but briefly and (hence) darkly, so that barren minds will declare it to be nonsense, rather than translate it into a nonsense that they can comprehend. For mean, vulgar minds have an ugly facility for seeing in the profoundest and most pregnant utterance only their own everyday opinion.' (PTG, p.64f.)[22]

So aphoristic writing and metaphorical style distinguish men from one another and keep at a distance the common run, the 'democratic' plebs, those who are not clean [*propres*] because they have no proper. Metaphor and proper are not opposites. Metaphor is the 'proper' insofar as it is a unique appropriation of the world, the property of those who are 'clean' ["*propres*"]. But the proper does not belong to a specific social class, the aristocracy. Nobility is genealogically determined: the 'proper' describes a certain structure of the soul, a specific hierarchy between the drives, a certain relation of forces. However, the proper can never be a 'pure' 'proper', for the unique perspective is never quite unique; it repeats evaluations which have already taken place (eternal return in difference). Different metaphors can repeat the same evaluations by another name, just as an identical term can contain varying interpretations. The eternal return is what introduces a certain unity to the points of view in 'aristocratic' style. Radical originality is impossible since 'the individual is nothing, the species everything': 'How wonderful and new and yet how gruesome and ironic I find my position vis-à-vis the whole of existence in the light of my insight! I have *discovered* for myself that the human and animal past, indeed the whole primal age and past of all sentient being continues in me to invent, to love, to hate, and to infer' (GS 54).

Thus, despite all their differences, the philosophies which share the same language all have an air of kinship about them and stand in a relation of genealogical affiliation to one another:

> The most diverse philosophers unfailingly fill out again and again a certain basic scheme of *possible* philosophies. Under an invisible spell they always trace once more the identical orbit: however independent of one another they may feel, with their will to criticism or systematism [...]. Where there exists a language affinity it is quite impossible, thanks to the common philosophy of grammar – I mean thanks to unconscious domination and directing by similar grammatical functions – to avoid everything being

prepared in advance for a similar evolution and succession of philosophical systems. (BGE 20)

So to be fully metaphorical, or 'proper', a writing would have to invent a unique code, an impossible original language containing evaluations which had never taken place. A minimum of writing, speaking, and making oneself heard, despite being misheard – of vulgarizing oneself ever so slightly – is an ineluctable fate; otherwise one falls into silence and/or madness.

Accepting to write, in the knowledge that the whole human race also writes in us,[23] means not taking *ourselves* 'seriously' any more, that is the wisdom of the *gay science* combined with laughter, lightness, and dance. A mocking and deconstructive laugh, the echo of a more serious[24] laugh, for 'we can destroy only as creators', and Nietzsche's 'yes' is louder than all the 'no's and all the 'perhaps'...

Appendix:
Genealogy, Interpretation, Text

However enriching a reading of Jean Granier's *Nietzsche*[1] might be, one is nevertheless led to some reflections of a critical nature, primarily because of his misuse of concepts taken from philosophies foreign to Nietzsche's.

Although the author – especially by means of typography (Granier, p.54) – makes a point of distinguishing the meanings of concepts which Nietzsche condemns from the meanings he himself deploys in speaking of Nietzsche's philosophy, the language he uses results in an ambiguity which is all the more regrettable because the distinction he establishes sometimes does not appear clearly until quite late in the work. Thus Granier misuses the terms 'Being', 'existential', 'ontological', 'essence', and 'intuition', Heideggerian expressions ('unveiling of Being', 'availability to Being', the distinction between Being and being), and ethico-religious language (the concepts of evil, guilt, the sacred).[2] Now all these expressions are fraught with metaphysical significance, and Nietzsche, far from ever using them on his own account, condemns them as obfuscatory, substituting for them concepts which seem to him more appropriate and less equivocal. Nietzsche never speaks of 'Being', or even of 'being', but of 'Nature' or 'life', the 'World' or 'Experience', 'phenomena' or 'appearance';[3] he substitutes for the concept of ontology that of 'psychology' (BGE 23). Granier does not ask himself enough questions about the meaning of these substitutions; thus although he recognizes that being for Nietzsche is an interpreted being, he seems to want to give an ontological interpretation of Nietzsche's thought at all costs, and the concept of will to power is for him 'the originary truth of Being'.

The difficulty Granier has in speaking of Nietzsche using Nietzsche's own concepts is symptomatic of the hold metaphysical language has over him. As a result he confines Nietzsche to the metaphysical camp and effaces the radical novelty and originality of Nietzsche's thought and project, which aims to burst the bounds of metaphysical thought, even if it means introducing concepts which are more mythical than rational – although the former actually operate more rigorously than the latter, which are illusory products of a substantialist logic. Now if Nietzsche essentially substitutes the concept of 'Life' for that of Being, it is to indicate straightaway that being is merely interpretation. For to live is to evaluate. Every evaluation is the positing of meanings which are symptomatic of the living being that has evaluated. Nietzsche's question is not an ontological but a psychological one, if by psychology one means 'morphology and the *development-theory of the will to power*' (BGE 23), as Nietzsche defines it – what he proclaims 'the queen of the sciences' (ibid.), the way to the fundamental problems.

Psychology so defined differs from classical psychology, whether introspective or psychoanalytical, and Granier is right in saying that Nietzsche's philosophy is no 'reductive psychologism' (cf. pp.16 and 17). If Nietzsche thus introduces a new type of psychology, it is because the old one seems to him to be superficial and not self-sufficient.

Nietzsche's aim is not to describe psychological phenomena but to decipher them as significations referring to the signified which is the body, itself a hierarchy of forces, and the organization of which is indicative of 'health' or '*illness*' – i.e. in the last resort, of the affirmation or negation of life. Psychical phenomena are symbols and symptoms, and the 'true' psychologist must also be a philologist and a physician. In this sense Nietzsche's question is not an ontological but a genealogical one: he questions the value of the value posited by spontaneous evaluations. *The genealogical method* is not simply genetic, as in classical English psychology; it is an axiological genesis which, at the same time as revealing every phenomenon as an interpretation, reveals the necessary multiplicity of interpretations and inaugurates a hierarchy in interpretation. This hierarchy is not based on an equivalence of value and being; contrary to what Granier says, it is not referred to 'a truth of being', but rather to the nobility or baseness of the evaluating will, the unconscious intention of this will and its ultimate goal. It is this goal which for each will constitutes the meaning of being, and it is to this goal that one must refer in order to judge the being which is evaluating:

> The question: what is the *value* of this or that table of values and 'morals'? should be viewed from the most divers perspectives; for the problem 'value *for what?*' cannot be examined too subtly. Something, for example, that possessed obvious value in relation to the longest possible survival of a race [...] would by no means possess the same value if it were a question, for instance, of producing a stronger type. The well-being of the majority and the well-being of the few are opposite viewpoints of value [...]. – All the sciences have from now on to prepare the way for the future task of the philosophers: this task understood as the solution of the *problem of value*, the determination of the *order of rank among values*. (GM I, concluding note)

The value of evaluations cannot be referred to a truth of being or an essence of being since, on the contrary, essence and 'truth' are constituted by the interpretations which appropriate being. Thus, for example, in the *Genealogy* (III,1) Nietzsche shows there is no essence of the ascetic ideal and that there is just a multiplicity of meanings which vary depending on the type of will which embodies it; similarly, in the Second Essay (GM II,12) he shows that one must not confuse the origin of an institution, such as, for example, punishment, with its goal, for there is no one proper goal corresponding to an essence, but there are as many goals as forces appropriating and interpreting it: 'all [...] becoming master involves a fresh interpretation'. Essence becomes, and its history obeys neither an internal logic nor a dialectic; it is linked solely to the chance encounters of forces and their relations of mastery. Which is why one cannot say that 'Nietzsche's psychology is [...] a technique for doing ontological research' (Granier, p.17) since, on the contrary, it is the 'essence' of being which is constituted by the 'psychology' of each being. With Nietzsche one cannot separate ontology and psychology. But it is ontology which is subordinated to psychology (in the sense defined above by Nietzsche) and not the other way round. The advantage of substituting the term 'life' for being, despite the danger which Nietzsche's philosophy thus courts of being wrongly interpreted as a biologism, is that it avoids cutting being off from its interpretations, from the multiple evaluations which constitute it as a text. Nietzsche is essentially interested not in 'man's structures of being' (Granier, p.163), but in whether the structuring process is given an affirmative or a negative sense by 'beings', in relation to the goal they aim at, whether near or far. It is the far-off goal, the advent of a higher human type, that is the ultimate intention guiding his new art of interpretation.

I have always taken pains to prove the *innocence of becoming*: in this way I should probably like to gain the

feeling of complete irresponsibility, – make myself
independent of all approval and disapproval, the
whole past and present: in order to pursue goals which
relate to the future of humanity. (OP 621. Cf. GOA
XIV, ii, 141, both quoted Granier, p.112)

Thus, contrary to Granier's thesis,[4] value is never referred
to truth, for Nietzsche, but truth is measured against value.

In fact initially, as is well demonstrated by Granier in the
first part of his work, the demystification of metaphysics
by Nietzsche consisted in showing that truth was but a
fiction necessary to certain living things and their conditions of existence, that the question concerning truth had to
be not ontological but axiological or genealogical in nature.
Nietzsche's great innovation was the idea that knowledge
itself has to be referred to life, and truth to the will to truth.
Nietzsche's question is not: 'What is the essence of the
Truth?', but 'What does the will which wants the Truth
want?' for the will to truth is in turn but a symbol and a
symptom (cf. BGE 1).

Searching for the truth would imply having a criterion
for truth and would presuppose knowledge of the real: a
knowledge which Nietzsche refutes as impossible, thereby
prohibiting any ontological interpretation of his work.

Are the axioms of logic adequate to reality or are they
a means and measure for us to *create* reality, the
concept 'reality', for ourselves? – To affirm the
former one would, as already said, have to have a
previous knowledge of being – which is certainly not
the case. (WP 516)

In fact, each living thing affirms itself as such by its
idiosyncratic and perspectivistic positing of truth. Each
species calls its own perspectives 'true', and it calls others'
'false' because they do not allow it to survive. Each species
dismisses as false what is refuted by life (cf. WP 204, 540,

565; GOA XI, ii, 80, XII, i, 37, XII, i, 111, XII, ii, 7, XIII, 202). Thus, to speak of true values or false values, to refer value to truth, as does Granier, is at the very least challengeable. A value is neither true nor false, nor is it based on the need to establish an equivalence with being or the failure to achieve it. It is not referred to anything outside itself, which is why it is more a question of judging 'truth' or being according to their axiological coefficient than of judging value according to its 'coefficient of ontological truth' (Granier, p.65). Refuting a value as false is absurd since, as Nietzsche puts it, conditions of existence cannot be refuted, they can only be changed (cf. GOA XII, ii, 149). No living thing can be converted to a different morality from that which it has 'chosen'. So values are all necessary, and referring value to truth means forgetting to place oneself 'beyond good and evil'.

> These opposite forms in the optics of value are *both* necessary: they are ways of seeing, immune to reasons and refutations. One cannot refute Christianity; one cannot refute a disease of the eye. It was the height of scholarly idiocy to fight that pessimism like a philosophy. The concepts 'true' and 'untrue' have, as it seems to me, no meaning in optics. – What alone should be resisted is that falseness, that deceitfulness of instinct which *refuses* to experience these opposites as opposites. (CW, 'Epilogue'. Cf. TI, 'The Problem of Socrates', 2, TI, 'Morality as Anti-Nature', 5; WP 682; GOA XII, i, 75, XII, i, 88, XIII, 320, XIV, i, 24)

All values, when judged from the point of view of life – contrary to what Granier says, and to use his language – have the 'same coefficient of ontological truth', because they are all affirmative of the living things which posit them. Value posits its right to be valid by the fact of its affirmation, by the will to power which it manifests.

All values are such *de facto*. Nietzsche nevertheless does not end up with an undifferentiated pluralism, a positivism of values, or a historicism – as is well demonstrated by Granier. For while it is true that all values are values (in this sense there is neither a true value nor a false one), all values are not equivalent, and the values which prevail '*de facto*' are not those which are most valuable '*de jure*'. Although for Nietzsche there are but values immanent to being since being is but evaluation, Nietzsche establishes a hierarchy of values. So what is the principle of hierarchical ordering if it is not, as Granier claims (pp.165–69), the 'coefficient of ontological truth'? Is Nietzsche referring to 'a new unconditional', as Granier puts it, quoting Jaspers? For Granier there seems to be no possible middle way between an undifferentiated pluralism and a hierarchy established in accordance with a criterion external to the evaluations themselves, that of ontological truth.[5] Now if it is true that 'the truth of Being' is not measured by Nietzsche against its value for a certain type of living things, against 'the pragmatism of life' or 'useful error' (cf. Granier, p.496), that is not because ontological truth is the foundation of values, but because such a truth does not exist. If Nietzsche introduces a distinction between true and false values it is not in the name of the truth of life or the truth of value, but of value for life, of a certain type of life and its future. True values are such for Nietzsche because they are not mystificatory, because they show a will which is strong enough either not to need untruthfulness or else to recognize lucidly that it needs illusion. They are also true because they are valid for man's future, allowing him to overcome himself in the direction of the overman. It is the man of the future who refutes the values of the 'last man' and can propose only a goal which is destructive of humanity, the 'real' goal of which is the condition of the overman.

False values are such because they veil their idiosyncratic origins and set themselves up as absolutes, thereby preventing the strongest living things from flourishing, since, in order to live, these latter must take as their yardstick their own evaluations and not obey any universal morality. The 'hypocrisy', 'deceitfulness of instinct' (cf. CW text quoted above), 'distortion of meaning' (BGE 22), and the injustice which consists in the will to level down without respecting the difference in evaluations: these are the signs of 'falsity', in other words the non-value of the values of certain living things, because they are not really alive. Injustice lies in refusing to justify life in all its forms and in its differentiated pluralism. It means opting for death, or at the very most for the preservation of the species. False values are those which make life ugly, narrow it down and impoverish it; true values are those which beautify life and make possible *amor fati*. The value of value – that which constitutes its truth or falsity – always depends on the valorization or devalorization of life, not its truth; on its ascent or its decadence, on the profusion or poverty of life in whoever is evaluating. In each case, the former allows one to see clearly the necessity of things, the latter shrinks everything to its own image. At all events, neither the one nor the other is adequate to being, for 'being' is neither beautiful nor ugly.[6] Beauty is just the projection into the world of a superabundance of forces in the being which is evaluating, and a sign of them. Ugliness, on the other hand, is the symbol of the powerlessness of the power which is evaluating (cf. CW, 'Epilogue', NCW, 'We Antipodes', TI, '"Reason" in Philosophy', 6, TI, 'Expeditions of an Untimely Man', 19; GS 276).

In the final analysis, then, what allows one to establish a hierarchy between values is the diversity of types of life which the different evaluations engender, some affirming life and humanity and others negating them. The criterion for hierarchization is indeed pragmatic, but its pragmatism is directed towards a use which is yet to come. It is possible to adopt this criterion by comparing the different types of life, because – by chance and in exceptional circumstances – certain spontaneous evaluations by a certain type of man have already managed to produce the ideal type of man, the overman, whom Nietzsche proposes to educate. Nietzsche's 'refutation' of God uses the same criterion. One must be an atheist not because one cannot prove the existence of God – 'if this God of the Christians were *proved* to us to exist, we should know even less how to believe in him' (AC 47; cf. WP 251, quoted Granier p.155, n.2) – but because such a God is absurd, a veritable '*crime against life*' (AC 47). Such a God is a sign of weakness and can serve to maintain only weak, negating lives;[7] as Granier says (p.203), Nietzsche discredits the ideal and condemns its axiological fragility. Here value is usurped value, pseudo-value, not because it is inadequate to the 'ontological truth', but because it has no value, since it negates life and its highest expressions. This non-value is symptomatic of the powerlessness of the evaluating being.

The affirmation of life, the criterion for the value of value, is not '[a participation in Being] which fulfils Being at the same time as we fulfil ourselves in and through Being. Our "yes" and our "no" have real weight in the balance of the world; by their own energy they inflect the movement of Being in the direction of advancement or regression' (Granier, p.167f.). What is in question for Nietzsche is not man's ability to alter the movement of Being, but its positive evaluation. Such an evaluation makes possible *amor fati* by allowing it to be beautified, but it does not modify the necessity of the world. Granier's formulation is obscure, mystical, almost Pauline, and it constitutes a metaphysical subversion of Nietzsche's thought.

Nor will we accept as a genealogical test of value 'the ontological density of the ideal' (Granier's formulation, p.169). For the ontological nullity or plenitude of an ideal cannot be measured. The ideal is symptomatic of the power of the evaluating will – of its value, not its being; or rather, its being is exactly that. Every ideal is affirmative; even negative ideals are affirmative of the evaluating being; they are means for it to stay alive, even if that is to the detriment of the strongest lives and the future of humanity. 'The genealogical test of the hammer' refers value to the type of evaluating will, to its power to affirm itself, life, and its ultimate goal, whether near or far.

That it should indeed be the future of man that Nietzsche is ultimately aiming for is also revealed by the self-limitation of knowledge, which only makes sense in relation to humanity. The imperative to 'unveil Being and master it' is not 'an ambiguity essential to Being'; its 'duplicity' (Granier, pp.532, 534), its imperatives are such only for man, who needs the 'pragmatism of life' and yet, having reached the final degree of power, is capable of surpassing it so as to will truth – in other words so as to become aware of the absence of the truth of being, and of the enigma which is life, a life that thus offers an indefinite multiplicity of possible interpretations. The conflict between knowledge and life takes place on an anthropological level. So the hierarchy of values established by Nietzsche and the value of the hierarchy correspond not, as Granier says (p.601), to an 'ontological care', but to an axiological one, to the task of educating the man of the future which Nietzsche sets himself.

But what then do the idea of a rigorous and upright philosophy, 'truthfulness', 'the spirit of justice', and the 'passion for knowledge' mean for Nietzsche? Do truthfulness and a rigorous method allow one to arrive at an ontological truth to which values can then be referred? Is philology situated beyond perspectivistic evaluations of life, thus allowing one to discriminate between the different interpretations and hierarchize them? In which case, what might be its status? Or does rigorous philology merely provide us with a new interpretation of being? In which case, what criterion allows one to adjudge it more rigorous than any other?

Granier (p.464) presents rigorous philology as a self-overcoming by the will to power. Since the 'essence' of the will to power is for him self-overcoming, it was necessary for the pragmatism of life to overcome itself in the direction of the 'passion for knowledge'. He argues that the passion for knowledge is characterized by an intellectual probity situated 'beyond any consideration of utility or interest'. It results, says Granier, in 'an unveiling of Being in its truth'. Irreproachable philology no longer manifests the plastic energy of willing (p.465) – it is sufficient to 'listen out for Being'. The passion for knowledge, and rigorous philology, imply a mode of relation to being radically different from the pragmatism of life (p.490). Probity demands absolute respect for the 'text' of being (p.502). One can and must separate the text from its interpretations, which implies a 'mutation', a 'real conversion' (p.502) of the will.

Now even if we accept – although it might perhaps be debatable – that the essence of will to power is transcendence, the transition from pragmatism to 'the passion for knowledge' is not a self-overcoming. For the pragmatism of life is the mode proper to the scientific and technical knowledge which the human species needs in order to humanize nature and feel secure in it. In this sense one might say it cannot be overcome. Fundamental error cannot be overcome; and individual errors come and add themselves to this background of universal errors proper to the human universe. The search for truth can only be carried out against a background of error:

> For there to be any degree of consciousness in the world, an unreal world of error had to be produced: beings which believed in permanence, in individuals, etc. Only once an imaginary world in conflict with eternal flux had been produced could *knowledge* be built *on this foundation*, – in short one can perceive the fundamental error on which everything is based (for contradictions can be *thought*), but this error can only be destroyed if one destroys life itself: the ultimate

truth, that things are in flux, will not stand being *incorporated* by us; our *organs* (necessary to *life*) are set up for error. And so the wise man experiences a *conflict between life* and his ultimate decisions; his drive [*Trieb*] to attain knowledge is conditional on his believing and living in error. Life is the condition of knowledge. Error is the condition of life – and I mean the most fundamental error. Knowing one is mistaken does not cancel [*aufheben*] the mistake! There is nothing bitter about this! We must love error and tend it; it is the matrix of knowledge. Art in the service of illusion – such is our form of worship. Loving and fostering life for the sake of knowledge, loving and fostering error and illusion for the sake of life. Giving existence an aesthetic meaning, *increasing our taste for it*, is the basic condition of the passion for knowledge. So here, too, we discover that we need night and day as a condition of life for *us*: wanting to know and wanting to err are the ebb and the flow. If *one* of the two reigns absolutely, man perishes and *the ability in question goes with him*. (GOA XII, i, 89. Cf. GOA XII, i, 10)

Man cannot stop himself dreaming, but he who has the 'passion for knowledge' knows that he is dreaming, and that is the paradox.

> I suddenly woke up in the midst of this dream, but only to the consciousness that I am dreaming and that I must go on dreaming lest I perish. (GS 54)
> Among all these dreamers, I, too, who 'know', am dancing my dance. (ibid. Cf. also GS 58)

But how does one make the transition from the pragmatism of life to 'the passion for knowledge', which is not absolute knowledge but awareness of error, and which allows one thus to be aware of being under an illusion without perishing thereby? In *The Gay Science*, Nietzsche shows that the intellectual condition of this overcoming was to register the multiplicity of opinions and their contradiction. An awareness of the plurality of truths leads to scepticism: 'this subtler honesty and scepticism came into being wherever two contradictory sentences appeared to be *applicable* to life' (GS 110) – and at the same time to be questionable or opposable in their utility for life – until there appeared 'new propositions' which, 'though not useful for life, were evidently not harmful to life: in such cases there was room for the expression of an intellectual instinct for play, and honesty and scepticism were innocent and happy like all play'. Utility was then no longer the only gain from the opposition between the two 'truths', for there was also the pleasure in 'the intellectual fight'. This pleasure in struggling for knowledge is a new form of the will to power and consequently a new need in life. Without it, 'scrutiny, denial, mistrust, and contradiction' would never have 'bec[o]me a *power*'.

So the passion for knowledge does not institute a radically new relationship between man and being, where man is placed 'without any consideration of utility or interest'. Contrary to what Granier says, there is neither a 'mutation' nor a 'conversion' here. The new intellectual conditions are still the mark of the power of the will, and they remain subordinate to the conditions of life: it is only when knowledge was able to free itself from the pressing need to preserve the species that it could stop being a 'means' to life and instead turn life into a means to knowledge.

As a result, the transition from the 'pragmatism of life' to the 'passion for knowledge' is indeed an overcoming of life, but one mediated through different wills. Only the nobles are capable of being aware of the absence of truth without perishing, only they can will themselves into illusion, will themselves as a unique and falsifying perspective, different from the others. For this uniqueness is again the sign of the power of 'affirmation of the will', whereas the weak would perish if they admitted to themselves the relativity of their perspectives, an admission which would oblige them to recognize the legitimacy of other evaluations, especially of those which condemn them. For the strong, veiling illusion from themselves is no longer useful to life, which is why they can reflect their perspective as a perspective. Truthfulness here becomes necessary to life, as proof of the valour of the soul which bears it. Though necessary to life it is speculatively useless, since becoming aware of one's perspective still does not allow one to overcome it in the direction of an absolute knowledge. It only allows one to compare perspectives, to hierarchize and multiply them. Overcoming is not an overcoming of life by knowledge, but rather it is still life which is mastering itself through knowledge. For if the will to power can indeed master itself, it is always by informing the real, hence by transforming it. It is an overcoming not in the direction of the essence of being, but of a new perspective, or the recognition of interpretation as the primary fact – the recognition of the existence not of an originary essence, but of initial texts. One cannot separate the moment of 'information' from that of overcoming, since it is only by multiplying perspectives that one will be able to become aware of perspective as such.

To argue that rigorous philology brings into play a will which is no longer plastic but merely 'receptive', Granier uses the following text of Nietzsche's: 'Learning to *see*, as I understand it, is almost what is called in unphilosophical language "strong will-power": the essence of it is precisely *not* to "will", the *ability* to defer decision. All unspirituality, all vulgarity, is due to the incapacity to resist a stimulus' (TI, 'What the Germans Lack', 6). Now this text in no way means that one must adopt a contemplative attitude, that one must 'listen out for Being' or 'give Being back its power to call out to human thought'. Not willing means not letting *one* conscious will speak – in a language which results from 'secondary rationalizations', simplification, and reduction – but letting the desires in their plurality speak, by multiplying perspectives through a change in the centre of perspective, by a different hierarchization of the drives:

> Our serious endeavour, though, is to understand everything as becoming, to deny our status as individuals, to see the world through the *greatest possible* number of eyes, to *live* in our drives and our activities so as to acquire eyes, to abandon ourselves *temporarily* to life, so as then to let our gaze rest temporarily on it: to foster the drives, as the foundation of all knowledge, but to know when they become the enemies of knowledge: *in summa*, it is to *wait* and see how far *knowledge and truth can assimilate each other*. (GOA XII, i, 21)

Though absolute error cannot, then, be overcome, because point of view cannot be overcome, it can be exposed if one contrasts interpretations, and it allows first opinions, 'foreground' opinions, to be negated if one accepts the plurality of evaluations. But in the final analysis the 'passion for knowledge' is in the service of superior life. Its goal remains a strong *will* which posits a certain number of evaluations to see *how far* they can lead. The final goal remains

> a Dionysian affirmation of the world as it is, without subtraction, exception, or selection. (WP 1041)
> In place of belief, which we no longer find possible, we set a strong *will* over ourselves – one which maintains a provisional series of fundamental evaluations – as an heuristic principle: so as to see *how far* it takes us. [...] In truth even the old 'belief' as a whole was no different: but formerly *spiritual discipline* was too weak to be able to withstand our *splendid prudence*. (GOA XIV, ii, 155)

In other words intellectual probity does not lead us to grasp an ontological truth inscribed in a text which exists independently of philological interpretation. Now, having granted that the 'text' of nature, its meaning, is constituted by the different perspectives on being of the forces which appropriate it and constitute it as a text, Granier nevertheless affirms that there is an original text of being independent of interpretations. It is precisely this text which rigorous philology would decipher and which would allow one to distinguish interpretations from one another, to describe certain ones as 'good' and others as 'bad' (cf. e.g. BGE 22).

If this were so, then rigorous philology would arrive at the essence of being, and Nietzsche's philosophy would be an ontology which it would be hard to tell apart from a demystified form of dogmatic metaphysics. As Heidegger has it, Nietzscheanism would then be nothing but an inverted Platonism.

Indeed Nietzsche certainly writes, when speaking of the French Revolution, that *'the text disappeared beneath the interpretation'* (BGE 38, quoted Granier p.316, n.2). But nevertheless that does not mean to say the first text itself should not already be an interpretation. If Nietzsche speaks of the Revolution as a text, it is to indicate straightaway that there is no brute historical fact, that in a general way 'there are no facts but merely interpretations'. History is a version of versions, so what is called 'text' is just the original version. The goal of rigorous philology is therefore not to separate the text from its interpretations – which is impossible since the text is constituted by them – but to distinguish a certain type of interpretation from other interpretations, to distinguish the first interpretations, which result from spontaneous evaluation by the drives, from the second – secondary – interpretations which often mask them. So being is not 'confusedly intelligible', a 'shimmering of sense', a series of 'discreet allusions'. It is not of itself equivocal (Granier, p.316f.). It is interpretations which constitute it as a text and as intelligible; it is they that are multiple, confused, and contradictory, and they that a good philology must disentangle.

The second text to which Granier refers (p.321f.) is a crucial one, since this time Nietzsche is speaking of a text of nature. Granier writes:

> Nietzsche is so loth to dissolve the 'text' in the whirlpool of different interpretations because, on the contrary, he wants to teach philosophers 'the invaluable art of reading well' and wants to teach them the principles of *rigorous philology*. He calls for a return to the text of nature and seeks to lay bare *homo natura*.

He uses the text:

> To translate man back into nature; to master the many vain and fanciful interpretations and secondary meanings which have been hitherto scribbled and daubed over that eternal basic text *homo natura*; to confront man henceforth with man in the way in which, hardened by the discipline of science, man today confronts the *rest* of nature, with dauntless Oedipus eyes and stopped-up Odysseus ears, deaf to the siren songs of old metaphysical bird-catchers. (BGE 230)

And Granier comments: 'Nietzsche demands that we now detach real "facts" from "beliefs", that we separate the text from its "interpretations", which obscure its primary meaning.' In fact Nietzsche demands that we separate not the 'text' from its 'interpretations', but the text, i.e. the originary interpretation as uncovered by philological probity, from certain specific interpretations, only those which he describes as 'vain and fanciful', those which have been 'scribbled and daubed' - interpretations which mask their nature as such and which mask the fact that the text is a product of an interpretation. If Nietzsche writes that one must refer to the 'eternal basic text' in man, to *homo natura*, it is essentially in order to set himself against a metaphysical interpretation of man. If one must have stopped-up Odysseus ears, it is so as not to be seduced by interpretations from a certain type of living thing which needs them. If one must have 'dauntless Oedipus eyes', it is to 'dare the truth', the tragic and inadmissible truth which must be discerned through the secondary interpretations, the primary interpretation by the drives which reveals the truth of secondary interpretation to be non-truth, falsification, a mask for the primary, unconscious interpretations. So it is to the first text to be constituted, the ultimate meaning of all the others, that one must refer in order to understand and perhaps demystify them.

Now if this primary text is not a given meaning but is constituted by spontaneous evaluations,[8] that immediately makes it multiple. For Nietzsche there is no 'ontological pluralism' but an originary pluralism of meanings[9] and values. What Nietzsche here calls nature is not 'the ground of Being' (Granier, p.379). 'Reading well', which is the goal of rigorous philology, means deciphering behind all the secondary interpretations the initial interpretations, which are symptomatic of the type of will that is evaluating – so it indeed means referring to a 'text' of nature, but the text is constituted, not given.

If Granier attaches such importance to preserving an originary text independent of interpretations, it seems to be in order to prevent Nietzscheanism from being interpreted as a philosophy of the absurd advocating the 'cult of unrestrained passion, of blind desire' (p.310).[10] Thus he writes 'that the refusal to equate reason with being', insofar as reason is a product of the pragmatism of human life, 'nevertheless does not mean that Being is unreason – Being sanctions only one affirmation, namely that there is rationality in the world'. In fact there is no rationality in the world; the world is indeed absurd, but it lends itself to a multiplicity of interpretations. Man alone can introduce into the innocence of becoming and into chance the law of

reason. Even in terms of *The Birth of Tragedy*, Apollo for
Nietzsche is never the symbol of rationality but of
organization, of beautiful form, and he implies the
Dionysian intoxication of which he is but a manifestation.
It seems that it is now easy to understand what Nietzsche
means when he speaks of the text of Nature, though it is
true that the ambiguity of the notion explains the misin-
terpretations that have been able to arise. Speaking of 'text'
indeed implies that being is constituted as meaning, for
there is no text without meaning, and meaning exists only
for the one who constitutes or reads the text. Without an art
of interpretation, the text is just brute matter. But furthermore, the 'text' is what one refers to in order to judge the
truth or non-truth of interpretations, or rather their value
or non-value; the 'text' is thus the guard-rail against any
interpretation which might be pure fabrication or falsification. In this instance it is indeed the final referent for any
reading and any commentary. One is then tempted to think
that it is an object in itself, independent of the originary
interpretation which constituted it, and one arrives at an
ontological position by cutting the text off from its
interpretations, as does Granier.

Now for Nietzsche interpretation is not a commentary
on a pre-existing text; what exists before the interpretation
is not text but chaos. This chaos is absurd, and that is the
truth of being, which is a lack of meaning and truth. So the
'true' world is the 'deceptive', illusory world of life. This
truth is not a 'truth' but a pure reality. Strictly speaking,
'truth' already belongs to the world of meaning, i.e. to the
world of interpretation.

> There is only *one* world, and this is false, cruel,
> contradictory, seductive, without meaning ... A
> world thus constituted is the real world. *We have need
> of lies* in order to conquer this reality, this 'truth', that
> is, in order to *live*. (WP 853. Cf. WP 602)

This chaos is, moreover, a 'pure abstraction', because it is always mastered and interpreted by the living things which appropriate it. That is why interpretation is indeed the primary fact – which Granier recognizes (p. 142) – and it is because being is always already interpreted that Nietzsche speaks of it as a text. The 'given' is just a 'pretext' for the constitution of a text. So being is indissolubly being *and* meaning because it is but interpretation, even though as pretext it is situated beyond any unique interpretation and is liable to receive a multiplicity of interpretations.[11] But what Nietzsche calls originary text is constituted by the spontaneous interpretations of the drives, and it is what will serve as a referent to judge the value or non-value of the other texts constituted by other arts of interpretation. One can thus understand how for Nietzsche the notion of text preserves the double meaning which we indicated above: on the one hand it is a constituted meaning, a multiplicity of meanings; on the other hand it is a unique referent which, if cut off from its constitutive interpretation, appears as an absolute and as the 'ontological truth'.

The relation which exists between the text of being and its interpretations is identical to that which Nietzsche establishes between the body and consciousness. Consciousness is just a symbolism of the body.[12] Everything which appears to consciousness is interpretation. The psychological text is the product of an elaboration, a simplification, a schematization. It is the symbolic signifier of the signified which is the body, itself an organization which is determined by a hierarchy of forces seeking power, and which institutes a first level of meaning, an initial text. The conscious text is a simplified text and is unaware that it is an interpretation. One can say the same of all phenomena. The only text of being is that which is produced by the different interpretations, which are simplifications, schematizations, and approximations of it. But behind the interpretations there is no *absolute* text to which one can refer in order to judge the truth of interpretations. A text without interpretation is no longer a text.

So philological probity, truthfulness, and the spirit of justice do not demand 'absolute respect for the "text" of Being cut off from its interpretations'. Contrary to what Granier says (p.325), 'philology properly understood' does not lead to an originary truth because it, too, is an 'art of interpretation'. When Granier speaks of 'philology' he concentrates above all on the qualities which Nietzsche ascribes to it – 'truthful', 'good', 'rigorous', 'just' – and says very little about the concept of philology, which is nevertheless essential. In fact this concept immediately implies a fundamental correlation between phenomenon and meaning; it emphasizes that the primary fact is not a 'fact' but a text, that the relation between living things and Being is not one of cognition but of interpretation. Nietzsche's philology does not provide us with 'an intuition of the Essence of Being'; it is simply an art of interpretation motivated by a different intention from those arts which have had currency hitherto.[13]

If these latter are 'bad philologies' it is primarily because, 'motivated by futile pride', they claim to speak the truth of being. They do not refer interpretations to their 'authors', unlike the 'new philology', which reveals 'ulterior motives'. For example, if the physicists' mechanistic interpretation of the world is bad, this is primarily because it is 'naïve'; it does not reflect its own nature as interpretation. What is more it is unfair: it is a 'humanitarian adjustment and distortion of meaning' (BGE 22), i.e. the mechanistic interpretation is a rational construction which veils both the spontaneous evaluations of natural forces and its own initial evaluations, both kinds of evaluation referring in the last resort to a will to power. If this philology is bad, it is, finally, because it reveals (to anyone who is capable of deciphering in accordance with good philology) that its ultimate intention is the desire to level down powers, the refusal of any superiority. That is why the mechanistic interpretation of the world is a 'more astute form of atheism'. It is symptomatic of weak wills, which negate the boundlessness and unreserved power of nature. The interpretation which Nietzsche proposes, on the other hand, is the result of a rigorous, truthful, honest, and just philology.

It is honest and truthful because it presents its interpretation as such and because its own reading is devoid of the 'human, all-too-human perspective'; it is correct and rigorous because behind every interpretation it reads the initial interpretation which constitutes the text of nature – not because it takes as its yardstick a 'truth of the world', which does not pre-exist it, but because it deciphers genealogically, i.e. by reading behind every constituted text the ultimate intentions of its author (which are in the last resort always moral); by deciphering phenomena as symptoms of the health or sickness of whoever interprets them. This interpretation is guided by an ultimate intention contrary to what precedes it: the affirmation of life. It is in this sense that the new philology is motivated by 'the spirit of justice'. Not because it gives us being in its rectitude, but because it justifies being in all its plenitude. It is not an unveiling[14] but a justification of Being, and it results in *amor fati*.

So between a complete pluralism of interpretations and the dogmatism of a unique text with an unequivocal meaning, there is room for a pluralism of meanings which are not all equivalent – equivalence being measured not by reference to a truth of being (since, whatever the interpretations, they reveal the will of whoever is interpreting, hence in this sense the being of life) but by reference to the value given to life by the one who is interpreting. 'Good philology' gives an interpretation which allows life to be enriched and embellished (cf. GS 301).

'Justice' does not exist without a creative act which embellishes all things. The just man does not judge in truth, he judges beyond true and false, beyond good and evil. He judges artistically by projecting on to the world his superabundance of life. 'Justice' is not a gnosiological concept. It means simply the justification of life in all its forms. It indicates essentially the gratitude of a certain type of life towards life.

So it is indeed true that rigorous philology arrives at 'the text of nature', a text for which no human, all-too-human term can account (cf. BGE 22), and this text is indeed that of the will to power. Yet does that mean Nietzsche claims to have arrived at the essence of being? No, for Nietzsche relates this 'text of nature' to the art of interpretation which enabled it to be read, an art of interpretation motivated by a specific intention.

The witticism which ends section 22 of *Beyond Good and Evil* is not simply a witticism: it indicates that for Nietzsche the will to power is just a necessary heuristic hypothesis[15] to account for all phenomena. This hypothesis can be posited only by one who has been able to multiply perspectives and compare them, one who has noticed that interpretation as such, in its differentiated multiplicity, is made possible only by a hypothesis like this. The hypothesis of the will to power is not just one hypothesis among many, like any other; it is an unhypothetical hypothesis because it accounts for the actual necessity of any hypothesis as such, and for the difference between hypotheses. It accounts for interpretation as interpretation; it is situated beyond the moral prejudices which constitute dogmatic truths, and is symptomatic of the force of will of the philologist who gives this interpretation. For to posit that Being is will to power is to admit that there is no truth but only interpretations. If 'truth kills us', it is because it teaches us there is no truth, that life is enigmatic and allows an indefinite questioning, an indefinite multiplicity of hypotheses.

Rather has the world become 'infinite' for us all over again, inasmuch as we cannot reject the possibility that *it may include infinite interpretations.* Once more we are seized by a great shudder. (GS 374)

The supreme measure of force: how far a man can live by *hypotheses* and not by belief, in other words venture out on limitless seas! (OP 314, quoted Granier, p.448)

Phrasing which is 'not right' can really be confirmed in countless cases; phrasing which is right, hardly ever. [...] The premise on which they [the 'phrasers'] build – that there *is* a correct, that is, *one* correct exposition – seems to me to be psychologically and experimentally *wrong*. [...] In short, the old philologist says, on the basis of his whole philological experience: *there is no sole saving interpretation.* (Letter to Carl Fuchs, 26 August 1888 (SL, p.306f.), quoted Granier, p.323)

So the idea of interpretation does not, as Granier has it (p.325), lead as far as a radical ontological problem. It leads on the one hand to pragmatist perspectivism and on the other to the possibility of hierarchizing perspectives. Rigorous philology unveils interpretation as interpretaion in the name of another interpretation which does not claim to grasp the essence of being but gives a reading which reveals an affirmative will to life. This interpretation allows man to overcome initial absurdity whilst still preserving the innocence of becoming. By showing that one cannot tear oneself away from perspectivism, Nietzsche nevertheless does not condemn his own philosophy, because he does not present it as a dogmatic ontology, rather as a new interpretation. And because all interpretations are not equivalent, he can present a new philosophy without contradicting his own presuppositions. Granier writes that it is hard to understand the status for Nietzsche of the secondary interpretation of interpretation as interpretation (p.605). Is this status not precisely that of rigorous philology, which is made possible by the multiplication of perspectives and their comparison, and which allows one to become aware of one's perspective as such without, however, being able to overcome it? For 'knowing one is mistaken does not cancel the mistake' (GOA XII, i, 89).

So while it is true that for Nietzsche the concept of will to power is not an ontological concept but a pure heuristic hypothesis, it remains to be seen whether it is really a concept that is necessary in order to make different phenomena intelligible, if it is really an operative concept – and if it is even a real concept at all. It is because Nietzsche cannot ultimately give a rational account of it, and because it is for him a pure principle of interpretation, that he speaks of it mythically in the form of Apollo and Dionysus: mythical language is another attempt to overcome metaphysical language. Now although Granier ponders a good deal over the meaning of these two figures, he does not demonstrate well enough the need for resorting to myth. Nietzsche's symbolism is not 'a poetic equivalent of an ontological intuition', but by itself it signifies the nature of being as interpreted being. Through his language and symbols as well as his aphorisms, Nietzsche indicates the need for a recourse to rigorous philology, to a reading which is a genealogical decipherment. Thus Nietzsche indicates to his reader precisely that he is providing him not with an intuition but an interpretation, and that he in turn must devote himself, when reading Nietzsche, to an effort of interpretation.

Hence while it is true that Dionysus is the Antichrist, with him Nietzsche is not substituting a Greek god for the God of the Christians; he is substituting a symbol, symptomatic of an ideal of a certain type, for another symbol, symptomatic of another ideal. Thus we will not follow Granier when he says there is no atheism in Nietzsche (p.29), and that through the symbolism of Dionysus Nietzsche sets off in search of a 'new non-metaphysical approach to the sacred itself' (p.72).

Nietzsche is indeed an atheist, even if he does not accept the refutation of God given by the majority of atheists. For there are multiple ways of refuting God. Nietzsche's philosophy is indeed a terrestrial philosophy with nothing 'sacred'. Everything sacred is introduced by man, and Nietzsche's philosophy is no humanism.

Author's Acknowledgements

This work reproduces in slightly modified form two texts previously published in *Critique*: 'Généalogie, interprétation, texte' (26/275 (April 1970), 359–81) and 'L'oubli de la métaphore' (27/291–92 (August–September 1971), 783–804); as well as one text published in *Poétique*, 5 (1971): 'Nietzsche et la métaphore' (77–98). Here I wish to thank Jean Piel, Tzvetan Todorov, and Gérard Genette.

A first version of this work was presented to Jacques Derrida's seminar on metaphor at the École Normale Supérieure (1969–1970).

Notes

I AN UNHEARD-OF AND INSOLENT PHILOSOPHY

1 Translator's Note (hereafter 'TN'). 'Inouï' corresponds to the German 'unerhört', and both, as in English, connote that which has never yet been physically heard: the first heading thus already contains a buried metaphor, which Kofman will shortly unearth and activate. Nietzsche uses the epithet in the self-description (EH, 'Why I Write Such Excellent Books', 4), which Kofman paraphrases in this section, and it forms part of the extended metaphorical complex derived from the sense of hearing, which is one of the most important under discussion (cf. section VI below, especially part 3). Kofman uses the term again to describe Jacques Derrida in her first published essay on him: cf. the section 'Un philosophe "inouï"' (pp.23–33) in 'Un philosophe "unheimlich"' (in *Écarts: Quatre essais à propos de Jacques Derrida*, by Lucette Finas, Sarah Kofman, Roger Laporte, and Jean-Michel Rey (Paris: Fayard, 1973), pp.107–204, reproduced in Sarah Kofman, *Lectures de Derrida* (Paris: Galilée, 1984), to which all further reference will be made). David B. Allison echoes the formulation in his 'Preface' to *The New Nietzsche: Contemporary Styles of Interpretation* (ed. by David B. Allison (New York: Dell, 1977), p.ix), when he writes of the need to reassess Nietzsche's project: 'it is an adventure, then, with an urgency that is strictly speaking, *unheard of.*'

2 TN. I have used 'drives' for the French 'instincts' (Freud's 'Triebe') throughout. Cf. Jean Laplanche and J.-B. Pontalis, *The Language of Psycho-Analysis*, 2nd edn, trans. by Donald Nicholson-Smith (New York and London: Norton, 1973), p.214.

3 TN. An untranslatable pun: 'Se jouer de l'écriture mais aussi jouer avec elle.' There is a good deal of 'play' in the words 'jouer' and 'jeu'

themselves, which are thus highly problematic to the translator, not least because 'play' is such a key notion in Kofman's reading of Nietzsche (cf. e.g. section II, parts 3–4 below) and in post-structuralist criticism in general (cf. Derrida, 'Structure, Sign, and Play in the Discourse of the Human Sciences' (in *Writing and Difference*, trans. by Alan Bass (London and Henley: Routledge and Kegan Paul, 1978), pp.278–93) and 'Plato's Pharmacy', part II, section 9: 'Play: From the Pharmakon to the Letter and from Blindness to the Supplement' (in *Dissemination*, trans. by Barbara Johnson (Chicago: University of Chicago Press; London: Athlone, 1981), pp.156–71). The main problem is the ambiguity of 'jeu', which translates as 'play' or 'game': as a rule I have used the former, less restrictive meaning, with exceptions made for 'the game of writing', the Heraclitean motif, 'Zeus's game', and the 'conceptual game of dice'.

4 TN. The play on 'entendre' as 'hear' and 'understand' begins here, with 'mal entendu' and its implicit homonym 'malentendu' ('misunderstanding'), which provides the title for section VI, part 3 below.

5 Extra Note for the English translation (hereafter 'EN'). I elaborate on this point in *Explosion II: Les enfants de Nietzsche* (Paris: Galilée, 1993).

6 TN. Cf. Eric Blondel, 'Les guillemets de Nietzsche: Philologie et généalogie', in *Nietzsche aujourd'hui?*, 2 vols (Paris: Union Générale d'Éditions ('10/18'), 1973), II ('Passion'), pp.153–78. Derrida writes of Nietzsche's 'epochal regime of quotation marks' (*Spurs: Nietzsche's Styles/Éperons: Les styles de Nietzsche*, trans. by Barbara Harlow (Chicago and London: University of Chicago Press, 1979), p.107).

7 TN. Another pun: '"genres"' ('genres', 'genders', or 'genera').

II METAPHOR, SYMBOL, METAMORPHOSIS

1 TN. By a similar argument, Nietzsche writes in BT 4 of 'the dream as a *mere appearance of mere appearance*' and 'the naïve work of art' as 'likewise only "mere appearance of mere appearance"'.

2 TN. Nietzsche himself develops the notion of the supplement in passages such as P 111: '*Music* as a *supplement* to *language*', though Kofman is here alluding to an essentially Derridean thematic. Cf. *Of Grammatology*, trans. by Gayatri Chakravorty Spivak (Baltimore and London: Johns Hopkins University Press, 1976), especially part II, section 2: '" ... That Dangerous Supplement ... "' (pp.141–64) and section 4: 'From/Of the Supplement to the Source: The Theory of Writing' (pp.269–316), and 'Speech and Phenomena: Introduction to the Problem of Signs in Husserl's Phenomenology', in *Speech and Phenomena, and Other Essays on Husserl's Theory of Signs*, trans. by

David B. Allison (Evanston, Ill.: Northwestern University Press, 1973), especially part 7: 'The Supplement of Origin' (pp.88–104).

3 Since this work was written, Philippe Lacoue-Labarthe's important text 'Le détour (Nietzsche et la rhétorique)' has been published (in *Poétique*, 5 (Spring 1971),* 53–76 ['The Detour', trans. by Gary M. Cole, in *The Subject of Philosophy*, ed. by Thomas Trezise (Minneapolis and London: University of Minnesota Press, 1993), pp.14–36]). Although in agreement with mine in its broad outline, it nevertheless differs in several slight respects, notably in the place given to musical rhythm at the time of *The Birth of Tragedy*. For Lacoue-Labarthe, the second chapter of this work unequivocally identifies melody and harmony with the Dionysian, and rhythm with the Apollinian. He argues, moreover, that this amounts to a privileging of sound, accent, and dynamism – the commonplace of Romantic aesthetics and the crux of Wagnerian theory and practice – and that rhythm does not achieve pre-eminence for Nietzsche until after the separation from Wagner (cf. op.cit., p.71 [p.31] in particular). It seems to me nevertheless difficult to make such clear-cut distinctions in Nietzsche's text: there are numerous passages in *The Birth of Tragedy* which place rhythm, harmony, and dynamics on the same level – passages which already indicate that the Dionysian and the Apollinian are not so alien to one another. The Dionysian dithyramb is a 'total dance which forces every member into rhythmic movement'. 'The Greek Music Drama', which dates from approximately the same period, gives as characteristics of ancient music the poverty of its harmony and the richness of its means of rhythmic expression.

 * TN. The same issue of *Poétique* contained not only the second and concluding part of Derrida's 'La mythologie blanche: La métaphore dans le texte philosophique' ['White Mythology: Metaphor in the Text of Philosophy'] (1–52), and the French translation, by Lacoue-Labarthe and Jean-Luc Nancy, of selections from Nietzsche's notebooks ('Rhétorique et langage' ['Rhetoric and Language'], 99–142; cf. section III, n.15, below), but also the first, abridged version of 'Nietzsche et la métaphore' (77–98).

4 TN. Cf. Appendix, n.5 below, where Kofman returns to the notion of valour ('vaillance'/'Tapferkeit') and relates it to value.

5 TN. This is the first appearance of the crucial opposition of metaphor to 'proper' which runs through the rest of the text. In French, 'le sens propre' is 'proper' or 'literal meaning' ('à proprement parler': 'strictly speaking'; 'proprement dit': 'proper' (postpositionally)), but 'le propre' as a noun on its own is a highly ambiguous term which implies propriety (appropriateness) and decency but more especially distinctiveness and (self-)ownership: the self as one's

own property, in the sense in which Nietzsche uses the Latin term
'*proprium*' (cf. e.g. GS 370 or AC 31). Indeed, David B. Allison
consistently translates Kofman's use of the term in this sense as 'self'
(cf. 'Mdtaphor, Symbol, Metamorphosis', in *The Ndw Ncetzsche*
(pp.201–14), e.g. pp.205, 206). I have preferred to use 'proper' as a
noun throughout, despite occasional awkwardness, and follow Alan
Bass in his translations of Derrida: cf. 'Tympan' (in *Margins of
Philosophy* (Chicago: University of Chicago Press; Brighton: Harvester, 1982)), p.xi, n.4 and 'Différance' (ibid.), p.4, n.1.

'Propre' is undoubtedly the most ambiguous term in the book, and
Kofman deliberately puns on it where possible (cf. especially section
V, part 1 below: 'Proper, Appropriation, Property', and the dictionary definition of 'approprier' in section V, part 1, n.2). Moreover, the
adjective 'propre' on its own, as well as *meaning* 'own', also means
'clean' or 'neat' - resonances which will come into play especially
later, when Kofman discusses the ascetic ideal in GM III and the
priestly obsession with cleanliness/neatness (cf. section III, part 8,
especially p.51-2).

Finally, let us note that in the 'Tympan' to *Margins of Philosophy*,
Derrida will spectacularly conflate the question of the proper and the
metaphor of hearing, broadening the question out still further and
taking his cue from the Nietzschean notion of 'How to Philosophize
with a Hammer' (cf. TI): 'If Being is in effect a process of
reappropriation, the "question of Being" can never be percussed
without being measured against the absolutely coextensive question
of the proper. [...] The *proprius* presupposed in all discourses on
economy, sexuality, language, semantics, rhetoric, etc., repercusses
its absolute limit only in sonorous representation. Such, at least, is the
most insistent hypothesis of this book' (*Margins of Philosophy*, p.xix,
quoted by Kofman in 'Un philosophe "unheimlich"' (*Lectures de
Derrida*, p.23)).

6 TN. Metaphor has a 'relation' to the proper which is analogous to
that of writing to speech in Derrida's various discussions on the
subject, and the reversal hinted at here is 'akin' to the filial revolt
charted in 'Plato's Pharmacy', especially part II, section 8: 'The
Heritage of the Pharmakon: Family Scene' (*Dissemination*, pp.142–
55). For a new twist to the motif, cf. also section V, part 2 below, on
the relation between the 'weak', 'derived' sense of a concept and the
originary, 'strong' one: 'The moral meaning expresses the strong
meaning only metaphorically, just as the daughter cannot give birth
to the mother' (p.89).

7 One could draw a parallel between Nietzsche, who is aiming to
liberate the music from the text, and Artaud, for whom the theatre as
a total art form, integrating music and dance, can provide a liberation

from the tyranny of the text. The theatre of cruelty is also a theatre without spectators, without anyone to enjoy it. Cf. J. Derrida, 'La parole soufflée' (in *Writing and Difference*, pp.169–95).
[TN. Cf. also Camille Dumoulée, *Nietzsche et Artaud: pour une éthique de la cruauté* (Paris: P.U.F., 1992).]
    EN. Elsewhere, Nietzsche shows how Rossini – composer of a *Cat Duet* which takes 'miaow' as its sole text – understood very well that in opera it is not the words which count but the sounds, and that every word could easily be replaced by 'tra la la'. Cf. GS 80.

8 EN. I develop this point in *Explosion II: Les enfants de Nietzsche*, in my reading of *The Birth of Tragedy*.

9 TN. Cf. APO, A5: 'Aeschylus as a total artist [*Gesammtkünstler*] [...] *Aeschylus depicted as pentathlos*'. The Wagnerian derivation of the notion of 'total art' ('*Gesammtkunst*') which Nietzsche is using here should also not be forgotten.

10 TN. Cf. section III, part 5 below for Nietzsche's use of the metaphor of the Chladni figures.

11 This text, like many others of Nietzsche's from this period, might appear to be very close to the thinking of Bergson, for whom language is but a miserable stopgap which is nevertheless necessary in order to express intuition. But for Nietzsche, 'intuition' itself is only a metaphor: it is impossible to arrive at the essence of being. Moreover, whereas Bergson attributes a single, pragmatic origin to language, Nietzsche shows that the appropriation of language for utilitarian purposes is achieved by the weak, and results from a transformation in the relations of forces. Like the empiricists, Bergson reads cultural and psychical phenomena 'perversely' and traces a genealogy against the grain.

12 In *The Poetics* 1457b, Aristotle defines metaphor thus: 'Metaphor is the application of a strange term either transferred from the genus and applied to the species or from the species and applied to the genus, or from one species to another or else by analogy' (μεταφορὰ 'δέστιν ὀνόματος ἀλλοτρίον ἐπιφορά) (trans. by W. Hamilton Fyfe (London: Heinemann; Cambridge, Mass.: Harvard University Press, 1973)).

13 TN. Cf. 'The Metaphors for Metaphor' below (section III, part 5).

14 TN. 'The Philosopher's Book' was a project which Nietzsche intended as a companion piece to *The Birth of Tragedy*, and on which he worked periodically from 1872 until definitively laying it aside in 1875 (cf. Daniel Breazeale, *Philosophy and Truth: Selections from Nietzsche's Notebooks of the early 1870's* (Atlantic Highlands, NJ: Humanities Press; Hassocks: Harvester, 1979), pp.xxii–xxvii). Excerpts were published in a German/French parallel edition in 1969 as *Das Philosophenbuch: Theoretische Studien/Le livre du philosophe:*

Études théoriques, trans. by Angèle Kremer-Marietti (Paris: Aubier-Flammarion), which Kofman reviewed, along with the earlier Bianquis translations of *The Birth of Tragedy* and *Philosophy in the Tragic Age of the Greeks*, in a review article for *Critique* (27/291–292 (August–September 1971), 783–804). The review, entitled 'L'oubli de la métaphore' ['The Forgetting of Metaphor'], uses material from both the second and third sections of the present work.

15 TN. 'Juste': another ambiguous term, meaning both 'accurate' and 'just' or 'fair'. Cf. below, section III, parts 4a ('Concept and Language') and 6 ('Genesis of the Concept and Genesis of Justice') for the concept of justice. I have generally translated 'juste' as 'accurate', since 'right' would bring too many extraneous meanings into play.

16 EN. In *Ecce Homo* ('Why I Write Such Excellent Books', UM, 3), however, Nietzsche writes of the Third and Fourth *Untimely Meditations* that at that stage he was using Schopenhauer and Wagner as simple rhetorical signs or metaphorical props. I develop this point in the 'Introduction' to *Explosion I* (Paris: Galilée, 1992), pp.23–24, and in the chapter of *Explosion II* devoted to the *Untimely Meditations*, 'Accessoires', ['Props']. In these *Ecce Homo* texts, the notion of metaphor recovers the meaning it had for Nietzsche in the *Philosophenbuch* and the *Untimely Meditations*.

17 '*Against images and similes.* – With images and similes one can persuade and convince, but not prove. That is why there is such an aversion to images and similes within science; here the persuasive and convincing, that which makes things *credible*, is precisely what is *not* wanted; one challenges, rather, the coldest mistrust, and does so even in the means of expression one employs and the bare walls it presents: because mistrust is the touchstone for the gold of certainty' (WS 145).

18 Another genealogical test is to ask oneself if the author of a book knows how to dance and if he is capable of making his reader dance:

> We do not belong to those who have ideas only among books, when stimulated by books. It is our habit to think outdoors – walking, leaping, climbing, dancing, preferably on lonely mountains or near the sea where even the trails become thoughtful. Our first questions about the value of a book, of a human being, or a musical composition are: Can they walk? Even more, Can they dance? We read rarely, but not worse on that account. How quickly we guess how someone has come by his ideas; whether it was while sitting in front of his inkwell, with a pinched belly, his head bowed low over the paper – in which case we are quickly finished with his book, too! Cramped intestines betray themselves

[...] no less than closet air, closet ceilings, closet narrowness. (GS 366)

19 'Whoever rejoices in great human beings will also rejoice in philosophical systems, even if completely erroneous. They always have one wholly incontrovertible point: personal mood, colour. They may be used to reconstruct the philosophic image, just as one may guess at the nature of the soil in a given place by studying a plant that grows there. "So this has existed – once, at least – and is therefore a possibility, this way of life, this way of looking at the human scene." The "system" is a growth of this soil' (PTG, p.23f.).

[TN. Cf. also below, section VI, part 2 for Nietzsche's use of the metaphor of the tree, and its 'heritage'.]

20 'One of the great qualities of the Hellenes is their inability to turn the best of themselves into reflection. In other words they are *naïve*: a word in which simplicity and depth are united' (CP, p.352).

'They lost their naïve impartiality thanks to Socrates. Their myths and tragedies are much wiser than the ethics of Plato and Aristotle, and their "*Stoics* and *Epicureans*" are *impoverished* in comparison with their earlier poets and statesmen' (SW 196).

21 TN. For Nietzsche's classic analysis of the function of '*ressentiment*', cf. GM I, *passim*. For a classic discussion of it, cf. Gilles Deleuze, *Nietzsche and Philosophy*, trans. by Hugh Tomlinson (London: Athlone, 1983), chapter 4, pp.111–46.

22 EN. I have expanded on everything concerning Heraclitus and his enigmatic obscurity in 'Nietzsche and the Obscurity of Heraclitus' (trans. by Françoise Lionnet-McCumber, *Diacritics*, 17/3 (Fall 1987), 39–55).

23 TN. In this Heraclitean 'artists' metaphysics' (BT, 'Attempt at a Self-Criticism', 5), Nietzsche is also echoing Friedrich Schiller's aesthetic 'Spieltrieb' ('play drive' – cf. the *Aesthetic Letters*). Kofman will return to Nietzsche's thematization of play in order to contrast Nietzsche with Freud on this account: cf. section IV, n.15 below.

24 Cf. Book A of *The Metaphysics*; for example, at 985a, 10: 'These thinkers then, as I say, [...] seem to have grasped two of the causes which we have defined in the *Physics*: the material cause and the source of motion; but only vaguely and indefinitely. They are like untrained soldiers in a battle, who rush about and often strike good blows, but without science; in the same way these thinkers do not seem to understand their own statements' (trans. by Hugh Tredennick (Cambridge, Mass.: Harvard University Press; London: Heinemann, 1980)).

I have expanded on the relationship between Aristotle and the Pre-Socratics in my *Freud and Fiction* (trans. by Sarah Wykes (Cambridge: Polity, 1991)), pp.9–19.

25 TN. 'En abîme': the term is heraldic, from the practice of reproducing the design of a coat of arms in miniature in the fesse-point of a shield – which has the effect of a recursive *pars pro toto*. The use of 'en abîme' here is particularly significant since 'abîme' ('fesse-point') also means 'abyss' (for which Kofman uses 'gouffre', however).

26 Like Montaigne, Nietzsche prefers Diogenes Laertius to more erudite specialists: 'Who, for example, can clear the history of the Greek philosophers of the soporific miasma spread over it by the learned, though not particularly scientific and unfortunately all too tedious, labours of Ritter, Brandis, and Zeller? I for one prefer reading Diogenes Laertius to Zeller, because the former at least breathes the spirit of the philosophers of antiquity, while the latter breathes neither that nor any other spirit' (UM III, 8).

27 This does not contradict the idea that the condition of possibility for metaphor is the stripping-away of individuality. To express oneself metaphorically one must simultaneously be outside oneself and express oneself, whereas the concept is the deliberate concealment of the personality in the interest of speaking 'properly' and objectively.

III THE FORGETTING OF METAPHOR

1 TN. 'Usage et usure'. The French term 'usure', which means both 'wearing away' and 'usury', keeps the connection between the two still manifest, whereas in English one needs to carry out a genealogical dig into the etymology of the latter to unearth traces of the former sense, and in German the root of the term lies in an altogether different ground ('Wucher'). Derrida begins 'White Mythology' (in *Margins of Philosophy*, pp.207–71) with a bout of punning on this couplet and a number of our other themes:

> Thus we will content ourselves with a chapter, and for usage we will substitute – subtitle – *usure*. And first we will be interested in a certain *usure* of metaphorical force in philosophical exchange. [...] What could be the *properly named usure* of a word, a statement, a meaning, a text? Let us take all the risk of unearthing an example (and merely an example, as a frequent type), of this metaphor of (the) *usure* (of metaphor), the ruining of the figure [*l'abîmé de cette figure*], in *The Garden of Epicurus*. (p.209)

2 'Truths are illusions which we have forgotten are illusions; they are metaphors that have become worn out and have been drained of sensuous force, coins which have lost their embossing and are now considered as metal and no longer as coins' (TL, p.84).

3 Just as the effacement of the effigy on a coin masks the forgetting of the genesis which produced it. Cf. J.-J. Goux, 'Numismatics: An

Essay in Theoretical Numismatics', in *Symbolic Economies: After Marx and Freud* (trans. by Jennifer C. Gage (Ithaca, NY: Cornell University Press, 1990), pp. 9–63), and 'Marx et l'inscription du travail', *Tel Quel*, 33 (Spring 1968), 77–94. Cf. also G. Bataille, 'Jean Babelon' (in *Œuvres Complètes*, ed. by Denis Hollier, 12 vols (Paris: Gallimard, 1970–88), I, p. 121) and J. Derrida, 'White Mythology'.

4 This rhythmic play is later specified as being similar to that of a pendulum. Cf. GM I, 16: the play between Rome and Judaea.

5 Cf. TL, p. 88f.: 'The drive toward the formation of metaphors is the fundamental human drive, which one cannot for a single instant dispense with in thought, for one would thereby dispense with man himself.'

GOA XIV, i, 57: 'The laws of thought as the result of organic development; – we must accept the existence of a force which posits and creates fictions; – similarly the fact that these fictions are hereditary and perpetuated.'

Cf. also BGE 192: 'one is much more of an artist than one realizes.'

6 Each species possesses a metaphorical activity by which it remakes the world in its image. Here again, Nietzsche is setting himself up in opposition to Aristotle, for whom the ability to make metaphors is just as proper to man as is the power of reason: metaphor is reason in potential, already in the grip of meaning; which is why it is important to be able to excel in metaphors: 'That alone cannot be learnt; it is the token of genius. For the right use of metaphor means an eye for resemblances' (*The Poetics* 1459a).

7 TN. Cf. section III, part 6 for a discussion of Nietzsche's derivation of the notion of sublimation from chemistry. For an application of the notion, cf. GM II, 6–7 on the sublimation of cruelty.

8 Cf. WP 646, where Nietzsche establishes an analogical relationship between our memory and 'another kind' of memory, which operates on the organic level:

There are analogies; e. g. a memory analogous to our memory that reveals itself in heredity and evolution and forms. An inventiveness in the application of tools to new ends analogous to our inventiveness and experimentation, etc.

That which we call our 'consciousness' is innocent of any of the essential processes of our preservation and our growth; and no head is so subtle that it could construe more than a machine – to which every organic process is far superior.

Cf. GOA XIII, 585: 'So far *neither* of the two explanations for organic life has worked: neither the mechanical one, *nor the mental one*. I emphasize *this last point*. The mind [*Geist*] is more superficial than we think. The organism is governed in such a way that neither the mechanical *nor* the mental world can serve other than as its *symbolic* explanation.'

9 It is interesting to recall that Marx, in *The German Ideology*, also uses the *camera obscura* as a model to describe the process of ideological transposition – which makes us see men and their relations upside down – as resulting naturally from their historical life-process: 'just as much [...] as the inversion of objects on the retina does from their physical life-process' (*Karl Marx and Frederick Engels: Collected Works* (London: Lawrence and Wishart, 1976), V (trans. by W. Lough), 36).

One can see how Nietzsche and Marx revaluate the traditional model for knowledge, the eye: to know is no longer to contemplate the essence of things, but merely – and necessarily – to have a simple perspective on them, an 'inverted' point of view. Whereas for Marx it is ideology alone and not science which is like a *camera obscura*, though, for Nietzsche it would be impossible to have an eye any different. Science, too, is a form of art which not only deforms reality but constitutes it as such.

For a similar image, cf. TL, p.80:

What does man actually know about himself? Is he, indeed, ever able to perceive himself completely, as if laid out in a lighted display case? Does nature not conceal most things from him – even concerning his own body – in order to confine and lock him within a proud, deceptive consciousness, aloof from the coils of the bowels, the rapid flow of the bloodstream, and the intricate quivering of the fibres! She threw away the key. And woe to that fatal curiosity which might one day have the power to peer out and down through a crack in the chamber of consciousness and then suspect that man is sustained in the indifference of his ignorance by that which is pitiless, greedy, insatiable, and murderous – as if hanging in dreams on the back of a tiger.

Cf. also HH I, 141: 'And yet here truth is stood completely on its head: which is in the case of truth particularly unbecoming.'

For the metaphor of the *camera obscura*, cf. my *Camera obscura, de l'idéologie* (Paris: Galilée, 1973), [EN:] two chapters of which have been published in English translation in the Canadian journal *Public*.

10 P 63: 'In any case, this production of forms, by means of which the memory of something occurs, is something *artistic. It throws this form into relief* and strengthens it thereby. Thinking is a process of throwing into relief.' Cf. P 64.

11 Cf. Lacoue-Labarthe, 'The Detour'.

12 TN. 'Esprit': along with its German counterpart, 'Geist', this is a notoriously difficult term to translate into English, and finds itself

caught between the two stools of 'mind' and 'spirit' (especially in any translation of Hegel's *Phenomenology*). Derrida's study of the notion in Heidegger (*De l'esprit: Heidegger et la question* (Paris: Galilée, 1987)) is translated as *Of Spirit* (trans. by Geoffrey Bennington and Rachel Bowlby (Chicago and London: Chicago University Press, 1989)); I have used both 'mind' and 'spirit' as seemed appropriate.

13 Freudian concepts are essential here. The advantage of 'repression' over 'forgetting' is that it no longer belongs to the vocabulary of traditional psychology. Like 'forgetting' as conceived of by Nietzsche, it stands opposed to a linear conception of time and, like Nietzsche's 'forgetting', implies a conflict between a play of forces.

14 'Knowledge, strictly speaking, has only the form of tautology and *is empty.* All the knowledge which is of assistance to us involves the *identification of things which are not the same*, of things which are only similar. In other words, such knowledge is essentially illogical.

Only in this way do we obtain a concept. Then afterwards we behave as if the concept, e.g. the concept "man", were something factual, whereas it is surely only something which we have constructed through a process of ignoring all individual features' (P 150).

15 Cf. 'Rhétorique et langage' ['Rhetoric and Language'], translated [from German into French] by P. Lacoue-Labarthe and J.-L. Nancy (in *Poétique*, 5, 99–142):* 'All dealings between men stem from this: each seeks to read the soul of the other; and common language is the expression in sound of a common soul. The more intimate and sensitive these dealings, the richer the language, for it grows or withers with this collective soul. Speech is ultimately the question I ask my fellow man to find out if he has the same soul as me' ('Lire et Écrire' ['Reading and Writing'], p.139).

*TN. A selection of Nietzsche's notes from the early 1870s, published in French translation in 1971. The first and largest group was entitled 'Cours sur la rhétorique' ['Course on Rhetoric'] (*Poétique*, 5, 104–30) and consisted of sections 1 (abridged), 2–6, and 7 (abridged) from the total of sixteen sections making up the lecture course which Nietzsche prepared for the winter semester 1872–73 at the University of Basle. These were published in an English translation by Carole Blair as 'Nietzsche's Lecture Notes on Rhetoric: A Translation' (in *Philosophy and Rhetoric*, 16/2 (1983), 94–129), although the complete German text for the whole course has recently been made available for the first time, in a parallel edition with English translation, as: 'Darstellung der antiken Rhetorik: Description of Ancient Rhetoric', in *Friedrich Nietzsche on Rhetoric and Language*, ed. and trans. by Sander L. Gilman, Carole Blair, and David J. Parent (Oxford and New York: Oxford University Press,

1989), pp.2/3–192/3. The other sections in 'Rhétorique et langage' from which Kofman quotes were entitled: 'Fragments sur le langage' ['Fragments on Language'] (132–35) and 'Extraits de "Lire et Écrire"' ['Extracts from "Reading and Writing"'] (139–42).

16 Nietzsche might appear to be giving language a pragmatic origin, in a way which is scarcely different from Bergson or the empiricists. But the language we are dealing with here is already a decadent language. The 'Course on Rhetoric' and the 'Fragments on Language' posit the hypothesis of an original language harbouring within it the seeds of all other languages. This language 'was certainly poor in words and contained only sensory concepts' (p.132). The more ancient a language, he maintains, the richer it was in sonorities:

and indeed it is often impossible to separate language from song. The more ancient languages were poorer in words, and general concepts were lacking; it was passions, needs, and feelings that were expressed in sonority. It could almost be argued that they were not so much languages of words as languages of feelings; at any rate the feelings formed the sonorities and the words, in each people according to its individual character, and the movement of feeling provided the rhythm. Gradually language became separated from the language of sonorities. (p.133)

Nietzsche is very close here to Rousseau, in particular to the first four chapters of the *Essay on the Origin of Language*. For Rousseau, 'the first languages were lilting and impassioned before they became simple and methodical' and 'figurative language was the first to be born; proper meaning was discovered last'. For both writers, music and the voice are given privileged positions characteristic of a certain metaphysics, and tropes also have primacy over the 'proper'.* As against Cicero and Quintilian, for whom the metaphorical mode was born of discourse, of the pressure of neediness exerted after the 'proper', original meaning had been fixed, Nietzsche appeals to Jean Paul (*Vorschule der Ästhetik* (in *Sämmtliche Werke* (Berlin, 1861), II, ix, §50, p.179)):

Just as in writing, where writing with hieroglyphics was older than writing with the letters of the alphabet, so it was that in speaking, the metaphor, insofar as it denotes relationships and not objects, was the *earlier* word, which had only to fade into the *proper expression*. The besouling and the embodiment still constituted a unit, because I and world were still fused. Thus, with respect to spiritual relationships, each language is a dictionary of faded metaphors. (p.132; DAR, p.53)

Finally, in a passage from 'Reading and Writing' he directly opposes a pragmatic conception:

For it is not true that language is born of neediness; at any rate, not of individual neediness, and at the outside that of a whole horde or tribe [...]. And do people really believe they hear in the sovereign sonorities of a language the echo of the neediness which is supposed to have been its mother? Is everything not born in joy and exuberance, freely, and under the sign of profundity of spirit, of contemplative spirit? What could ape-like man make of our languages! A people which has six cases and conjugates its verbs with a hundred forms possesses a soul which is entirely collective and overflowing, and any people which was able to create for itself such a language has passed on the plenitude of its soul to posterity: for in the periods which follow, the same forces, thanks to the poets, musicians, actors, orators, and prophets, come to throw themselves into form. But it was these forces, when they were still in the overflowing plenitude of first youth, that engendered the creators of languages [*Sprachbildner*]. These were the most fertile men of all time, and they designated what the musicians and the artists have subsequently always designated: their soul was greater, more full of love, more collective. (p.140)

Though Nietzsche indeed deletes the opposition between a metaphorical language and a 'proper', conceptual language – since the concept is a condensate of forgotten metaphors – he nevertheless preserves the opposition between a 'noble', artistic language which does not shy away from waste, and a language of the herd born of neediness. The originary language which is transformed by becoming ever more abstract must be interpreted as a myth whose significance is typological, for there is no one linear historical evolution of one language starting from one origin: the two types of language have always already existed.

The eternal return prevents what is said in the 'Course on Rhetoric' being conceived literally. In truth the notion had hardly been elaborated at the time of the 'Course', though a later text, from *The Gay Science*, shows the constancy of Nietzsche's thought in this respect:

it seems to me as if the subtlety and strength of consciousness always were proportionate to a man's (or animal's) *capacity for communication* and as if this capacity in turn were proportionate to the *need for communication*. [...] Where need and distress have forced men for a long time to communicate and to understand each other quickly and subtly, the ultimate result is an excess of this strength and art of communication – as it were, a capacity that has gradually been accumulated and now waits for an heir who might squander it. (Those who are called artists are these heirs; so are orators, preachers, writers – all of them people who always come at the end of a long chain, 'late born' every one of them in the best sense of that word and, as I have said, by their nature squanderers.) Supposing that this observation is correct, I may proceed to the surmise that *consciousness has developed only under the pressure of the need for communication*; that from the start it was needed and useful only between human beings (particularly between those who commanded and those who obeyed); and that it also developed only in proportion to the degree of this utility. Consciousness is really only a net of communication between human beings [...]. Man, like every living being, thinks continually without knowing it; the thinking that rises to *consciousness* is only the smallest part of all this – the most superficial and worst part – for only this conscious thinking *takes the form of words, which is to say signs of communication*, and this fact uncovers the origin of consciousness. (GS 354. Cf. GS 111; cf. also UM IV, 5 and IV, 9)

★ TN. For a more extended analysis of these themes in Rousseau, cf. Derrida, *Of Grammatology*, part II, especially 'The Originary Metaphor' (section 4, pp.270–80).

17 TN. For the link between equilibrium and justice, cf. the discussion of WS 22 in section III, part 6 below.

18 Cf. BGE 19: 'what happens here is what happens in every well-constructed and happy commonwealth: the ruling class identifies itself with the successes of the commonwealth. In all willing it is absolutely a question of commanding and obeying, on the basis, as I have said already, of a social structure composed of many "souls".'
On the evidence of such a text one would be justified in drawing a parallel between the metaphysical fictions which Nietzsche deconstructs, and ideology as Marx conceives it. In both cases the genesis of the conscious processes, the work of the unconscious forces, is forgotten. Nevertheless, as far as the play of social forces is concerned there remain some fundamental differences. Marx envisages the possibility of a classless society without hierarchical distinction, whereas for Nietzsche hierarchical differences are part of life itself. They are what are hidden in the fictions created by the herd-man – the metaphysician and democratic animal. For Nietzsche, the primary relations between men are not relations of profit or production, but those founded on the pathos of distance which establishes hierarchy – a pathos of distance which is independent of

any specific economic structure. The body of society and the living body are both governed by the will to power:

life itself is *essentially* appropriation, injury, overpowering of the strange and weaker, suppression, severity, imposition of one's own forms, incorporation and, at the least and mildest, exploitation – but why should one always have to employ precisely those words which have from of old been stamped with a slanderous intention? Even that body within which [...] individuals treat one another as equals – this happens in every healthy aristocracy – must, if it is a living and not a decaying body, itself do all that to other bodies which the individuals within it refrain from doing to one another: it will have to be the will to power incarnate, it will want to grow, expand, draw to itself, gain ascendancy – not out of any morality or immorality, but because it *lives*, and because life *is* will to power. On no point, however, is the common European consciousness more reluctant to learn than it is here; everywhere one enthuses, even under scientific guises, about coming states of society in which there will be 'no more exploitation' - that sounds to my ears like promising a life in which there will be no organic functions. 'Exploitation' does not pertain to a corrupt or imperfect or primitive society: it pertains to the *essence* of the living thing as a fundamental organic function, it is a consequence of the intrinsic will to power which is precisely the will of life. – Granted this is a novelty as a theory – as a reality it is the *primordial fact* [*Urfaktum*] of all history: let us be at least that honest with ourselves! (BGE 259)

19 In BGE 19 Nietzsche pastiches Cartesian analytical method – in order to expose its limits the better – as a culinary method which puts together a process by combining supposedly simple elements like so many ingredients.

For the relation between Nietzsche and Descartes, cf. my 'Descartes Entrapped' (trans. by Kathryn Aschheim, in *Who Comes After the Subject?*, ed. by Eduardo Cadava, Peter Connor, and Jean-Luc Nancy (New York and London: Routledge, 1991), pp.178–97).

20 For fetishism as a projection into the world of the will conceived as cause, cf. TI, '"Reason" in Philosophy', 5: 'we find ourselves in the midst of a rude fetishism when we call to mind the basic presuppositions of the metaphysics of language – which is to say, of *reason*. It is *this* which sees everywhere deed and doer; this which believes in will as cause in general; this which believes in the "ego", in the ego as being, in the ego as substance, and which *projects* its belief in the ego-substance on to all things – only thus does it *create* the concept

"thing". ... Being is everywhere thought in, *foisted on*, as cause; it is only from the conception "ego" that there follows, derivatively, the concept "being".'

Cf. my 'Baubô: Theological Perversion and Fetishism' (trans. by Tracy B. Strong, in *Nietzsche's New Seas: Explorations in Philosophy, Aesthetics, and Politics*, ed. by Michael Allen Gillespie and Tracy B. Strong (Chicago and London: University of Chicago Press, 1988), pp.175–202).

21 For the implicit mythology hidden in language and grammar, cf. GM I, 13 and WS 11: 'A philosophical mythology lies concealed in *language* which breaks out again every moment, however careful one may be otherwise.'

22 TN. 'As distinguished from a litigation, a differend [*différend*] would be a case of conflict, between (at least) two parties, that cannot be equitably resolved for lack of a rule of judgement applicable to both arguments' (Jean-François Lyotard, *The Differend: Phrases in Dispute*, trans. by Georges Van Den Abbeele (Minneapolis: University of Minnesota Press; Manchester: Manchester University Press), 1988, p.xi).

23 TN. Of course this does not apply to English at all; nor indeed does it strictly apply to Nietzsche's German, where the neuter 'gender' is also used. This whole passage, though, is a paraphrase of TL, p.82.

24 TN. The notion of communication in this sense is a Leibnizian one and recalls the windowless monads of the *Monadology*. For the relationship between Nietzsche and Leibniz, cf. Walter Kaufmann on 'Nietzsche's "monadology"', in *Nietzsche: Philosopher, Psychologist, Antichrist*, 3rd edn (New York: Vintage, 1968), pp.263–64. Cf. also section VI, part 1, n.4 below.

25 Cf. A. Kremer-Marietti's note in *Le livre du philosophe* (p.250, n.7): the Chladni figures are 'figures in sand which represent the fundamental and the higher modes of vibrations: for example, in the case of a standardized sheet covered with powder, when the sheet vibrates the powder accumulates in the zones of minimal amplitude, and the number of nodes increases with the frequency.'

Thomas Mann refers to the Chladni figures in *Doctor Faustus*, chapter 3.

26 These two metaphors and their meaning show the continuity of Nietzsche's thought from *The Birth of Tragedy* onwards.

27 TN. 'Penser, c'est peser.' In German, 'Mensch' is the standard term for 'person', or 'man' in the generic sense of 'mankind' ('Menschheit'). Cf. Zarathustra: '"Man", that is: the evaluator' (Z I, 'Of the Thousand and One Goals').

28 TN. 'right of retribution'.

29 TN. For more on the image of the doorkeeper, and its associations for Nietzsche with memory and the *camera obscura*, cf. *Camera obscura* (p.48).

30 TN. Kofman will expand on this rich concentration of metaphors below. For further discussion of the seductive nakedness of the concept (as mask), cf. section V, part 3; for the concept as a mummification and a preservation, cf. section IV, part 1c.

31 For the distinction between the two types of forgetting, cf. G. Deleuze, *Nietzsche and Philosophy*, pp.112–14.

32 TN. '*Dé-figure*': a pun which conveys both 'disfigurement' and 'unfiguration', a reduction of metaphorical to conceptual meaning.

33 These chasms recall the abyss which separates Heraclitus from Aristotle.

34 'Every elevation of the type "man" has hitherto been the work of an aristocratic society – and so it will always be: a society which believes in a long scale of orders of rank and differences of worth between man and man and needs slavery in some sense or other. Without the *pathos of distance* such as develops from the incarnate differences of classes, from the ruling caste's constant looking out and looking down on subjects and instruments and from its equally constant exercise of obedience and command, its holding down and holding at a distance, that other, more mysterious pathos could not have developed either, that longing for an ever-increasing widening of distance within the soul itself, the formation of ever higher, rarer, more remote, tenser, more comprehensive states, in short precisely the elevation of the type "man", the continual "self-overcoming of man", to take a moral formula in a supra-moral sense' (BGE 257).

35 EN. In *Ecce Homo*, Nietzsche claims that the instinct for cleanliness is his essential characteristic. Does this mean that he belongs typologically to the same caste as the priests? Cf. the chapter in *Explosion I*, 'L'instinct de propreté' ['The instinct for cleanliness'] (pp.263–69).

36 Let us recall that Freud establishes an analogical relationship between obsessional neurosis and religion: the former is like a caricature of the latter (cf. in particular *Totem and Taboo* (SE, XIII, 1–161)). Freud insists on the phobia of touch as characteristic of the obsession, in tandem with the prohibition on sexual contact. Both Nietzsche and Freud see prohibitions as defences, as means of protection: but for Freud they are also substitutive realizations of repressed wishes, and punishments for these realizations.

37 With this thesis of a single force, affirmative even in illness, and by excluding all negativity, Nietzsche stands radically opposed to Freud with his hypothesis of the death drives. However, Freud, too, sees in the pathological only an exaggeration of normal processes, and

establishes between the two only a difference of degree. Freud wavers between dualism and monism.

38 I have borrowed this translation of 'Aufhebung' from J. Derrida.* But Nietzschean 'Aufhebung', which implies no work of the negative, has nothing to do with Hegelian 'Aufhebung'. In Nietzsche's case there is a parodic revaluation of this metaphysical concept.

*TN. For Derrida's 'rendering' of this essentially Hegelian concept, cf. 'From Restricted to General Economy: A Hegelianism without Reserve' (in *Writing and Difference*, pp.251–77), especially pp.257 and 275, and 'The Pit and the Pyramid: Introduction to Hegel's Semiology' (in *Margins of Philosophy*, pp.69–108), especially pp.88–95: '*Relever* – What Talking Means'. Cf. also Alan Bass's informative note in his translation of 'Différance' (*Margins of Philosophy*, p.19, n.23).

39 TN. 'La maladie est une "relève" de la santé': a pun on Derrida's version of 'Aufhebung', 'relève', which conveys the two basic meanings 'relief' (as in relieving a guard on watch, rather than pain relief) and 'lift'. For further discussion of the question of illness and health in Nietzsche, in the context of *Ecce Homo*, cf. *Explosion I*, 'Un malade en bonne santé' ['An Invalid in Good Health'], pp.181–88.

40 TN. 'Vivre, c'est jouer sous peine d'être joué': a new twist to the earlier pun (cf. section I, n.3).

41 TN. Freud points to an analogous historical link between the divinization of women and their corresponding loss of real power. Cf. Kofman's discussion in the recent interview 'Subvertir le philosophique *ou* Pour un supplément de jouissance', *Compar(a)ison*, 1 (1993), 9–26 (p.15).

42 Cf. Theognis, *Elegies*, vv.54–58, 63–68: 'in former days, there was a tribe who knew no laws nor manners, but like deer they grazed outside the city walls, and wore the skins of goats. These men are nobles (ἀγαθοί), now. The gentlemen of old (οἱ δὲ πρὶν ἐσθλοί) are now the trash (δειλοί) [...] Pretend, my Kurnos, that you love them all, but when it comes to something serious, stay clear; for in their pitiable hearts you'll find no honour, and their love, you'll learn, is all for mischief, for a cruel joke; their faith, like that of souls already doomed.'

v.1025: 'gentlemen (ἀγαθοί) can stand up straighter still.'

v.1167–8: 'A good man answers well (ἐσθλή) and his acts are good; the bad man's worthless words fly on the wind' (trans. by Dorothea Wender, in *Hesiod: Theogony, Works and Days; Theognis: Elegies* (Harmondsworth: Penguin, 1973)).

43 The rest of the text shows how Christian love comes from Judaic hatred, and how Christianity merely results from Judaism being

pushed to the limit and ending up being inverted. I have studied the relation between Christianity and Judaism in 'Métamorphose de la volonté de puissance du Judaïsme au Christianisme d'après "L'Anté-christ" de Nietzsche' ['Metamorphosis of the Will to Power from Judaism to Christianity in Nietzsche's *The Antichrist*'], *Revue de l'enseignement philosophique*, 18/3 (February–March 1968), 15–19.

44 It should be noted that the metaphor of stiffening and hardening takes up the Platonic image of *Glaucus the sea-god* in inversion. For Plato it is the soul that is no longer recognizable, hardened as it is by feasts and banquets which cover it like so much seaweed and so many shells. Here it is the stream of images which is, as it were, petrified and ossified. Cf. *Republic* X, 611d.

IV METAPHORICAL ARCHITECTURES

1 This is what Marx does, for example: 'a bee puts to shame many an architect in the construction of her cells. But what distinguishes the worst architect from the best of bees is this, that the architect raises his structure in imagination before he erects it in reality' (*Capital: A Critical Analysis of Capitalist Production*, ed. by Friedrich Engels, trans. by Samuel Moore and Edward Aveling, 3 vols (London: Lawrence and Wishart, 1970), I, 174).

2 Cf. SW 193: 'The false opposition between *vita practica* and *vita contemplativa* is something Asiatic. The Greeks understood the matter better.'

3 Cf. P 103 and P 77. Nietzsche's texts on science as a semiology and a symptomatology are countless. The following are the most impor-tant: P 50, 78, 80, 95, 101; GS 112, 121, 246, 373; BGE 21; TI, '"Reason" in Philosophy', 3 and 6, 'The Four Great Errors', 3; AC 15; WP 488, 524, 555, 558, 565, 625, 636; GOA XII, i, 37, XII, i, 66, XII, i, 351, XIII, 166, XIII, 202, XIV, i, 69, XIV, i, 85, XIV, i, 86.

4 Here Nietzsche takes up again the biblical metaphor, which Leibniz had already reiterated, in order to revaluate it.* For Leibniz it was actually a matter of constructing a scholarly, unequivocal, and universal language so as to put an end to the diversity and equivocation of natural languages: 'For we have the option of fixing significations, at least in some learned language, and of agreeing on them, so as to pull down this Tower of Babel' (*New Essays on Human Understanding*, ed. and trans. by Peter Remnant and Jonathan Bennett (Cambridge: Cambridge University Press, 1981), III, 9, p.337). By taking up again this same metaphor but applying it to science, Nietzsche effaces the opposition between artificial and natural language, between common and scientific language.

*TN. The French translation which Kofman is using (*Par-delà le*

Bien et le Mal, trans. by Geneviève Bianquis (Paris: Aubier, 1963)) is more explicit here than the German (or R.J. Hollingdale's English translation, which follows it closely) and actually names the Tower of Babel.

5 Cf. GOA XIV, i, 39: 'What disaster lies just in the mummified error that the word "abstraction" conceals! As if what it designates were produced by omitting something rather than by emphasizing, highlighting, and strengthening it! Every image, every form in us is produced by a similar coarsening which makes it possible!'

6 The metaphor of the pyramid is a parodic repetition of the metaphor Hegel uses for the sign in the *Encyclopaedia* (§458): 'The sign is some immediate intuition, representing a totally different import from what naturally belongs to it; it is the pyramid into which a foreign soul has been conveyed, and where it is conserved' (*Hegel's Philosophy of Mind*, trans. by William Wallace (Oxford: Clarendon Press, 1971), p.213). Cf. J. Derrida's commentary on this passage in 'The Pit and the Pyramid', in particular:

> The sign, as the unity of the signifying body and the signified ideality, becomes a kind of incarnation. Therefore the opposition of soul and body, and analogically the opposition of the intelligible and the sensory, condition the difference between the signified and the signifier, between the signifying intention (*bedeuten*), which is an animating activity, and the inert body of the signifier. [...] Hegel knew that this proper and animated body of the signifier was also a *tomb*. The association *sōma/sēma* is also at work in this semiology, which is in no way surprising. The tomb is the life of the body as the sign of death, the body as the other of the soul, the other of the animate psyche, of the living breath. But the tomb also shelters, maintains in reserve, capitalizes on life by marking that life continues elsewhere. [...] It consecrates the disappearance of life by attesting to the perseverance of life. Thus, the tomb also shelters life from death. It *warns* the soul of possible death, warns (of) death of the soul, turns away (from) death. This double warning function belongs to the funerary monument. The body of the sign thus becomes the monument in which the soul will be enclosed, preserved, maintained, kept in maintenance, present, signified. At the heart of this monument the soul keeps itself alive, but it needs the monument only to the extent that it is exposed – to death – in its living relation to its own body. (*Margins of Philosophy*, p.82f.)

From this metaphor, Nietzsche retains the idea that inside the tomb the presence of life is maintained, and that this monument serves to safeguard life against death. But whereas for Hegel the metaphor of the pyramid presupposes the opposition between signifier and signified (a discontinuity marked in the *Aesthetics* by the fact that here the pyramid is the symbol for symbolic art and no longer for the sign, as in the *Encyclopaedia*), it is introduced by Nietzsche precisely to deconstruct the whole system of metaphysical oppositions. Thus this metaphor is itself erased by those which precede or succeed it: no metaphor could be *the* sign itself for the sign, the *proper* sign for the sign.

[TN. Cf. also BT 15 for a link between 'the *dying Socrates*' and 'the amazingly high pyramid of knowledge [*Wissenspyramide*] in our own time'.]

7 TN. There is a pun here on 'suprême', which conveys more explicitly than in English the temporal sense of 'final', 'last' (i.e. at the moment of death) as well as 'supreme'.

8 Aristotle already saw society as a game of backgammon, where each piece had to move according to predetermined rules at the risk of being taken out of the game: the πόλις is a game where the opponents take numerous pieces from each other. The squares on a draughts board were called 'cities' and the pieces 'dogs'. The tyrant, who has no definite place in the game, is analogous to the gods or an animal. Cf. *The Politics* 1253a:

From these things therefore it is clear that the city-state is a natural growth, and that man is by nature a political animal, and a man that is by nature and not merely by fortune citiless is either low in the scale of humanity or above it (like the 'clanless, lawless, heartless' man reviled by Homer, for one by nature unsocial is also a 'lover of war') inasmuch as he is solitary, like an isolated piece at draughts. (Trans. by H. Rackham (London: Heinemann; New York: Putnam, 1932))

Cf. also J.-P. Vernant, 'Ambiguity and Reversal: On the Enigmatic Structure of *Oedipus Rex*' (in Jean-Pierre Vernant and Pierre Vidal-Naquet, *Myth and Tragedy in Ancient Greece*, trans. by Janet Lloyd (New York: Zone Books, 1988), pp.113–40), in particular p.437, n.123, where he refers to Suetonius: "'*polis* is also a type of dice game in which the players took each other's pieces, positioned as in draughts [*pettenticos*] on squares drawn with intersecting lines. These squares were, quite wittily, called cities [*poleis*], while the pieces of the opposing player were called dogs [*kunes*]".' So Nietzsche once more takes up a traditional metaphor – the city as a game – but he does so in order to bring into question the very idea of a game by generalizing the notion and deleting the opposition between game-playing and seriousness.

9 Cf. BGE 5, where the geometrical construction of the *Ethics* is
assimilated to a shield behind which the invalid Spinoza shelters: 'that
hocus-pocus of mathematical form in which, as if in iron, Spinoza
encased and masked his philosophy – "the love of *his* wisdom"', to
render that word fairly and squarely – so as to strike terror into the
heart of any assailant who should dare to glance at that invincible
maiden and Pallas Athene – how much personal timidity and
vulnerability this masquerade of a sick recluse betrays!'
   EN. I have commented on BGE 5 in *Nietzsche et la scène
philosophique* (Paris: Union Générale d'Éditions ('10/18'), 1979; 2nd
edn: Galilée, 1986), in the section 'Les jongleries de Spinoza'
['Spinoza's Juggling'], pp.313–16.

10 Cf. Freud, *New Introductory Lectures*, 'Revision of the Theory of
Dreams' (SE, XXII, 24), where the spider is deciphered as symbolic
of the phallic mother.

11 EN. Cf. GM III, 9 where Nietzsche contrasts the Greek point of
view with the 'modern' one (a 'technological' one – and thus a pre-
emptive response to Heidegger's reading of Nietzsche as the last
metaphysician), writing: 'our attitude toward God as some alleged
spider of purpose and morality behind the great captious web of
causality, is *hubris* – we might say, with Charles the Bold when he
opposed Louis XI, *"je combats l'universelle araignée"* [I fight the
universal spider]'.

12 Cf. BGE 230, where Nietzsche applies the same metaphor to the
seductive song of the 'metaphysical bird-catchers': 'to confront man
henceforth with man in the way in which, hardened by the discipline
of science, man today confronts the *rest* of nature, with dauntless
Oedipus eyes and stopped-up Odysseus ears, deaf to the siren songs
of old metaphysical bird-catchers who have all too long been piping
to him "you are more! you are higher! you are of a different
origin!"'.

13 Cf. TI, '"Reason" in Philosophy', 1 and 'Expeditions of an
Untimely Man', 23; in *Philosophy in the Tragic Age of the Greeks*, truth,
from Parmenides onwards, is said to inhabit a castle made of spider's
web, in the company of a philosopher who is as bloodless as an
abstraction: 'A spider at least wants blood from his victims. The
Parmenidean philosopher hates most of all the blood of his victims,
the blood of the empirical reality which was sacrificed and shed by
him' (PTG, p.80).

14 TN. A pun on the homophones 'sens' ('meaning', 'sense') and 'sang'
('blood').
   Perhaps surprisingly, Kofman makes no reference here to the
section in *Zarathustra* entitled 'Of the Tarantulas' (Z II), on which
Gilles Deleuze bases his thematization of the spider, e.g. in his second

Nietzsche (Paris: P.U.F., 1965), p.44. In 'Un philosophe "unheimlich"' (*Lectures de Derrida*, p.16), Kofman again discusses the spider motif, this time in the context of writing and Derrida's 'Qual Quelle: Valéry's Sources' (in *Margins of Philosophy*, pp.273–306).

15 'And as children and artists play, so plays the ever-living fire. It constructs and destroys, all in innocence. Such is the game that the aeon plays with itself. [...] The child throws its toys away from time to time – and starts again, in innocent caprice. But when it does build, it combines and joins and forms its structures regularly, conforming to inner laws.

Only aesthetic man can look thus at the world, a man who has experienced in artists and in the birth of art objects how the struggle of the many can yet carry rules and laws inherent in itself, how the artist stands contemplatively above and at the same time actively within his work, how necessity and random play, oppositional tension and harmony, must pair to create a work of art' (PTG, p.62).

The notion of play, fundamental in Nietzsche, implies successive constructions and deconstructions of worlds without the need for a negative force. It allows Nietzsche to do without the death drives which feature in Freud's hypothesis. When Freud seeks to prove the necessity of positing a principle beyond the pleasure principle, he takes as his first example the child's game, which is far from innocent. But the rest of the text rejects this example, which is considered to be hardly a convincing justification for something beyond the pleasure principle. Cf. *Beyond the Pleasure Principle* (SE, XVIII, 14–17).

16 This 'other channel for its activity' can be compared to the Freudian metaphor of sublimation, which also represents a diversionary pathway.

17 For the metaphorical writing of dream and art as a return to the archaic, cf. WS 194:

The dream. – Our dreams are, on the rare occasions when they are for once successful and perfect – usually the dream is a bungled product – chains of symbolic scenes and images in place of the language of poetic narration; they paraphrase our experiences or expectations or circumstances with such poetic boldness and definiteness that in the morning we are always astonished at ourselves when we recall our dreams. In dreaming we use up too much of our artistic capacity – and therefore often have too little of it during the day.

Cf. also HH I, 13:

Logic of the dream. [...] In the dream this piece of primeval humanity continues to exercise itself, for it is the basis upon which higher rationality evolved and continues to evolve in every human being: the dream takes us back again to remote stages of human culture and provides us with a means of understanding them better. We now find dream-thinking so easy because it is in precisely this imaginative and agreeable form of explanation by means of the first plausible idea that strikes us that we have been so well drilled over such enormous periods of human evolution. To this extent the dream is a relaxation for the brain, which has had enough of the strenuous demands in the way of thinking such as are imposed by our higher culture during the day.

Cf. also UM IV, 4; BGE 193. This whole conception of dream, art, and their interrelation is very close to Freud's. Freud himself, in *The Interpretation Of Dreams*, VII B, 'Regression' (SE, V, 549), quotes Nietzsche when he wants to show that the analysis of dreams can lead us to a knowledge of the archaic heritage innate in every man. Cf. my *The Childhood of Art* (trans. by Winifred Woodhull (New York: Columbia University Press, 1988)), in particular chapter 2.
18 Cf. GS 54:

I suddenly woke up in the midst of this dream, but only to the consciousness that I am dreaming and that I must go on dreaming lest I perish [...]. Appearance is for me that which lives and is effective and goes so far in its self-mockery that it makes me feel that this is appearance and will-o'-the-wisp and a dance of spirits and nothing more – that among all these dreamers, I, too, who 'know', am dancing my dance; that the knower is a means for prolonging the earthly dance and thus belongs to the masters of ceremony of existence; and that the sublime consistency and interrelatedness of all knowledge perhaps is and will be the highest means to *preserve* the universality of dreaming and the mutual comprehension of all dreamers and thus also *the continuation of the dream*.

19 For Spinoza, too, the fictions created by knowledge of the first kind are 'supplements' added to Nature by the insane. Nature, a full and infinite totality, needs nothing, but the delirium which men owe to their truncated, mutilated, incomplete knowledge makes Nature delirious in turn: here again men project their own powerlessness externally. Nature thus appears as a blind force able to oppose divine laws if need be, and a miracle is a special intervention by God in favour of man – an authority within an authority – to fill a natural deficiency. The ignorant man thus introduces a fictional opposition between nature and God which becomes a transcendent force, a

stopgap for human deficiencies. Cf. in particular chapter 6 of the *Tractatus Theologico-Politicus*, where Spinoza shows that natural causes are never *lacking*, but that men believe in miracles because, either wilfully or through ignorance, they *omit* certain circumstances: 'If anything be found in Scripture which can be conclusively proved to contravene the laws of Nature, or which could not possibly follow from them, we have to believe that this was inserted into Holy Scripture by sacrilegious men' (trans. by Samuel Shirley (Leiden: Brill, 1989), p.134).

For Nietzsche, as for Spinoza, this fiction implies that Nature is separated from its own powers and the nature of desire is falsified.

20 Cf. also WP 574: 'Senselessness of all metaphysics as the derivation of the conditioned from the unconditioned.

It is in the nature of thinking that it thinks of and invents the unconditioned as an adjunct to the conditioned; just as it thought of and invented the "ego" as an adjunct to the multiplicity of its processes; it measures the world according to magnitudes posited by itself – such fundamental fictions as "the unconditional", "ends and means", "things", "substances", logical laws, numbers, and forms.'

21 Cf. HH II, 32:

Alleged 'real reality'. – When he describes the various professions [...] the poet poses as *knowing* of these things to the very bottom; indeed when it comes to the conflict of human actions and destinies he acts as though he had been present at the weaving of the whole nexus of the world; to this extent he is a deceiver. And he practises his deception only before those who *do not know* – and that is why his deception is successful: the latter commend him for his profound and genuine knowledge and in the end induce in him the delusion that he really does know these things as well as do the individuals he is describing, indeed as well as the great world-spider itself. Thus at last the deceiver becomes honest and believes in his own veracity. People of sensibility, indeed, even tell him to his face that he possesses a *higher* truth and veracity – for they are for a time tired of reality and accept the poetic dream as a benevolent relaxation and night for head and heart. What this dream shows them now seems to them more *valuable*, because, as remarked, they find it more beneficent: and men have always believed that that which seems more valuable is the truer and more real.

Cf. GS 57: 'That mountain there! That cloud there! What is "real" in that? Subtract the phantasm and every human *contribution* from it, my sober friends! [...] There is no "reality" for us – not for you either, my sober friends.' Cf. also GS 59 and TL, p.80.

22 TN. As Daniel Breazeale points out, Nietzsche actually misquotes *pensée* 386 and omits the 'almost' (cf. *Philosophy and Truth*, p.89, n.31)!

23 *The Gay Science* also has the air of a festival following on from a long period of slavery: '"Gay Science": that signifies the Saturnalia of a spirit who has patiently resisted a terrible, long pressure – patiently, severely, coldly, without submitting, but also without hope – and who is now all at once attacked by hope, the hope for health, and the *intoxication* of convalescence. [...] This whole book is nothing but a bit of merry-making after long privation and powerlessness' (GS 'Preface', 1).

24 According to Aristotle, anyone who talks for the sake of talking is like a vegetable. Cf. *Metaphysics*, Γ 1006a.

25 Cf. Ovid, *Metamorphoses*, II, 17, 833–75 ('Jupiter and Europa', in *Ovid: Metamorphoses*, trans. by A.D. Melville (Oxford and New York: Oxford University Press, 1986), p.49f.).

26 Cf. Herodotus, *The History*, I, §60 (trans. by David Grene (Chicago and London: University of Chicago Press, 1987), p.59).

27 Nietzsche's texts on the Stoics are numerous. Besides the admirable BGE 9, a veritable masterpiece of deconstruction where all the Stoic themes are taken up again to be revaluated and deciphered genealogically, let us quote GOA XII, i, 253:

I think Stoicism is misunderstood. The essence of this disposition (which is what it is even before it is annexed by philosophy) is an attitude towards pain and the representations of displeasure: a certain *weight*, *pressure*, and *inertia* are intensified in the extreme so as to attenuate the feeling of pain; *rigidity* and *coldness* are the trick, in other words anaesthetics. The main aim of Stoic education: to stop you becoming *easily aroused*, and increasingly to restrict the number of things worthy of *moving* you; to lead you to consider contemptible and of little value the majority of things which arouse you; to cultivate hatred and hostility towards arousal, towards passion itself, as if it were an illness or something unworthy; to direct your attention to all the ugly or uncomfortable manifestations of passion – *in summa*: *petrifaction* as a remedy for pain; and then the statue is attributed all the lofty names of the divine, of virtue. What does it matter if you embrace a statue in winter when you have become insensitive to the cold? – what does it matter when one statue embraces another! Once the Stoic has reached the state to which he aspires (*usually he brings it with him, which is why he chooses this philosophy!*), he has the *compressive force of a bandage*, which produces insensitivity. – I find this way of thinking highly repugnant: it underestimates the value of *pain* (which is as useful and beneficial as pleasure), the value of *arousal* and of *passion*. In the end the Stoic is forced to say: everything is fine by me as it is, and I want nothing to be different, – *he can no longer deal with an emergency* because he has killed off his sensitivity to emergencies. He expresses this in religious terms, as an agreement with all the acts of the divinity (e.g. in Epictetus).

Cf. also WP 435; GOA XI, ii, 230, XIII, 79; BGE 21, 44, 188, 198, 211, 227; GM II, *passim*; GS 109, 306, 359.

For a reading of BGE 9, cf. the chapter, 'La comédie du stoïcisme' ['The Play-Acting of Stoicism'] in *Nietzsche et la scène philosophique*, pp.165–87.

V NAKEDNESS, DRESS

1 TN. For a discussion of the notion of culture as clothing in Nietzsche, cf. Kofman's paper to the 1972 'Colloque de Cerisy' ('Le/ Les "concepts" de culture dans les *Intempestives* ou la double dissimulation' ['The "Concept(s)" of Culture in Nietzsche's *Untimely Meditations*, or: The Double Dissimulation', in *Nietzsche aujourd'hui?*, II, pp.119–46, reproduced in *Nietzsche et la scène philosophique*, pp.337–71), especially pp.345–47 and p.368.

2 Cf. *Le Petit Robert*, under 'approprier' [to appropriate]: '1) attribute as proper [*en propre*] to someone; 2) make appropriate [*rendre propre*], suited to a use, a purpose; 3) appropriate [*s'approprier*], make one's own, claim ownership [*propriété*] of something.'

3 By deciphering it genealogically, Nietzsche resurrects the metaphor effaced in 'Begriff'. Cf. what Hegel says on this in the *Aesthetics* (trans. by T.M. Knox, 2 vols (Oxford: Clarendon Press, 1975), I, pp.404–05) and J. Derrida's commentary in 'White Mythology' (*Margins of Philosophy*, pp.224–26).

Cf. also Marx who, in *The German Ideology*, calls Saint Max's assimilation of 'Eigentum' to 'Eigenschaft' a 'bourgeois play on words' (*Karl Marx, Frederick Engels: Collected Works* (London: Lawrence and Wishart, 1976), V (trans. by Clemens Dutt), 231).

Cf. also P. Valéry in his 'Address to the Congress of Surgeons' (in *The Collected Works of Paul Valéry*, ed. by Jackson Mathews, 15 vols (London: Routledge and Kegan Paul, 1958–75), XI, trans. by Roger Shattuck and Frederick Brown, pp.129–47): 'Just consider our vocabulary of the most abstract words. Among terms indispensable to mental activity are many which must have been furnished by simple hand movements: *to put forward, to take, to grasp, to hold, to seize, to place*. Then again: *synthesis, thesis, hypothesis, comprehension, supposition*. ... *Addition* refers to giving: *multiplication* and *complexity* to folding' (p.142).

4 Cf. BGE 9, where Nietzsche proposes the Stoic as prime example of the will to power of the philosopher: the will to be the first cause of the world and of himself.

5 Nietzsche is doubtless thinking of Aristotle, for whom the 'proper' meaning of a term is κυρίος: it is the meaning which dominates, the master meaning, the sovereign meaning. It commands the other meanings as the master commands the slave, and it is imposed by the masters of thought, the philosophers. These turn the potential 'truths' which are locked up confusedly in common opinions and myths into action. Finally, only the master has the right to speak, and the word is always *sovereign*.

6 Cf. GS 58:

> [...] to realize that what things *are called* is incomparably more important than what they are. The reputation, name, and appearance, the usual measure and weight of a thing, what it counts for – originally almost always wrong and arbitrary, thrown over things like a dress and altogether foreign to their nature and even to their skin – all this grows from generation unto generation, merely because people believe in it, until it gradually grows to be part of the thing and turns into its very body. What at first was appearance becomes in the end, almost invariably, the essence and is effective as such. How foolish it would be to suppose that one needs only to point out this origin and this misty shroud of delusion in order to *destroy* the world that counts for real, so-called *reality*. We can destroy only as creators. – But let us not forget this either: it is enough to create new names and estimations and probabilities in order to create in the long run new 'things'.

7 Cf. GS 83, where Nietzsche shows how the Romans *translated* the Greeks by seizing their works and *conquering* them, deleting the author's name so as to put their own in its place.

8 ἔτυμος means true, accurate. Plato mocks those who think etymology leads them to the truth. In the *Cratylus*, Socrates has fun giving the most widely divergent etymologies of the same term, as an invitation to seek truth not in words but in things themselves. Etymology is impugned in the name of essences. With Nietzsche there is an inversion: precisely because there is no essence one must turn to etymology.

9 TI, 'The "Improvers" of Mankind', 1: 'moral judgement is never to be taken literally [*wörtlich*]: as such it never contains anything but nonsense [*Widersinn*]. But as *semiotics* [*Semiotik*] it remains of incalculable value: it reveals, to the informed man at least, the most

precious realities of cultures and inner worlds which did not *know* enough to "understand" themselves. Morality is merely sign language [*Zeichenrede*], merely symptomatology: one must already know *what* it is about to derive profit from it'.

10 G. Bataille, a direct heir to Nietzsche, writes on the relation between laughing and writing in 'The "Old Mole" and the Prefix *Sur* in the Words *Surhomme* [Superman] and *Surrealist*' (VE, pp.32–44): 'He [Nietzsche] even went so far as to give greatest value from the perspective of philosophical truth to outbursts of laughter (may any truth that has not made you burst out laughing at least once be seen by you as false). It is nonetheless true that the opposing tendency quickly gained the upper hand, that laughter, brutal expression of the heart's baseness, became along with truth something elevated, weightless, Hellenic' (p.39).

11 For this whole passage, cf. my 'Genealogy, Interpretation, Text' (Appendix, pp.120–45 below).

12 The idea of truth as unveiling implies the opposition between reality and appearance. Nietzsche deletes such an opposition by generalizing the notion of surface, giving a good demonstration of how the removal of masks does not take one to the deepest level. To philosophize is not to dis-cover: the 'truth' is like a woman who must not be unveiled lest one find she has nothing to hide. She is but this veil itself, and so shame is *de rigueur*. But a veil which hides nothing is no longer even a veil. Cf. GS, 'Preface', 4:

We no longer believe that truth remains truth when the veils are withdrawn; we have lived too much to believe this. Today we consider it a matter of decency not to wish to see everything naked, or to be present at everything, or to understand and 'know' everything. 'Is it true that God is present everywhere?' a little girl asked her mother; 'I think that's indecent' - a hint for philosophers! One should have more respect for the bashfulness with which nature has hidden behind riddles and iridescent uncertainties. Perhaps truth is a woman who has reasons for not letting us see her reasons? Perhaps her name is - to speak Greek - *Baubô*? Oh, those Greeks! They knew how to live. What is required for that is to stop courageously at the surface, the fold, the skin, to adore appearance, to believe in forms, tones, words, in the whole Olympus of appearance. Those Greeks were superficial - *out of profundity*.

For 'Baubô', cf. 'Baubô: Theological Perversion and Fetishism'.

13 TN. Once more, there is a pun on 'figure' as 'figure' (of speech) and 'face'.

14 Cf. WP 327: 'One should reduce and limit the realm of morality step
    by step: one should bring to light and honour the names of the
    instincts that are really at work here after they have been hidden for
    so long beneath hypocritical names of virtue.'
15 'In the end, it is not merely permitted to make this experiment: it is
    commanded by the conscience of *method*. Not to assume several
    kinds of causality so long as the experiment of getting on with one
    has not been taken to its ultimate limits (– to the point of nonsense, if
    I may say so): that is a morality of method which one may not
    repudiate nowadays – it follows "from its definition", as a mathe-
    matician would say' (BGE 36).
16 Cf. also BGE 5, where the 'abstract' writing of the philosopher
    appears as a cover which masks desire, the real 'inspiration' of the
    work: 'They pose as having discovered and attained their real
    opinions through the self-evolution of a cold, pure, divinely
    unperturbed dialectic (in contrast to the mystics of every rank, who
    are more honest and more stupid than they – these speak of
    "inspiration"): while what happens at bottom is that a prejudice, a
    notion, an "inspiration", generally a desire of the heart sifted and
    made abstract, is defended by them with reasons sought after the
    event'.
17 TN. The target here is Martin Heidegger, as is made explicit in a
    similar passage below (Appendix, p.135). Heidegger's lectures on
    Nietzsche were published in German in 1961 (*Nietzsche*, 2 vols
    (Pfullingen: Neske)), and their influence spread rapidly in France,
    especially after the publication in 1971 of Pierre Klossowski's French
    translation (*Nietzsche*, 2 vols (Paris: Gallimard)). Kofman's resistance
    to Heidegger's reading of Nietzsche is made indirectly apparent in
    her critique of Jean Granier's Heideggerian *Nietzsche* (see Appendix),
    but her explicit engagements with Heidegger are relatively rare. Cf.
    the Extra Note above (section IV, part 1d, n.11); 'Nietzsche and the
    Obscurity of Heraclitus', trans. by Françoise Lionnet-McCumber,
    Diacritics, 17/3 (Fall 1987), 39–55; and especially the 'Introduction' to
    Explosion I (pp.37–43). Cf. also, in the context of their conflicting
    readings of Plato, 'Method and Way', the final section of 'Beyond
    Aporia?' (trans. by David Macey, in *Post-structuralist Classics*, ed. by
    Andrew Benjamin (London and New York: Routledge, 1988), pp.7–
    44 (pp.40–42)).
18 The absence of shame can also betray a weak type of will which
    wants to know *everything*, discover *everything*. The majority of
    concepts suit the strong and the weak alike; but they have different
    meanings for each. Each term which a type of will appropriates is at
    the same time displaced and revaluated.

19 Cf. Freud, for whom woman invented weaving so as to hide the fact that she has nothing to hide (*New Introductory Lectures*, 'Femininity' (SE, XXII, 132)). UM IV, 5 argues along the same lines.

20 W. Gombrowicz's *Operetta* is entirely constructed around the opposition between dress and nakedness, and it might appear to illustrate Nietzsche's thought: all those who dress up are in fact people who fear nakedness because they are ugly; they are ashamed of their bodies and camouflage them, being prisoners of moral prejudices, whereas it is a young girl, beautiful and innocent as life, who praises nakedness. But on another level of reading the different costumes with their different fashions represent the different ideologies (Communism, Existentialism, Nazism) which, as such and in relation to nakedness, i.e. the very presence of unattainable truth, are presented as equivalent. The great couturier Master Fior, the master of ceremonies, who makes and unmakes fashion, is the embodiment of total scepticism, which is merely the obverse of disappointed dogmatism. The whole play seems to me to bask in a nostalgia for Being in its truth. For Nietzsche, on the other hand, in spite of the absence of truth different costumes are not equivalent: some make the wearer ugly, others beautify; some allow man to overcome himself, others, on the contrary, lead to nihilism. His is a virile scepticism which creates new forms. *Operetta*, whilst recognizing that nakedness is impossible, dreams of it nostalgically and considers it to have been defiled by clothing. At the end of the play, Fior says:

I curse man's clothing, I curse the masks.
Those bloodstained masks that eat into our bodies
I curse the cut of trousers and blouses
They've eaten too far into our flesh!
[...]
I, Fior,
I, the master of men's and women's fashion,
I place in this coffin that sacred –
But forever defiled by clothing –
Nudity of man!
(*Operetta*, trans. by Louis Iribarne (London: Calder and Boyars, 1971), p. 103).

21 Cf. WS 17: 'He who explains a passage in an author "more deeply" than the passage was meant has not explained the author but *obscured* him. This is how our metaphysicians stand in regard to the text of nature; indeed they stand much worse. For in order to apply their deep explanations they frequently first adjust the text in a way that

will facilitate it: in other words, they *spoil* it.' Cf. also GS 57. The *Genealogy* (III, 10) compares the mask of the ascetic ideal adopted by the priest to a travesty, a cocoon, an old cast-off. The new species of philosopher whom Nietzsche calls upon is not lacking in clothing but is metamorphosed from a caterpillar into a many-coloured butterfly: once the husk is cast off, philosophy does not unveil itself in its essential nakedness, but behind the mask one finds the 'original text' written by many-coloured drives, i.e. life-affirming drives, strong and bold enough not to be ashamed of themselves. Removing an article of clothing, one finds another which, in comparison with the first – a shameful and hypocritical travesty – appears as nakedness:

for the longest time philosophy would not have been *possible at all* on earth without ascetic wraps and cloak, without an ascetic self-misunderstanding. To put it vividly: the *ascetic priest* provided until the most modern times the repulsive and gloomy caterpillar form in which alone the philosopher could live and creep about. Has all this really *altered*? Has that many-coloured and dangerous winged creature, the 'spirit' which this caterpillar concealed, really been unfettered at last and released into the light, thanks to a sunnier, warmer, brighter world? Is there sufficient pride, daring, courage, self-confidence available today, sufficient will of the spirit, will to reponsibility, *freedom of will*, for 'the philosopher' to be hence-forth – *possible* on earth?' (GM III, 10)

22 EN. Cf. *Explosion I*, 'Le dernier disciple du philosophe Dionysos' ['The Last Disciple of the Philosopher Dionysus'] (pp.91–106), for a detailed commentary on BGE 295.

23 Cf. HH I, 270: '*The art of reading.* [...] the entire Middle Ages was profoundly incapable of a strict philological elucidation, that is to say of a simple desire to understand what the author is saying – to have discovered these methods was an achievement, let no one undervalue it! It was only when the art of correct reading, that is to say philology, arrived at its summit that science of any kind acquired continuity and constancy.' Cf. also NF 19 [1–6] (KGW IV₂, 428f.).

   For this art of reading with philology as its model, it is again Spinoza who provides Nietzsche with a forebear. Spinoza, however, does not read nature as one reads books, but rather he reads the biblical Book as one reads Nature: 'our enquiry is here confined to the teachings of Scripture, with [a] view to drawing our own conclusions from these, as from data presented by Nature' (*Tractatus Theologico-Politicus*, I, p.71). This involves removing from Nature the clothing of signs which covers it, and restoring to it its true power, just as for Nietzsche it is a case of doing away with fictional supplements. For Spinoza, nature does not signify but it expresses itself, just as for Nietzsche it is a power of affirmation which refers only to itself. For Spinoza, Scripture needs to have restored to it its symbolic meaning beyond the literal way men read it: Scripture is a collection of metaphors, symptomatic of the idiosyncrasy of its authors. Addressing itself, furthermore, to the imagination of its readers, it uses metaphors for didactic reasons. Spinoza's aim is not to find the true meaning of Scripture but the true meaning which it had for its authors: so Scripture must only be interpreted by Scripture. In the case of nature the imaginative covering needs to be removed, whereas it needs to be clearly highlighted in the case of the Book. If on the other hand it is the truth of Scripture and no longer its meaning that is to be judged, then each of the concepts must be deconstructed by relating them to the definitions in the *Ethics*. In relation to the text of Nature, Scripture then appears as a truncated, mutilated, and corrupt body of knowledge, just as the writing of consciousness is for Nietzsche a simplification, an abbreviation of the unconscious writing of the drives.

In the *Tractatus Theologico-Politicus* two methods are used: one is interpretative and essentially philological, analogous to Nietzsche's genealogical method; the other is deconstructive and reductive, whereby the biblical text is referred to an originary text – that of the *Ethics* or of Nature – which claims to be a true text and not an interpretation (this therefore distinguishes Spinoza from Nietzsche).

For the relation between sign and expression in Spinoza, cf. G. Deleuze, *Expressionism in Philosophy: Spinoza* (trans. by Martin Joughin (New York: Zone Books, 1990)).

[TN. For a further treatment of the question of reading and writing in Nietzsche, especially in the context of *Zarathustra*, cf. Jean-Michel Rey, *L'enjeu des signes: lecture de Nietzsche* (Paris: Seuil, 1971), chapter 4: 'Lecture et écriture' (pp.118–51).]

VI WRITING, READING

1 TN. For further discussion of the metaphor of the eye, cf. the section 'Le mauvais œil' ['The Evil Eye'], in *Nietzsche et la scène philosophique* (pp.99–136).

2 EN. I expand at length on what is entailed by the 'biographical' and the 'autobiographical' in my two books on *Ecce Homo: Explosion I* and *Explosion II*. Cf. also my *Autobiogriffures* (Paris: Christian Bourgois, 1976; Galilée, 1984. English trans. of 'La perte des plumes' (pp.89–141): 'No Longer Full-Fledged *Autobiogriffies*', trans. by Winnie Woodhull, *SubStance*, 29 (1981), 3–22).

3 This critique of 'representation' recalls Rousseau's in his 'Letter to M. D'Alembert on the Theatre' (in *Politics and The Arts*, trans. by Allan

Bloom (Ithaca: Cornell University Press, 1968). He has the same ideal
of authenticity as Nietzsche, even if for Rousseau the critique is
carried out in the name of a full and complete self-presence, but for
Nietzsche in the name of the affirmation of a strong life.
[TN. For a more detailed discussion of the notion of 'philological
probity' in Nietzsche, cf. Jean-Luc Nancy, '"Our Probity!"': On
Truth in the Moral Sense in Nietzsche', trans. by Peter Connor, in
Looking After Nietzsche, ed. by Laurence A. Rickels (Albany, NY:
State University of New York Press, 1990), pp.67–87. The term
Nancy explores is 'Redlichkeit' (his title comes from 'unsere
Redlichkeit' in GS 335), though Nietzsche also uses '*Probität*' (e.g. GS
366).]

4 EN. Since the publication of this book, G. Deleuze has analysed at
length in his fine book on Leibniz (*The Fold: Leibniz and the Baroque*,
trans. by Tom Conley (London: Athlone, 1993)) what Leibniz's
perspectivism entails and how it is different from Nietzsche's.

5 In the hierarchy which Hegel establishes between the different
senses, hearing comes first because it is the only one which is fully
ideal and theoretical, salvaging objectivity and interiority at the same
time (cf. the *Aesthetics*, II, pp.888–93, and J. Derrida, 'The Pit and the
Pyramid' (*Margins*, p.92f.)).

6 For vision as a model for knowledge one could refer to all the
philosopher-metaphysicians. For the parallel devaluation of smell as
a sense linked to the sexual function, cf. Aristotle, *On the Soul*. The
relationship between the repression of the sense of smell and sexual
repression is emphasized by Freud, especially in chapter 4 of
Civilization and its Discontents. The devaluation of the sense of smell
is here a consequence of mankind's vertical stance, and it jeopardizes
not only anal eroticism but sexuality as a whole. In the sexual process,
then, visual stimuli take over from olfactory sensations:

> The diminution of the olfactory stimuli seems itself to be a
> consequence of man's raising himself from the ground, of his
> assumption of an upright gait; this made his genitals, which were
> previously concealed, visible and in need of protection, and so
> provoked feelings of shame in him.
>
> The fateful process of civilization would thus have set in with
> man's adoption of an erect posture. From that point the chain of
> events would have proceeded through the devaluation of olfac-
> tory stimuli and the isolation of the menstrual period to the time
> when visual stimuli were paramount and the genitals became
> visible, and thence to the continuity of sexual excitation, the
> founding of the family and so to the threshold of human
> civilization. (SE, XXI, 99–100n.)

Cf. also the other note in the same chapter (SE, XXI, 105–07n.) and the 'Rat Man' ('Notes Upon a Case of Obsessional Neurosis' (SE, X, 151–249)).

7 Bataille adopts the same procedure, effacing the opposition between high and low; for him the eye is always at the same time a sex organ and the sex organ an eye, without the two 'opposites' ever being 'sublated' [*relevés*] into a third term. Only a prohibition prevents one looking into the face of the sun, turning it into a symbol of moral elevation and the highest level of knowledge; a symbol of the father whom one cannot look in the face for fear of castration. Once the prohibition has been transgressed, the sun is no longer a star but a disa-star [*le soleil n'est plus un astre mais un désastre*], a volcano which spews out its energy extravagantly, an ejaculation without reserve. Similarly, once the prohibition on sex is lifted, one finds the erect organ is directed upwards. Cf. in particular 'The Solar Anus' (VE, pp.5–9), 'The Language of Flowers' (VE, pp.10–14), 'Rotten Sun' (VE, pp.57–58), 'Corps célestes' ['Celestial Bodies'] (*Œuvres Complètes* I, 514–20), 'Base Materialism and Gnosticism' (VE, pp.45–52), 'Sacrificial Mutilation and the Severed Ear of Vincent Van Gogh' (VE, pp.61–72), etc.★

'The Solar Anus' is thus a burlesque parody (a term which for Bataille itself parodies the Platonic simulacrum) of 'creation', where Bataille substitutes for the traditional opposition of concepts an indefinite circularity of terms with no hierarchy. There is a circularity in the writing at the level of the signifier: the terms copulate with each other to arrive, at the end of the text, at an ejaculation without reserve. The verb 'to be' is now just the vehicle for amorous frenzy. The circularity of the signifier mimics and, parodically, coincides with sexual circularity, which breaks with the opposition between high and low, feminine and masculine. Sexual circularity is a metaphor for planetary and biological circularity. Nowhere is there a principle to interrupt the circularity and allow a hierarchy, a linear history, to be instituted. Bataille's writing is a burst of laughter which disseminates habitual meanings and the logic of reason; his is a text which mimics an insemination without reserve.†

For 'the low and the high' in Bataille, cf. R. Gasché, 'L'avorton de la pensée', in *L'Arc*, 44 (1971, special Bataille number), 11–27.

★TN. Bataille's recently published posthumous writings evidently became very rapidly canonical. Derrida lists exactly the same texts at the end of 'White Mythology' (*Margins of Philosophy*, p.271, n.87).

†TN. For another contextualization of this treatment of Bataille, within a discussion of Derrida and his essay, 'From Restricted to General Economy: A Hegelianism without Reserve', cf. 'Un philosophe "unheimlich"' (*Lectures de Derrida*, p.43).

8 TN. For an analysis of Nietzsche's 'tastes' as flaunted in *Ecce Homo*, 'Why I Am So Wise', 1, cf. 'Une nouvelle diététique' ['A New Dietetics'], in *Explosion I* (pp.271–93).

9 EN. Nietzsche is not saying anything different when he writes to Cosima Wagner (3 January 1889):

It is a prejudice that I am a man. But I have often lived among men already and I know everything they can experience, from the lowest to the highest. Among Indians I was Buddha, in Greece I was Dionysus, – Alexander and Caesar are my incarnations, as is the Shakespeare poet, Lord Bacon. Latterly I was Voltaire and Napoleon, perhaps Richard Wagner, too. ... But this time I come as the victorious Dionysus, who will make a feast day of the earth. ... Not that I have much time. ... The heavens are glad I am here. ... I hung on the cross, too ... (KGB III₅, 572f.)

Isolated from the context of Nietzsche's work as a whole, though, this letter has mistakenly been seen as insane. Cf. *Explosion I*, 'Introduction', p.27.

10 There are countless texts of Nietzsche's where metaphors taken from the sensory register overlap, or where at least one of the senses provides a model. For the metaphor of hearing, cf. among others HH I, 'Preface', 8: 'This *German* book, which has known how to find its readers in a wide circle of lands and peoples [...] and must be capable of some kind of music and flute-player's art by which even coy foreign ears are seduced to listen – it is precisely in Germany that this book has been read most carelessly and *heard* the worst.' Cf. also I 111, 126, 153.

For smell, cf. HH I, 217: 'the more attenuated the fragrant odour of "significance" becomes, the fewer there will be still able to perceive it.'

Cf. also HH I, 150: 'Wherever we perceive human endeavours to be tinted with a higher, gloomier colouring, we can assume that dread of spirits, the odour of incense, and the shadows of churches are still adhering to them.'

Cf. also HH I, 37.

11 TN. 'Sens "propre"': a pun this time on 'sens', since 'literal meaning' is the usual sense of 'sens propre' (i.e. *its* 'proper meaning').

12 Cf. G. Deleuze, *The Logic of Sense* (ed. by Constantin V. Boundas, trans. by Mark Lester with Charles Stivale (London: Athlone; New York: Columbia University Press, 1990)), p.7.

13 TN. 'le sens (au double sens du terme)': 'reason' and 'meaning' are implied, although the word has certainly by now picked up rather more resonances: 'direction' and 'sense' ('bodily faculty', as above, n.10) in particular.

14 Cf. e.g. Descartes' tree, a metaphor for philosophy as a system founded on metaphysics, the roots; illuminated by the light of reason, it bears the fruits of wisdom and happiness. The tree represents an irreversible order among the areas of knowledge (cf. the Preface to *The Principles of Philosophy* (in *The Philosophical Works of Descartes*, ed. and trans. by Elizabeth S. Haldane and G.R.T. Ross, 2 vols (Cambridge: Cambridge University Press, 1911)), I, p.211).

Even philosophers who seem no longer to belong to the metaphysical tradition can be found using 'the tree' as the privileged example which comes 'naturally'. Cf. Heidegger (*What is Philosophy?*, trans. by William Kluback and Jean T. Wilde (New Haven, Conn.: College and University Press, 1958)) and Sartre ('Une idée fondamentale de la phénoménologie de Husserl: L'Intentionnalité', in *Situations I* (Paris: Gallimard, 1947), pp.31–35; reproduced in *Situations philosophiques* (Paris: Gallimard, 1990), pp.9–12 (p.10)). For a new tree figure, very close to Nietzsche's, cf. G. Bataille: another tree, another sun, another path. Cf. in particular 'The Language of Flowers' (VE, pp.10–14). The flower challenges the vertical sweep from the roots to the top of the tree: its life is short and, like Van Gogh's sunflowers, it wilts. It is a symbol more of death than of love, or rather of the indissoluble links between the two. Hence the flower is no longer the opposite of the roots buried in the earth, down below – themselves principles of the tree's life, of a life dedicated to death. 'Flowers [...] die ridiculously on stems that seemed to carry them to the clouds' (p.12). They are very close to their 'perfect counterpart', the roots, 'swarming under the surface of the soil, nauseating and naked like vermin', and which, 'ignoble and sticky', 'wallow in the ground, loving rottenness just as leaves love light' (p.13). Cf. also 'The "Old Mole"' (VE, pp.32–44):

A man is not so different from a plant, experiencing like a plant an urge that raises him perpendicular to the ground. It will not be difficult to show that human morality is linked to the urge to an erect posture that distinguishes the human being from the anthropomorphic ape. But on the other hand, a plant thrusts its obscene-looking roots into the earth in order to assimilate the putrescence of organic matter, and a man experiences, in contradiction to strict morality, urges that draw him to what is low, placing him in open antagonism to all forms of spiritual elevation. Such urges have always been eloquently rebuked, confused in their aggregate with the most immediately nefarious of specific passions. (p.36)

Cf. also the *Manuel de l'Anti-chrétien* ['Anti-Christian's Handbook'] (*Œuvres complètes*, II, 375–99).

[TN. For another treatment of the tree motif in Nietzsche, cf. Alain Juranville, 'De l'arbre', in *Physique de Nietzsche* (Paris: Denoël/ Gonthier, 1973), pp.7–8 and 159–71. For a book-length analysis of the solar metaphor, cf. Bernard Pautrat, *Versions du soleil: Figures et système de Nietzsche* (Paris: Seuil, 1971).]

15 Cf. also GM, 'Preface', 3; PTG, p.23f. and HH I, 513: '*Life as the yield of life*. – No matter how far a man may extend himself with his knowledge, no matter how objectively he may come to view himself, in the end it can yield to him nothing but his own biography.'

16 For tree metaphors, cf. HH I, 29, 56, 111, 130, 159, 197, 210, 221, 224, 239, 250, 264, 285, 292; II, 189.

17 EN. I lay great stress on this point in *Explosion I*, especially in the 'Introduction' ('Otite, métaotite' ['Otitis, Metaotitis'], pp.11–21), and in *Explosion II* ('"Hallucination négative généralisée"' ['"Generalized Negative Hallucination"']).

18 TN. 'Mal-entendu': the pun on 'misheard'/'misunderstood' referred to in section I, n.4. In 'Un philosophe "inouï"' (*Lectures de Derrida*, pp.23–33), Kofman rehearses a number of Derrida's arguments concerning the ear, the 'third ear' (pp.30–33), and hearing in general (especially in 'Speech and Phenomena' and 'Tympan'). In *Spurs*, Derrida makes the claim that: 'All of Nietzsche's investigations, and in particular those which concern woman, are coiled in the labyrinth of an ear' (p.43), and in two further texts he develops the theme in a Nietzschean context: *Otobiographies: L'enseignement de Nietzsche et la politique du nom propre* (Paris: Galilée, 1984) and the expanded version, *The Ear of the Other: Otobiography, Transference, Translation: Texts and Discussions with Jacques Derrida*, ed. by Christie V. McDonald, trans. by Peggy Kamuf (New York: Schocken, 1985).

19 Cf. GS 371: '*We incomprehensible ones*. – Have we ever complained because we are misunderstood, misjudged, misidentified, slandered, misheard, and not heard? Precisely this is our fate – oh, for a long time yet! let us say, to be modest, until 1901 – it is also our distinction.'

20 Cf. also EH, 'Why I Am So Wise', 8:

May I venture to indicate one last trait of my nature which creates for me no little difficulty in my relations with others? I possess a perfectly uncanny sensitivity of the instinct for cleanliness, so that I perceive physiologically – *smell* – the proximity or – what am I saying? – the innermost parts, the 'entrails', of every soul. [...] My humanity consists, *not* in feeling for and with man, but in *enduring* that I do feel for and with him [...]. My entire Zarathustra is a dithyramb on solitude or, if I have been understood, on *cleanliness*.

... Fortunately not on *pure folly*. – He who has eyes for colours will call it diamond. – *Disgust* at mankind, at the 'rabble', has always been my greatest danger ...

Nietzsche then quotes a passage from *Zarathustra* (*A Book for Everyone and No One*), where Zarathustra and his friends build their eyrie on the tree of the future and have eagles bring them meats which the 'impure' cannot defile: 'we do not prepare a home here for unclean men!' (Z II, 'Of the Rabble').

21 Cf. GM, 'Preface', 7: '*gay science* – is a reward: the reward of a long, brave, industrious, and subterranean seriousness, of which, to be sure, not everyone is capable.' Cf. also 'Preface', 8 and UM IV, 1.

22 For this whole passage on the aphorism, cf. GS 381 and especially:

I approach deep problems like cold baths: quickly into them and quickly out again. That one does not get to the depths that way, not deep enough down, is the superstition of those afraid of the water, the enemies of cold water; they speak without experience. The freezing cold makes one swift. – And to ask this incidentally: does a matter necessarily remain ununderstood and unfathomed merely because it has been touched only in flight, glanced at, in a flash? Is it absolutely imperative that one settles down on it? that one has brooded over it as over an egg [...] as Newton said of himself? At least there are truths that are singularly shy and ticklish and cannot be caught except suddenly – that must be *surprised* or left alone. ... Finally, my brevity has yet another value: given such questions as concern me, I must say many things briefly in order that they may be heard still more briefly. For, being an immoralist, one has to take steps against corrupting innocents – I mean, asses and old maids of both sexes whom life offers nothing but their innocence. [...] How much a spirit needs for its nourishment, for this there is no formula; but if its taste is for independence, for quick coming and going, for roaming, perhaps for adventures for which only the swiftest are a match, it is better for such a spirit to live in freedom with little to eat than unfree and stuffed. It is not fat but the greatest possible suppleness and strength that a good dancer desires from his nourishment – and I would not know what the spirit of a philosopher might wish more to be than a good dancer. For the dance is his ideal, also his art, and finally also his only piety, his 'service of God'.

23 Thus – *and this seems to me crucial* – Nietzsche reiterates old metaphors rather than inventing new ones. It is the philistines who confuse an unheard-of metaphor with a new or modern one (cf. UM I, 11); let

us rather note the almost complete absence in Nietzsche of metaphors taken from the world of the machine and modernism. The
writing of the gay science is a repetition which displaces, takes old
constructions to pieces and recomposes them by connecting up what
is different and separating what is similar: a new ludic construction.
To write is to play, to parody. And primarily to parody 'creation': the
ex nihilo is a trap; the world is merely the eternal game of Heraclitus'
Zeus, which always *returns* but displaced, deconstructed and recon-
structed from the same elements. There are displacements,
deconstructions, and reconstructions in writing, too, but they
nevertheless do not transform the book into a 'soulless mosaic of
words'. The dismemberment of Dionysus is always followed by his
resurrection in unity, and even when it is composed of aphorisms,
the book remains a piece of architecture in the grand style: polemic
and plurality carry with them 'law and right'.

24 TN. In French, 'grave' also carries the meaning of 'deep(-voiced)',
although it is apparent from the passage Kofman quotes that for
Nietzsche, deepness and seriousness are in fact mutually exclusive
(cf. n.22, above).

APPENDIX: GENEALOGY, INTERPRETATION, TEXT

1 *Le problème de la vérité dans la philosophie de Nietzsche* (Paris: Seuil,
1966).
2 a) For the distinction Granier establishes in Nietzsche between
'Being' and 'being', cf. e.g. p.377: 'How can one dispute the fact, in
the face of such clear formulations, that Nietzsche registered
perfectly clearly the radical difference between being and Being?'
b) For the misuse of 'existential', cf. pp.147 and 162.
c) For the misuse of the term 'ontological', cf. pp.17, 30, 38, 81, 105,
115, 118, 154, 162, 169, 211, 226–28, 233–34, 296, 298, 304–07, 407,
436, 446, 450, 457, 566, 597. For example: 'This second stage, which
consists in regressing to *existential* conditions of possibility, i.e. in
Nietzsche's language, the *'hierarchy* of the drives' which defines the
ontological formula of a certain type of living thing, represents, in
the strictest sense of the word, the *genealogy of Morals* properly
speaking' (p.162). Why speak of an ontological formula when
Nietzsche, in *Beyond Good and Evil* and *On the Genealogy of Morals*,
calls the doctrine of the hierarchy of the drives 'psychology'? If
Nietzsche is deliberately using a different concept to that of
ontology here, it would be as well to ask oneself why he makes this
substitution.
d) For the use of ethico-religious concepts, cf. e.g. p.205: 'To act is
necessarily to dissolve the rigid dualism of good and evil, to

experience the complementarity of values and so, by assuming the negative, to accept being guilty.' For Nietzsche it is a question of placing oneself *beyond good and evil*, in a region where the concept of guilt no longer has any meaning. Instead, Nietzsche substitutes for it the concepts of the innocence of becoming and man's irresponsibility. Evil is no longer evil. Suffering exists, but it is no longer described in moral terms or justified in religious ones.

e) For 'the unveiling of Being', cf. e.g.: pp.167, 463, 464, 532. Cf. also p.314: 'revelation'; pp.598–99: 'availability to Being'; p.496: 'the will to power's ability to master itself indefinitely while preserving the availability which allows things to unveil themselves as such.'

3 a) Nietzsche's texts on this subject are numerous. For the record, let us cite *The Will to Power*: WP 298, 328, 407, 461, 476, 488, 507, 520, 552, 553, 555, 557, 566–69, 572–73, 576, 579, 583–84, 585A, 586, 588, 617, 708; GOA XII, i, 33, XII, i, 187, XIII, 79, XIII, 120–23, XIII, 160, XIV, i, 59.

b) Instead of 'Being', which only ever appears in order to be decried, Nietzsche uses the concepts of 'life', 'nature', 'lived experience', 'the world', 'becoming', 'experience', 'existence' or 'the real', in the following texts: TI, '"Reason" in Philosophy', 1, quoted Granier p.59; GS 373, quoted Granier p.85; GOA XIV, ii, 155 and XIV, ii, 267 (p.394f). (both quoted); GOA XIV, i, 6: 'Fanatical logicians have managed to turn the world into an illusion, and to find the path to 'being', to the 'absolute', only in thought. I, on the other hand, take pleasure in the world *even if* it is but illusion.'

[TN. For a more detailed discussion of the metaphorical character of 'being' for Nietzsche, cf. Rey, *L'enjeu des signes*, chapter 3: 'La métaphore de l'être' (pp.85–117).]

c) Granier (p.321, n.1) notes that Nietzsche very frequently resorts to the term 'world' to designate being, but he draws no conclusions and continues to use the ontological concepts which Nietzsche decries. For Nietzsche, the 'world' clearly indicates immanence as against any possible transcendent conception of being, and it lacks the equivocation of this latter concept. Moreover, the word 'world' is also introduced by the ascetic ideal, which opposes the vain character of this world to 'the other world'. This therefore proves once again that the term contains both an axiological and a genealogical meaning.

4 Cf. Granier, p.615: 'Beneath the critique of the value of values hides the question of the truth of values ... ' 'The origin of values is the being of value insofar as this being grounds the validity or non-validity of value according to its coefficient of ontological truth.' Or p.207: 'The value of value is necessarily *derived from Being*.'

5 The Nietzsche text which Granier quotes (p.497, n.3): 'How much truth can a spirit *bear*, how much truth can a spirit *dare*? that became

for me more and more the real measure of value' (EH, 'Foreword', 3) indicates that the criterion of value is not truth but the capacity to bear and to dare truth (if one looks at the preceding passage, this means the capacity to bear a 'virile scepticism', to bear having to generate hypotheses indefinitely, beyond any conviction or truth). In other words value is referred to the power of the spirit doing the evaluating. One cannot separate 'the extension of the *imperium*' from tragic courage in the face of truth, because if courage were not at the same time '*imperium*' it would result in scepticism and nihilism, not in virile scepticism. Value is thus essentially referred to the *valour* which is a measure of the power of the will. Now this valour reveals itself not only in overcoming in the direction of truth, but in any form of courage: 'the only thing that can prove today whether one is worth anything or not – that one endures' (WP 910). The truth which is absence of truth, and thus the discovery that life is infinite and permits an indefinite number of hypotheses, is a threat which reveals the 'valour' of anyone who accepts it. But it is not the only one. That is why one cannot say, with Granier, that 'overcoming in the direction of truth' is the truth of the power of the will to power.

6   The difference between human evaluations, and their lack of equivalence to 'Being', is well brought out by Nietzsche with the distinction he establishes between Nature and Life in BGE 9.

7   Cf. also Z IV, 'Retired from Service': 'There is also good taste in piety: *that* said at last: Away with *such* a god! Better no god, better to produce destiny on one's own account, better to be a fool, better to be God oneself!' So this 'good taste', this noble taste – which Granier (p.264) identifies with truthfulness and intellectual probity – brings out well the fact that truth, even at the level of probity, remains dependent on and subordinate to value.

8   Granier writes (p.319) that living things translate the text of Being in accordance with their own norms. It is actually a question not of translating being, but of constituting it as text.

9   Cf. WP 481: 'In so far as the word "knowledge" has any meaning, the world is knowable; but it is *interpretable* otherwise, it has no meaning behind it, but countless meanings.'

10   Apparently for the same reason, Granier places the emphasis in *The Will to Power* on self-overcoming and not on mastery, which would make it even more possible to turn the will to power into an unequivocal concept that can be applied to all types of will. Self-overcoming indicates a superior degree of mastery, and it is liable to give the highest feeling of power; but it can only exist in noble souls who, by dint of mastering the others and being at a distance from them, can take their distance from and despise themselves. That is why the noble is also a political concept for Nietzsche, even if it is not

only that. Like the majority of Nietzsche's concepts it is overdetermined: conquest and self-overcoming cannot be separated (cf. BGE 257).

11 Cf. GOA XII, i, 69: 'The senses provide us merely with slight causes and motives, on which we then elaborate'; 'but so far whenever a "that is" has been established, again and again a later and more refined period has discovered that this is nothing more than: "that means"' (GOA XIV, i, 38). Cf. WP 589.

12 Granier indeed sees this; cf. p.133, where he quotes two of Nietzsche's texts which are very important in this context: 'thoughts are the sign of a play and a struggle between the emotional impulses; through their hidden roots they remain always linked to them' (OP 321). 'All our conscious motives are surface phenomena: behind them the struggle between our drives and our states is played out: the struggle for power' (OP 325). On p.142, Granier writes: 'The real immediate datum is interpretation itself, i.e. the psychological "phenomenon" elaborated, abbreviated, schematized, rationalized.' But that is not the originary text which rigorous philology seeks to arrive at.

[TN. With the phrase 'symbolism of the body', Kofman takes us back again to the passage in BT 2 which formed the epigraph to section II (cf. p.6).]

13 Cf. BGE 22, and the whole analysis which follows it. Cf. GOA XIV, i, 59: 'My new interpretation will give the philosophers of the future – the masters of the earth – the necessary uninhibitedness.

The religious and moral interpretation seems to us impossible, not so much because it is "refuted" as because it is *incompatible* with what we now pre-eminently hold to be "true" and believe.'

14 Granier writes: 'The principle of justice will be to let becoming unveil itself in person' (p.511). He also writes 'that it consists in being available to Being' (p.504). For Nietzsche, justice does not consist in being passively attentive to being, but in changing one's passions and multiplying one's perspectives, which allows one to abandon any conviction without ever arriving at truth, merely at 'certainties and precisely calculated probabilities' (HH I, 637).

15 Nietzsche indicates that the will to power is just an interpretative hypothesis in a number of texts besides the fundamental BGE 22. Thus in GOA XIII, 121 he writes: 'So I do not posit "appearance" as the opposite of "reality"; on the contrary I take appearance to be the reality which resists being transformed into an imaginary "true world". A specific name for this reality would be "the will to power" – in other words a designation from within, not based on its elusive, fluid, protean nature.' The will to power is here a *name* which designates the foundation of things yet without providing us with

reality. Cf. GOA XII, ii, 381 and Z III, 'Of the Three Evil Things'. Moreover, on p.375 of his book Granier recognizes that all of Nietzsche's formulations are hypothetical. Why, then, does he continue to speak of an ontological intuition? It is hard to understand why Granier (p.367) should see only one alternative, and argue that the will to power is either the result of experimental induction or it is the product of ontological reflection *sui generis*. Why not admit the possibility of a mythico-transcendental reflection perhaps unique in the history of philosophy? (Cf. a number of Nietzsche's texts along these lines: WP 55, 254 and 424; GOA XIII, 589; BGE 36).

Sarah Kofman: A Complete Bibliography, 1963–1993

Compiled by Duncan Large
(with the assistance of Sarah Kofman)

This is the first comprehensive and systematic Sarah Kofman bibliography. Previously information of this kind could be gleaned only from the list of short titles provided by Éditions Galilée in each new Kofman book – a list which is not only particularly inadequate in its coverage of Kofman's articles, and includes no interviews, but is also occasionally unreliable.

The conventions observed are as follows: all books are published in Paris unless otherwise indicated; within each year, books precede articles and interviews; square brackets indicate that the title, subtitle, or description has been added by the compiler, who welcomes any information concerning possible additions and corrections.

1963

'Le problème moral dans une philosophie de l'absurde', *Revue de l'enseignement philosophique*, 14/1 (October–November), 1–7. Reproduced in *Séductions* (1990a), pp.167–81.

1968

'Métamorphose de la volonté de puissance du Judaïsme au Christianisme d'après "L'Antéchrist" de Nietzsche', *Revue de l'enseignement philosophique*, 18/3 (February–March), 15–19.

1969

'Freud et Empédocle', *Critique*, 25/265 (June), 525–50 [review article on Jean Bollack, *Empédocle* (Minuit, 1965) and Sigmund Freud, *Analyse terminée et analyse interminable*, trans. by A. Berman, *Revue française de psychanalyse*, 2 (1939)]. Revised republication in *Quatre romans analytiques* (1974a), pp.31–66.

1970

a) *L'enfance de l'art: une interprétation de l'esthétique freudienne*, Payot ('Bibliothèque scientifique'). 2nd edn: 'Petite bibliothèque Payot', coll. 'Science de l'homme' 250, 1975. 3rd edn: Galilée ('Débats'), 1985, includes 'Délire et fiction (à propos de *Délire et Rêves dans la* Gradiva *de Jensen* de Freud)' (cf. 1974c), pp.251–81.
   Spanish: *El nacimiento del arte: Una interpretación de la estética freudiana*, trans. by Patricio Canto (Buenos Aires: Siglo XXI, 1973).
   English: *The Childhood of Art: An Interpretation of Freud's Aesthetics*, trans. by Winifred Woodhull (New York: Columbia University Press ('European Perspectives'), 1988).

b) 'Généalogie, interprétation, texte', *Critique*, 26/275 (April), 359–81 [review article on Jean Granier, *Le problème de la vérité dans la philosophie de Nietzsche* (Seuil, 1966)]. Revised republication in *Nietzsche et la métaphore* (1972a), pp.173–206.

1971

a) 'Nietzsche et la métaphore', *Poétique*, 5 (Spring), 77–98. Revised and extended republication in *Nietzsche et la métaphore* (1972a).

b) 'L'oubli de la métaphore', *Critique*, 27/291–92 (August–September), 783–804 [review article on Nietzsche: *Das Philosophenbuch/Le livre du philosophe: Études théoriques*, trans. by Angèle Kremer-Marietti (Aubier-Flammarion, 1969); *La naissance de la tragédie*, trans. by Geneviève Bianquis, 12th edn (Gallimard, 1949); *La naissance de la philosophie à l'époque de la tragédie grecque*, trans. by Geneviève Bianquis, 7th edn (Gallimard, 1938)]. Revised and extended republication in *Nietzsche et la métaphore* (1972a).

c) 'Judith, ou la mise en scène du tabou de la virginité', *Littérature*, 3 (October), 100–16. Revised republication (as 'Judith') in *Quatre romans analytiques* (1974a), pp.67–98.

Dutch: 'Het Maagdelijkheidstaboe', trans. by Nel van den Haak, *Krisis*, 28 (September 1987), 97–123.

1972

a) *Nietzsche et la métaphore*, Payot ('Bibliothèque scientifique'). 2nd edn: Galilée ('Débats'), 1983. Includes 'Appendice: Généalogie, interprétation, texte' (cf. 1970b), pp.173–206.

Italian trans. of 'Écriture, lecture' (pp.147–71): 'La scrittura nietzscheana: gioco di gran stile', trans. by Alessandro Serra, *Il Verri*, 39–40 (November 1972), 147–64.

English trans. of 'Métaphore, symbole, métamorphose' (pp.15–37): 'Metaphor, Symbol, Metamorphosis', trans. by David B. Allison, in *The New Nietzsche: Contemporary Styles of Interpretation*, ed. by David B. Allison (New York: Dell, 1977; 2nd edn Cambridge, Mass. and London: MIT Press, 1985), pp.201–14.

Japanese: [*Nietzsche and Metaphor*], trans. by Hiroshi Udagawa (Tokyo: Asahi Shuppan-Sha, 1986).

English trans. of 'Architectures métaphoriques' (pp.87–117): 'Metaphoric Architectures', trans. by Peter T. Connor and Mira Kamdar, in *Looking After Nietzsche*, ed. by Laurence A. Rickels (Albany, NY: State University

of New York Press ('Intersections: Philosophy and Critical Theory'), 1990), pp.89–112.
English: *Nietzsche and Metaphor*, trans. by Duncan Large (London: Athlone; Stanford, CA: Stanford University Press, 1993).

b) 'Résumer, interpréter', *Critique*, 28/305 (October), 892–916 [review article on Sigmund Freud, *Délire et rêves dans la Gradiva de Jensen* (Gallimard ('Idées'), 1971)]. Revised republication (as 'Résumer, interpréter (*Gradiva*)') in *Quatre romans analytiques* (1974a), pp.99–134.

1973

a) *Camera obscura: de l'idéologie*, Galilée ('La philosophie en effet').
Spanish: *Cámara oscura: de la ideología*, trans. by Anne Leroux (Madrid: Taller ('Taller uno'), 1975).
Serbo-Croat: *Camera obscura ideologije*, trans. by Gordana Popović-Vujčić, ed. by Zoran Pavlović (Zagreb: Studentski centar svenčilišta ('Varteks'), 1977).
English trans. by Will Straw of 'Nietzsche: La chambre des peintres' (pp.47–69) and 'L'Œil de Bœuf: Descartes et l'après-coup idéologique' (pp.71–76): 'Nietzsche and the Painter's Chamber', and 'The Ox's Eye: Descartes and the Ideological After-Effect', in *Public*, 7 ('Sacred Technologies', 1993), 153–70.

b) 'Le/les "concepts" de culture dans les "Intempestives" ou la double dissimulation', in *Nietzsche aujourd'hui?* (Proceedings of the Colloque de Cerisy-la-Salle, July 1972), 2 vols, Union Générale d'Éditions ('10/18'), II ('Passion'), pp.119–46 (discussion to p.151; further S.K. interventions: I, pp.180, 182f., 215, 288, 367; II, pp.85 and 181). Reproduced (without the discussion) in *Nietzsche et la scène philosophique* (1979b), pp.337–71.
Portuguese: trans. by Milton Nascimento.

c) 'Un philosophe "unheimlich"', in *Écarts: Quatre essais à propos de Jacques Derrida*, by Lucette Finas, Sarah Kofman, Roger Laporte, and Jean-Michel Rey, Fayard

('Digraphe'), pp.107–204. Reproduced (with additional notes) in *Lectures de Derrida* (1984a), pp.11–114. Japanese: trans. in *Revue de la pensée contemporaine*, 11/12 (1983).

1974

a) *Quatre romans analytiques*, Galilée ('La philosophie en effet'). Includes: 'Freud et Empédocle', pp.31–66 (cf. 1969); 'Judith', pp.67–98 (cf. 1971c); 'Résumer, interpréter (*Gradiva*)', pp.99–134 (cf. 1972b); 'Le double e(s)t le diable: L'inquiétante étrangeté de *L'homme au sable* (*Der Sandmann*)', pp.135–81 (cf. 1974b). Spanish: *Cuatro novelas analíticas* (Buenos Aires: Trieb, 1978). English: *Freud and Fiction*, trans. by Sarah Wykes (Cambridge: Polity, 1991).

b) 'Le double e(s)t le diable: L'inquiétante étrangeté de *L'homme au sable* (*Der Sandmann*)', *Revue française de psychanalyse*, 38/1 (January-February), 25–56. Revised republication in *Quatre romans analytiques* (1974a), pp.135–81.

c) 'Délire et fiction (à propos de *Délire et Rêves dans la Gradiva de Jensen* de Freud)', *Europe*, 539 (March) (special number: 'Freud'), 165–84. Reproduced in *L'enfance de l'art* (3rd edn, 1985, pp.251–81) (cf. 1970a).

1975

a) 'Vautour rouge (Le double dans *les Élixirs du diable* d'Hoffmann)', in *Mimesis des articulations*, by Sylviane Agacinski, Jacques Derrida, Sarah Kofman, Philippe Lacoue-Labarthe, Jean-Luc Nancy, and Bernard Pautrat, Aubier-Flammarion ('La philosophie en effet'), pp.95–163.

b) 'Baubô (Perversion théologique et fétichisme chez Nietzsche)', *Nuova Corrente*, 68–9 (1975–6) (special number: 'Nietzsche'), 648–80. Revised republication in *Nietzsche et la scène philosophique* (1979b), pp.263–304.

Dutch: 'Baubo: theologische perversie en fetisjisme', trans. by Joke Hermsen and Henk van der Waal (Amsterdam: Picaron ('Cahiers de Kassandra'), 1987).
English (with new Postscript): 'Baubô: Theological Perversion and Fetishism', trans. by Tracy B. Strong, in *Nietzsche's New Seas: Explorations in Philosophy, Aesthetics, and Politics*, ed. by Michael Allen Gillespie and Tracy B. Strong (Chicago and London: University of Chicago Press, 1988), pp. 175–202.

1976

a) *Autobiogriffures*, Christian Bourgois. 2nd edn: *Autobiogriffures: Du chat Murr d'Hoffmann*, Galilée ('Débats'), 1984.
English trans. of 'La perte des plumes' (pp. 89–141): 'No Longer Full-Fledged *Autobiogriffies*', trans. by Winnie Woodhull, *SubStance*, 29 (1981), 3–22.
German: *Schreiben wie eine Katze: zu E.T.A. Hoffmanns 'Lebens-Ansichten des Katers Murr'*, trans. by Monika Buchgeister and Hans-Walter Schmidt (Graz and Vienna: Böhlau ('Passagen' 5), 1985).

b) '"Ma vie" et la psychanalyse (Janvier 76: Fragment d'analyse)', *Première Livraison*, 4 (February–March). Reproduced in *Trois*, 3/1 (Autumn 1987), 18 (cf. 1987c) and *La Part de l'Œil*, 9 (special number: 'Arts Plastiques et Psychanalyse II', 1993), 83.

c) 'Six philosophes occupés à déplacer le philosophique à propos de la "mimesis"', *La Quinzaine Littéraire*, 231 (16–30 April), pp. 19–22 (S.K., pp. 19–21) [group interview with Sylviane Agacinski, Jacques Derrida, Sarah Kofman, Philippe Lacoue-Labarthe, Jean-Luc Nancy, and Bernard Pautrat; questions from Jean-Louis Bouttes, Roger Dadoun, Christian Descamps, Gilles Lapouge, and Maurice Nadeau].

d) 'Tombeau pour un nom propre', *Première Livraison*, 5 (April–May). Reproduced in *Trois*, 3/1 (Autumn 1987), 20 (cf. 1987c) and *La Part de l'Œil*, 9 (special number:

'Arts Plastiques et Psychanalyse II', 1993), 84 (with 'Postscriptum – 1992').
English: 'Tomb for a proper name', trans. by Frances Bartkowski, in 'Autobiographical Writings', *SubStance*, 49 (1986), 6–13 (9–10).
Portuguese (with new Postscript): 'Tumulo para un nome proprio', in *Revista de comunicação e linguagens*, 10/11 (1990) (special number: 'O Corpo, O Nome, A Escrita'), 93–94.

1977

a) 'Philosophie terminée, Philosophie interminable', in *Qui a peur de la philosophie?*, by G.R.E.P.H. [= Groupe de Recherches sur l'Enseignement Philosophique], Flammarion ('Champs'), pp.15–37. Reproduced (with additional notes) in *Lectures de Derrida* (1984a), pp.153–84.
Italian: 'Filosofia terminabile, filosofia interminabile', trans. by Silvano Petrosino, in *Il corpo insegnante e la filosofia*, ed. by Gianfranco Dalmasso (Milan: Jaca Book, 1980), pp.137–61.

b) 'Sarah Kofman' [interview], in François Laruelle, *Le déclin de l'écriture, suivi d'entretiens avec Jean-Luc Nancy, Sarah Kofman, Jacques Derrida et Philippe Lacoue-Labarthe*, Aubier-Flammarion ('La philosophie en effet'), pp.260–66.

1978

a) *Aberrations: le devenir-femme d'Auguste Comte*, Aubier-Flammarion ('La philosophie en effet').

b) 'Qui a peur de la philosophie?', *Noroît*, 224–27 (January–April) [round-table discussion with Sylviane Agacinski, Roland Brunet, Jacques Derrida, and Sarah Kofman].

c) 'L'espace de la césure', *Critique*, 34/379 (December), 1143–50 [review article on Philippe Lacoue-Labarthe, *Hölderlin: L'Antigone de Sophocle, traduction française suivie de 'La césure du spéculatif'* (Christian Bourgois ('Première livraison'), 1978)]. Revised republication in *Mélancolie de l'art* (1985a), pp.71–86.

1979

a) *Nerval: Le charme de la répétition. Lecture de 'Sylvie'* (Lausanne: L'Âge d'Homme ('Cistre Essais' 6)). Portuguese trans. of 'Biographie et fiction' (pp.9–23): 'O contrato com o nome proprio', in *Revista de comunicação e linguagens*, 10/11 (1990), 143–51.

b) *Nietzsche et la scène philosophique*, Union Générale d'Éditions ('10/18'). 2nd edn: Galilée ('Débats'), 1986. Includes: 'Annexe: Baubô. Perversion théologique et Fétichisme', pp.263–304 (cf. 1975b); 'Appendice: Le/les "concepts" de culture dans les *Intempestives* ou *la double dissimulation*', pp.337–71 (cf. 1973b). English trans. of 'Descartes piégé' (pp.227–61): 'Descartes Entrapped', trans. by Kathryn Aschheim, in *Who Comes After the Subject?*, ed. by Eduardo Cadava, Peter Connor, and Jean-Luc Nancy (New York and London: Routledge, 1991), pp.178–97.

c) 'Nerval sur le divan' [interview with Lucette Finas on *Nerval: Le charme de la répétition* (1979a)], *La Quinzaine Littéraire*, 306 (16–31 July), p.17.

1980

a) *L'énigme de la femme: La femme dans les textes de Freud*, Galilée ('Débats'). 2nd edn, 1983. English trans. of 'La relève des mères' (pp.84–97): 'The Sublation of Mothers', trans. by Cynthia Chase, *enclitic*, 4 (1980), 17–28. English trans. of 'Supplément rhapsodique' (pp.253–72): 'Freud's "Rhapsodic Supplement" on Femininity', trans. by Christine Saxton, *Discourse*, 4 (Winter 1981–2), 37–51. Italian: *L'enigma donna: la sessualità femminile nei testi di Freud*, trans. by Luisa Muraro (Milan: Bompiani ('Saggi Bompiani'), 1982). Spanish: *El Enigma de la mujer*, trans. by Estela Ocampo (Barcelona: Gedisa ('Psicoteca mayor: Freudiana'), 1982).

English: *The Enigma of Woman: Woman in Freud's Writings*,
trans. by Catherine Porter (Ithaca, NY and London:
Cornell University Press, 1985).
English trans. of excerpts from 'L'Autre' (pp.39–42) and
'Criminelle ou hystérique' (pp.77–80): 'The Other'
(p.248) and 'Criminal or hysteric' (p.249f.), in *Feminisms: A Reader*, ed. by Maggie Humm (Hemel
Hempstead: Harvester Wheatsheaf), 1992.

b) 'La mélancolie de l'art', in *Philosopher: Les interrogations
contemporaines. Matériaux pour un enseignement*, ed. by
Christian Delacampagne and Robert Maggiori, Fayard,
pp.415–27. Revised republication in *Mélancolie de l'art*
(1985a), pp.9–33.

German: 'Die Melancholie der Kunst', trans. by Birgit
Wagner, in *Postmoderne und Dekonstruktion: Texte französischer Philosophen der Gegenwart*, ed. by Peter
Engelmann (Stuttgart: Reclam, 1990), pp.224–43.

c) 'Sacrée nourriture', in *Manger*, ed. by Christian Besson
and Catherine Weinzaepflen (Liège: Yellow Now;
Chalon-sur-Saône: Maison de la Culture), pp.71–74.
Reproduced in *Trois*, 3/1 (Autumn 1987), 17 (cf. 1987c)
and *La Part de l'Œil*, 9 (special number: 'Arts Plastiques et
Psychanalyse II', 1993), 85.

English: 'Damned Food', trans. by Frances Bartkowski, in
'Autobiographical Writings', *SubStance*, 49 (1986), 6–13
(8–9).

German: 'Geheiligte/Verfluchte Nahrung', trans. by
Ursula Beitz, in *Die Philosophin*, 2/3 (1991), 110–11.

d) 'La femme narcissique: Freud et Girard', *Revue française
de psychanalyse*, 44/1 (January-February), 195–210.
Revised republication in *L'énigme de la femme*, pp.60–80
(cf. 1980a).

English: 'The Narcissistic Woman: Freud and Girard',
trans. by George van den Abbeele, *Diacritics*, 10/3 (Fall
1980), 36–45, reproduced in *French Feminist Thought: A
Reader*, ed. by Toril Moi (Oxford: Blackwell, 1987),
pp.210–26.

1981

a) 'Ça cloche', in *Les fins de l'homme: À partir du travail de Jacques Derrida*, ed. by Philippe Lacoue-Labarthe and Jean-Luc Nancy, Galilée (Proceedings of the Colloque de Cerisy-la-Salle, 23 July–2 August 1980), pp.89–112 (discussion to p.116; further S.K. interventions: pp.16, 47, 86, 87, 184, 196f., 199, 310, 341, 365, 391, 392, 410, 480, 497, 650, 651). Reproduced (without the discussion but with additional notes) in *Lectures de Derrida* (1984a), pp.115–51.
English: 'Ça cloche', trans. by Caren Kaplan, in *Continental Philosophy II: Derrida and Deconstruction*, ed. by Hugh J. Silverman (New York and London: Routledge, 1989), pp.108–38.

b) [2 illus.] in Françoise Metz, 'Ombrelles, ou la puissance fantastique de l'écriture' [Review article on *Aberrations: le devenir-femme d'Auguste Comte* (1978a), *Nerval: Le charme de la répétition* (1979a), and *Nietzsche et la scène philosophique* (1979b)], *Avant-Guerre*, 2 (1981), 91.

1982

a) *Le respect des femmes (Kant et Rousseau)*, Galilée ('Débats').
English trans. of 'L'économie du respect: Kant' (pp.21–56): 'The Economy of Respect: Kant and Respect for Women', trans. by Nicola Fisher, *Social Research*, 49/2 (Summer 1982), 383–404.
Japanese trans. of 'L'économie du respect: Kant': ['The Economy of Respect: Kant'], in *Revue de la pensée contemporaine*, 13/1 and 13/3 (1985).
German trans. of 'L'économie du respect: Kant': 'Die Ökonomie der Achtung: Kant', trans. by Leonhard Schmeiser, in *Feministische Philosophie*, ed. by Herta Nagl-Docekal (Vienna and Munich: Oldenbourg ('Wiener Reihe: Themen der Philosophie' 4), 1990), pp.41–62.

b) 'La femme autrement dite', *Les Nouveaux Cahiers*, 70 (Autumn), 80 [review article on Catherine Chalier,

Figures du féminin: Lecture d'Emmanuel Lévinas (La Nuit surveillée, 1982)].

1983

a) *Comment s'en sortir?*, Galilée ('Débats'). English trans. of 'Cauchemar: En marge des études médiévales' (pp.101–12): 'Nightmare: At the Margins of Medieval Studies', trans. by Frances Bartkowski, in 'Autobiographical Writings', *SubStance*, 49 (1986), 6–13 (10–13). English trans. of 'Prométhée, premier philosophe' (pp.71–94): 'Prometheus, the First Philosopher', trans. by Winnie Woodhull, *SubStance*, 50 (1986), 26–35. English trans. of 'Aporie' (pp.9–100): 'Beyond Aporia?', trans. by David Macey, in *Post-structuralist Classics*, ed. by Andrew Benjamin (London and New York: Routledge ('Warwick Studies in Philosophy and Literature'), 1988), pp.7–44.

b) *Un métier impossible: Lecture de 'Constructions en analyse'*, Galilée ('Débats').

1984

a) *Lectures de Derrida*, Galilée ('Débats'). Includes: 'Un philosophe "unheimlich"', pp.11–114 (cf. 1973c); 'Ça cloche', pp.115–51 (cf.1981a); 'Annexe: Philosophie terminée. Philosophie interminable', pp.153–84 (cf. 1977a). German: *Derrida lesen*, trans. by Monika Buchgeister and Hans-Walter Schmidt, ed. by Peter Engelmann (Vienna: Passagen-Verlag and Böhlau ('Passagen' 14), 1988).

b) 'La ressemblance des portraits (À propos du *Salon de 1767* consacré à *La Tour*)', *L'Esprit Créateur*, 24/1 (Spring), 13–32. Reproduced in *Rencontres de l'École du Louvre*, September (special number: 'L'imitation'), 215–30; revised republication (as 'La ressemblance des portraits: l'imitation selon Diderot') in *Mélancolie de l'art* (1985a), pp.35–70.

c) 'Il y a quelqu'un qui manque', *Le temps de la réflexion*, 5, 430–41 [review article on Denis Hollier, *Politique de la*

prose: Jean-Paul Sartre et l'an quarante (Gallimard, 1982)].
Revised and extended republication (as 'Sartre: Fort! ou
Da?') in *Séductions* (1990a), pp.139–66.
English: 'Sartre: Fort! ou Da?', trans. by Arthur Denner,
Diacritics, 14/4 (Winter 1984), 9–18.

1985

a) *Mélancolie de l'art*, Galilée ('Débats'). Includes: 'La
mélancolie de l'art', pp.9–33 (cf. 1980b); 'La
ressemblance des portraits: l'imitation selon Diderot',
pp.35–70 (cf. 1984b); 'L'espace de la césure', pp.71–86
(cf. 1978c); 'Balthus ou la pause', pp.87–101.
German: *Melancholie der Kunst*, ed. by Peter Engelmann,
trans. by Birgit Wagner (Vienna and Graz: Böhlau
('Passagen' 9), 1986).

b) *Rousseau und die Frauen*, trans. by Ruthard Stäblin
(Tübingen: Rive Gauche (Konkursbuchverlag Claudia
Gehrke) ('Wegweisende Worte')). Includes 4 illus. by
S.K.
French: 'Les fins phallocratiques de Rousseau', in *Cahiers de
l'ACFAS*, 44 (special number: 'Égalité et différence des
sexes'), 1986, 341–58.
Portuguese: trans. by Amalia Aires and Teresa Caino, in
Revista de comunicação e linguagens, 5 (November 1987).
English: 'Rousseau's Phallocratic Ends', trans. by Mara
Dukats, in *Hypatia*, 3/3 (Winter 1989), 123–36, repro-
duced in *Revaluing French Feminism: Critical Essays on
Difference, Agency, and Culture*, ed. by Nancy Fraser and
Sandra Lee Bartky (Bloomington and Indianapolis: Indi-
ana University Press, 1992), pp.46–59.

1986

a) *Pourquoi rit-on? Freud et le mot d'esprit*, Galilée ('Débats').
German: *Die lachenden Dritten: Freud und der Witz*, trans. by
Monika Buchgeister and Hans-Walter Schmidt (Munich
and Vienna: Verlag der Internationalen Psychoanalyse,
1990).

b) 'Entrevista com Sarah Kofman conduzida por Chakè Matossian', *Revista de comunicação e linguagens*, 3 (June) (special number: 'Textualidades'), 143–47.

c) 'Nietzsche et l'obscurité d'Héraclite', *Furor*, 15 (October), 3–33. Revised and extended republication in *Séductions* (1990a), pp.87–137.

English: 'Nietzsche and the Obscurity of Heraclitus', trans. by Françoise Lionnet-McCumber, *Diacritics*, 17/3 (Fall 1987), 39–55.

German: 'Nietzsche und die Dunkelheit des Heraklit', trans. by Claire Baldwin and Thomas Nolden, in *Nietzsche heute: Die Rezeption seines Werkes nach 1968*, ed. by Sigrid Bauschinger, Susan L. Cocalis, and Sara Lennox (Berne and Stuttgart: Francke (Proceedings of the 15th Annual Colloquium on German Literature at Amherst, Mass., April 1986), 1988), pp.75–104.

1987

a) *Paroles suffoquées*, Galilée ('Débats').

German: *Erstickte Worte*, ed. by Peter Engelmann, trans. by Birgit Wagner, Preface by Jürg Altwegg (Vienna: Passagen-Verlag and Böhlau ('Passagen' 19), 1988).

b) *Conversions: Le Marchand de Venise sous le signe de Saturne*, Galilée ('Débats').

German: *Konversionen: 'Der Kaufmann von Venedig' unter dem Zeichen des Saturn*, trans. by Monika Buchgeister (Vienna: Passagen-Verlag and Böhlau ('Passagen' 24), 1989).

English: 'Conversions: *The Merchant of Venice* under the Sign of Saturn', trans. by Shaun Whiteside, in *Literary Theory Today*, ed. by Peter Collier and Helga Geyer-Ryan (Cambridge: Polity, 1990), pp.142–66.

c) 'Trois textes', in *Trois*, 3/1 (Autumn), 16–20. Includes 'Sacrée nourriture' (17, cf. 1980c); '"Ma vie" et la psychanalyse' (18, cf. 1976b); 'Tombeau pour un nom propre' (20, cf. 1976d). Includes 2 illus. by S.K. ('Surmoi', p.16, and 'La mort ou l'autisme', p.19).

d) [Interview with Christa Stevens], *Stoicheia*, 4 (December).

e) 'Sarah Kofman: de verleiding van een tegendraads filosofe' [interview with Christa Stevens], *Katijf*, 42 (December 1987–January 1988), 26–29. Includes illus. by S.K., p.28.

1988

a) 'Gesprek met de Franse filosofe Sarah Kofman: "de vrouw is de skeptika, zij weet dat er geen waarheid achter de sluiers is"' [interview with Karen Vintges], in *De Groene Amsterdammer*, 22 June, pp.20–21.

b) 'Miroir et mirages oniriques: Platon, précurseur de Freud', *La Part de l'Œil*, 4, 127–35. Revised republication in *Séductions* (1990a), pp.61–86.

c) 'Sarah Kofman' [excerpted interview with Alice Jardine], trans. by Patricia Baudoin, in 'Exploding the Issue: "French" "Women" "Writers" and "The Canon"? Fourteen Interviews', by Alice Jardine and Anne M. Menke, *Yale French Studies*, 75 (special number: 'The Politics of Tradition: Placing Women in French Literature'), 229–58 (S.K., 246–48); reprinted in *Displacements: Women, Traditions, Literatures in French*, ed. by Joan DeJean and Nancy K. Miller (Baltimore: Johns Hopkins University Press, 1990). Full interview in *Shifting Scenes* (1991f).

d) 'Shoah (ou la Dis-Grâce)', *Les Nouveaux Cahiers*, 95 (Winter 1988–9), 67. Reproduced in *Actes*, 67–8 (special number: 'Droit et humanité') (September 1989), 1.
German: 'Shoah (oder die Un-Gnade)', trans. by Ursula Beitz, *Die Philosophin*, 2/3 (1991), 7–8.

1989

a) *Socrate(s)*, Galilée ('La philosophie en effet').
English trans. of 'Les Socrate(s) de Nietzsche: "Qui" est Socrate?' (pp.291–318): 'Nietzsche's Socrates: "Who" is Socrates?', trans. by Madeleine Dobie, *Graduate Faculty Philosophy Journal*, 15/2 (1991), 7–29.

b) 'Autour de *Socrate(s)*: Rencontre avec Sarah Kofman' [interview with Ghyslaine Guertin], *La Petite Revue de Philosophie* (Spring) (special number: 'Psychologie et connaissance de soi'), 117–29.

c) 'L'efficace du simulacre', *Autrement dire*, 6 (special number: 'Simulacres'), 141–49. Extract from 'Séductions: essai sur *La Religieuse* de Diderot' in *Séductions* (1990a).

1990

a) *Séductions: De Sartre à Héraclite*, Galilée ('La philosophie en effet'). Includes: 'Séductions: essai sur *La Religieuse* de Diderot', pp.9–60 (cf. 1989c); 'Miroir et mirages oniriques: Platon précurseur de Freud', pp.61–86 (cf. 1988b); 'Nietzsche et l'obscurité d'Héraclite', pp.87–137 (cf. 1986c); 'Sartre: Fort! ou Da?', pp.139–66 (cf. 1984c); 'Appendice: Le problème moral dans une philosophie de l'absurde', pp.167–81 (cf. 1963).

b) 'Au-delà de la mélancolie' [reply to a questionnaire on Sartre], *Libération*, 23–24 June, p.25.

c) 'Un battu imbattable: Sur *Larmes de Clown* de Victor Sjörström', *Théâtre/public*, 92, 55.

1991

a) *Don Juan ou le refus de la dette*, by Sarah Kofman and Jean-Yves Masson, Galilée ('Débats'). Includes S.K.: 'L'art de ne pas payer ses dettes (Molière)', pp.63–121.

Japanese trans. of 'L'art de ne pas payer ses dettes (Molière)' (pp.63–121): trans. by Sumie Kôyama, *Revue de la pensée contemporaine*, 21/4 and 21/5 (1993).

b) *'Il n'y a que le premier pas qui coûte': Freud et la spéculation*, Galilée ('Débats').

German: 'Nun der erste Schritt, der Mühen kostet: Freud und die Spekulation', in *Entfernte Wahrheit: Von der Endlichkeit der Psychoanalyse*, ed. by Martin Kuster (Tübingen: Diskord, 1992), pp.10–62.

English: trans. by Sarah Wykes, in *After Freud: Speculations on Psychoanalysis, Philosophy and Culture*, ed. by Sonu

Shamdasani and Michael Münchow (London: Routledge, 1994).

c) 'Schreiben ohne Macht' [interview with Ursula Könnertz], *Die Philosophin*, 2/3 (1991), 103–09.

d) 'Tot, unsterblich', *Die Philosophin*, 2/3 (1991), 111–12.

e) 'Ecce mulier' [interview with Takashi Minatomichi], trans. by Sumie Kôyama, *Revue de la pensée contemporaine*, 19/11 and 19/12.

f) 'Sarah Kofman' [interview with Alice Jardine], trans. by Janice Orion, in *Shifting Scenes: Interviews on Women, Writing, and Politics in Post-68 France*, ed. by Alice A. Jardine and Anne M. Menke (New York and Oxford: Columbia University Press ('Gender and Culture')), pp.104–12.

1992

a) *Explosion I: De l' 'Ecce Homo' de Nietzsche*, Galilée ('La philosophie en effet').
Hungarian trans. of 'Introduction' (pp.9–43): 'Bevezetó az *Ecce homo* olvasásához', trans. by Balint Somlyo, *Athenaeum*, 1992/3, 214–41.
English trans. of 'Introduction' (pp.9–43), in *Diacritics* (forthcoming).
English trans. of 'Une généalogie fantastique' (pp.189–213), in *Nietzsche and the Feminine*, ed. by Peter Burgard (Charlottesville: University of Virginia Press, 1994).

b) 'La question des femmes: une impasse pour les philosophes' [interview with Joke Hermsen], *Les Cahiers du Grif*, 46 (Spring) (special number: 'Provenances de la pensée: Femmes/philosophie'), 65–74.

c) 'Nietzsche et Wagner: Comment la musique devient bonne pour les cochons', *Furor*, 23 (May), 5–28 (slightly modified version of 1993d).

1993

a) *Explosion II: Les enfants de Nietzsche*, Galilée ('La philosophie en effet').
English trans. of 'Le psychologue de l'Éternel féminin', in *Yale French Studies* (forthcoming).

b) 'Interview avec Sarah Kofman 22 mars 1991. Subvertir le philosophique *ou* Pour un supplément de jouissance' [interview with Evelyne Ender], *Compar(a)ison*, 1 (January), 9–26.

c) 'Un autre Moïse ou la force de la loi', *La Part de l'Œil*, 9 (special number: 'Arts Plastiques et Psychanalyse II'), 70–81.

d) 'L'idéal ascétique de Wagner selon Nietzsche', in *L'art moderne et la question du sacré*, ed. by Jean-Jacques Milles, Le Cerf, pp. 43–65 (first version of 1992c).

e) '"Naissance et renaissance de la tragédie" suivi de "Sagesse tragique"', *La métaphore (revue)*, 1 (Spring), 77–102 and 103–14. Pre-publication of two chapters from 1993a.

Index of Nietzsche's Works Cited

General Index

absolute (*absolutum*), 71, 187n.3b;
artistic experience, 12; centre,
111; concept, 50; distinction,
108; error, 134; knowledge,
133; norm, 2, 44; spirituality,
105; text, 139; value, 3, 36, 51,
56, 82, 88, 126; world of, 76
abstraction, 60, 67, 168n.13;
concept as, 19, 22, 39–40, 48,
79, 86; consciousness as, 93;
language and, 159n.16; as
mask, 176n.16; as mummified
error, 166n.5; originary chaos
as, 138; science as, 65
absurdity, 108, 128, 137–8, 143
abyss, 20, 24, 25, 49, 91, 154n.25,
163n.33
accuracy (correctness), 16–18, 42,
69, 71, 87–8, 101, 141, 143,
152n.15, 174n.8, 178n.23
Achilles, 51
Aeschylus, 13, 19, 24, 151n.9
aesthetic: chemistry, 47;
experience, 4, 12; relation, 42;
value of philosophy, 20. *See
also* artistic
affect, 53, 85, 103, 106. *See also*
emotion, passion
affirmation: of dominant drive,
103; of force, 76, 163–4n.37;
of living things, 125; of
power, 52; of will, 82, 129,

132; of the world, 134. *See also*
negation
affirmation of life: and *amor fati*,
102; and authenticity, 180n.3;
and the body, 122; and denial
of life, 64–5; by drives,
178n.21; and interpretation,
141, 143; Jews and, 55;
metaphor and, 19, 21; and the
new philosopher, 111; and
nihilism, 11; and science, 67;
and the value of value, 127–9;
and will to nothingness, 51
Albert, Henri, xiii
Alexander the Great, 182n.9
Allison, David B.: *The New
Nietzsche*, viii, xxv, 147n.1,
150n.5
amor fati, xxii, 102, 127, 128, 141.
See also fate
amor intellectualis dei, 73
anaemia, 30, 72, 168n.13. *See also*
blood
anaesthetization, 57, 172n.27
Anaxagoras, 19
anthropomorphism, 25, 33, 39,
58, 63, 65, 70, 183n.14
anticathexis, 35, 43, 50
Antichrist, The, x, 54–5
antithesis. *See* opposition

Apollinian and Dionysian, 6–13, 134, 138, 149n.3. *See also* Dionysian

Apollo and Dionysus, 13, 96, 138, 144. *See also* Dionysus

appearance, xii, 148n.1; and Being, 120–1; concept and, 35; and dream, 170n.18; and essence, 174n.6; and reality, 32, 66, 75, 175n.12, 189n.15. *See also* surface

appropriateness, 15–16, 33, 120, 149n.5. *See also* proper

appropriation, xii, 82–6, 173n.2; of being, 123, 135; of chaos, 139; conceptual language as, 36; and grasping, 83, 173n.3; and imitation, 36; and interpretation, 123; of language, 151n.11; metaphor as, 118; moral evaluations as, 50; of one's 'own', 114; of the 'proper', 33; the 'proper' as, 82, 102, 118. *See also* force, proper

arche, 21

architecture, 59–74 *passim*, 108, 165n.1, 186n.23; as rhetoric of power, 61

Ariadne, 97

aristocracy, 52–4, 57, 161n.18, 163n.34. *See also* hierarchy, nobility

aristocratic: evaluations, 50–4; meaning, 88–9; style, 112, 118. *See also* high, noble

Aristotle, 25, 153n.20, 172n.24; *On the Soul*, 180n.6; and the Pre-Socratics, 19–22, 153n.24, 163n.33; on 'proper' meaning, 174n.5; on society, 167n.8

art(s), 17, 18; as cult of the surface, 27–31; and dream, 46, 74, 77; and form, 27–30, 32–3, 156n.10; and happiness, 79; and idealization, 30; and illusion, 131; interrelation of, 11–13; and lying, 46, 64, 74–5; and metaphor, 27–33; and myth, 64, 74–5, 77–8; and nature, 30,

78; and philosophy, 1, 17, 19–20; and play, 30–1, 78, 169n.15; as 'proper' to man, 28; and rhetoric, 27, 32; and science, 23, 156n.9; symbolic, 167n.6; of waste, 3, 159–60n.16; will to power as, 17, 65, 82. *See also Gesamtkunst*, music, painting, poetry

Artaud, Antonin, xxi, 150–1n.7

artist, 12, 23, 29–32, 46, 84, 102; just man as, 142; of language, 40; man as, 25, 155n.5; philosopher as, 106; as squanderer, 159–60n.16. *See also* poet

artistic: creation, 56, 60, 65; force, 17, 25, 27–8, 74, 82, 116, 155nn.5–6; ideal, 57; judgement, 141–2; life as, 21, 60, 75; value, 20. *See also* aesthetic

ascetic ideal, 19, 20, 51, 57, 187n.3c; essence of, 84, 123; mask of, 178n.21; meaning of, 76, 123

ashes, 67, 78, 101

Assyrians, 54

atheism, 128, 141, 144

atoms, 72

Aufhebung. See sublation

authenticity, 8–9, 12, 16, 180n.3

author, 19, 101, 109, 152n.18, 177n.21

authorial intention, 114–16, 140–1, 178–9n.23

axe: philosophical, 107, 109

Babel. *See* tower

Bacon, Francis, 182n.9

Basle, xv

Bass, Alan, 150n.5, 164n.38

bastion, 64, 65. *See also* tower

Bataille, Georges, x, xxi, xxiv, xxviin.6, xxxixn.61, 74, 155n.3, 181n.7; 'The Language of Flowers', 183n.14; 'The "Old Mole"', xxviin.6, 175n.10, 183n.14; 'The Solar Anus', 181n.7

163n.34, 177n.20, 188–9n.10;
ownership, 149n.5; under-
standing, 175n.9
semiology: morality as, 87, 174–
5n.9; science as, 62, 65, 165n.3;
and symptomatology, xii, xiv,
xxxiiin.33, 87, 165n.3, 174–
5n.9. *See also* sign
senses, 10–12, 28, 35, 38, 45–7,
52, 70–3, 105–8, 182n.10,
189n.11. *See also* hearing,
smell, taste, touch, vision
sensory: and intelligible, 52,
166n.6
seriousness, 61, 119, 185n.21; and
play, 18, 53, 69, 74–5, 80, 104,
115, 167n.8. *See also* gravity
sex organ(s), 105, 180n.6, 181n.7
shame, 2, 65, 96–8, 175n.12,
176n.18, 178n.21, 180n.6. *See
also* disgrace
shield, 65, 102, 168n.9. *See also*
protection
sickness. *See* illness
sight. *See* vision
sign(s), xii, xxxvn.43, 81; body
and, 26, 121–2; chain, 85;
communication through, 2;
consciousness as system of, 26;
Derrida on, 166n.6; Hegel on,
166–7n.6; language, 46, 87;
music as system of, 10; spheres
of, 40; and truths, 83; words
as, 7. *See also* semiology,
symbol
silence, 79, 119
sirens, 72, 136, 168n.12
skeleton, 66, 81. *See also* bones
slave: and free man, 60, 75, 95,
172n.23; and master, 77–8, 88–
9, 163n.34, 174n.5; morality,
88. *See also* hierarchy
smell (odour, scent), 16, 104–5,
107, 112–13, 180n.6, 182n.10,
184n.20. *See also* senses
'snake', 39
social: distance, 90; equilibrium,
43–6; hierarchy, 37, 55, 95,
160–1n.18; justice, 43;

memory, 43, 47; norm, 47;
organization, 43–5. *See also*
political
society, 43–8, 95, 113; Aristotle
on, 167n.8; classless, 160–
1n.18; as game, 167n.8;
language and, 36–7. *See also*
city, politics
Socrates, xxxviiin.56, 11, 19,
153n.20, 167n.6, 174n.8
Socratic, 73; culture, 10
soil, 22, 24, 103, 109–11, 153n.19.
See also plant, tree
solitude. *See* isolation
song, 4–5, 11, 13, 19, 41–2,
168n.12; language and,
158n.16. *See also* music, opera
Sorbonne (Paris I), xviii
soul(s): aristocratic, 89–91; and
body, 11, 26, 108, 166n.6;
collective, 157n.15, 159n.16;
eternal, 87; new, 4–5; noble,
188n.10; Plato on, 165n.44;
structure of, 118
sound. *See* Chladni sound figures,
hearing, music
space, 27–8; as fundamental
metaphorical schema, 40
specialization, 11, 51–3, 104, 107
speculation, 32, 62, 105
speech, 1, 4, 6, 13, 77–8, 119,
157n.15; common, 112;
metaphorical and 'proper', 17;
and silence, 79; sovereign,
174n.5; and writing, 7, 101,
150n.6, 158n.16
spider, 69–73, 168–9n.14; Freud
on, 168n.10; God as, 168n.11,
171n.21. *See also* insect
spider's web, 60, 69–72, 74, 75,
168n.13
Spinoza, Benedict (Baruch) de,
xxiv, 66, 79; *Ethics*, 168n.9,
179n.23; as spider, 69, 71, 73;
Tractatus Theologico-Politicus,
170–1n.19, 178–9n.23
spirit, 178n.21; free, 51–2, 115,
185n.25; honey-gatherers of the,
63; 'life' and, 94; profundity of,

159n.16; 'pure', 71; and truth,
187–8n.5. *See also* mind
spiritual: discipline, 134; elevation, 183n.14; meaning, 51–2
spirituality, spiritualization, 105,
113
staging, 34, 103–4. *See also* theatre
statue: Stoic as, 172n.27. *See also*
petrifaction
Stoics, 79, 153n.20, 172–3n.27,
174n.4. *See also* pleasure,
suffering
stomach, 26, 81, 152–3n.18. *See
also* digestion
stronghold, 60, 64–6. *See also*
tower
style, 99, 114; aristocratic, 112,
118; art of, 2; grand, 3, 61, 74,
186n.23; Heraclitus', 117; 'in
itself', 2; metaphorical, 1, 19,
112–13, 117, 119; original, 74;
philosophical, 2–3, 17, 19;
poetic, 3. *See also* language,
writing
subject, 37–9; knowing, 105; and
object, 42, 94; permanent, 38–
9; and ruler, 90
subjectivity, 28, 102. *See also*
objectivity
sublation, 53, 131, 164nn.38–9,
181n.7
sublimation, 26, 43, 46–7, 51, 74,
155n.7; Freud on, 169n.16. *See
also* volatilization
sublime, 20, 110, 113, 170n.18;
abortion, 75
substance, 36–8, 161n.20, 171n.20
SubStance, viii
substitution(s), 17, 19, 22, 120–1,
123; for metaphor, 16–17, 82;
metaphorical, 8–9, 33, 41, 60,
74, 106, 144
Suetonius, 167n.8
suffering, 79–80, 89, 111,
187n.2d. *See also* pleasure,
Stoics
sun, 59, 108–11, 178n.21, 181n.7,
184n.14. *See also* light
superficiality, 49, 115, 121; of
consciousness, 25, 87, 160n.16;

of the mind, 155–6n.8. *See also*
surface
supplement, 7, 76, 96, 148–9n.2,
170n.19, 179n.23
surface, xxii; and appearance, 64,
78; art and, 27–31; consciousness as, 28, 189n.12; and depth,
91, 115; generalization of,
175n.12; reading and, 116. *See
also* depth, superficiality
syllogism, 39. *See also* logic
symbol(ism), 6–17, 33, 52, 96, 99,
139, 144; of the body, 6, 11,
139; and dream, 169n.17; and
sign, 167n.6; and symptom, 99,
122, 124, 144
symbolic: art, 167n.6; explanation, 155–6n.8; expressivity,
26; faculties, 6; languages, 7–
15, 35, 41–2, 87; meaning,
179n.23
symptom, 19, 61, 86, 94; and
symbol, 99, 122, 124, 144
symptomatology: and semiology,
xii, xiv, xxxiiin.33, 87, 165n.3,
174–5n.9

taste(s), 2, 104–8; of architects,
60–1, 74; bad, 11–12, 65, 74;
common, 2, 112, 114;
decadent, 58; for life, 131;
Nietzsche's, 182n.8; noble,
188n.7; philosophy and, 106–7;
of science, 65. *See also* senses
technology, 168n.11
teleology, 70, 85–6
text, 120–45 *passim*; of being,
123, 130, 135, 139–40, 188n.8;
and body, 87, 92; as clothing,
69; of consciousness, 99, 139;
and interpretation, xxiii, 16,
82, 92–4, 116, 123, 130, 133,
135–44; of life, 93, 96, 109,
129; as mask, 69; of morality,
87; of nature, 98–9, 135–8,
141–2, 177–8n.21; original,
instinctive, 33, 90–4, 137, 139,
178n.21, 179n.23, 189n.12; and
philology, 86, 98–9, 135–6; and